KAFFE FASSETT'S

Quilts in an English Village

featuring

Liza Prior Lucy

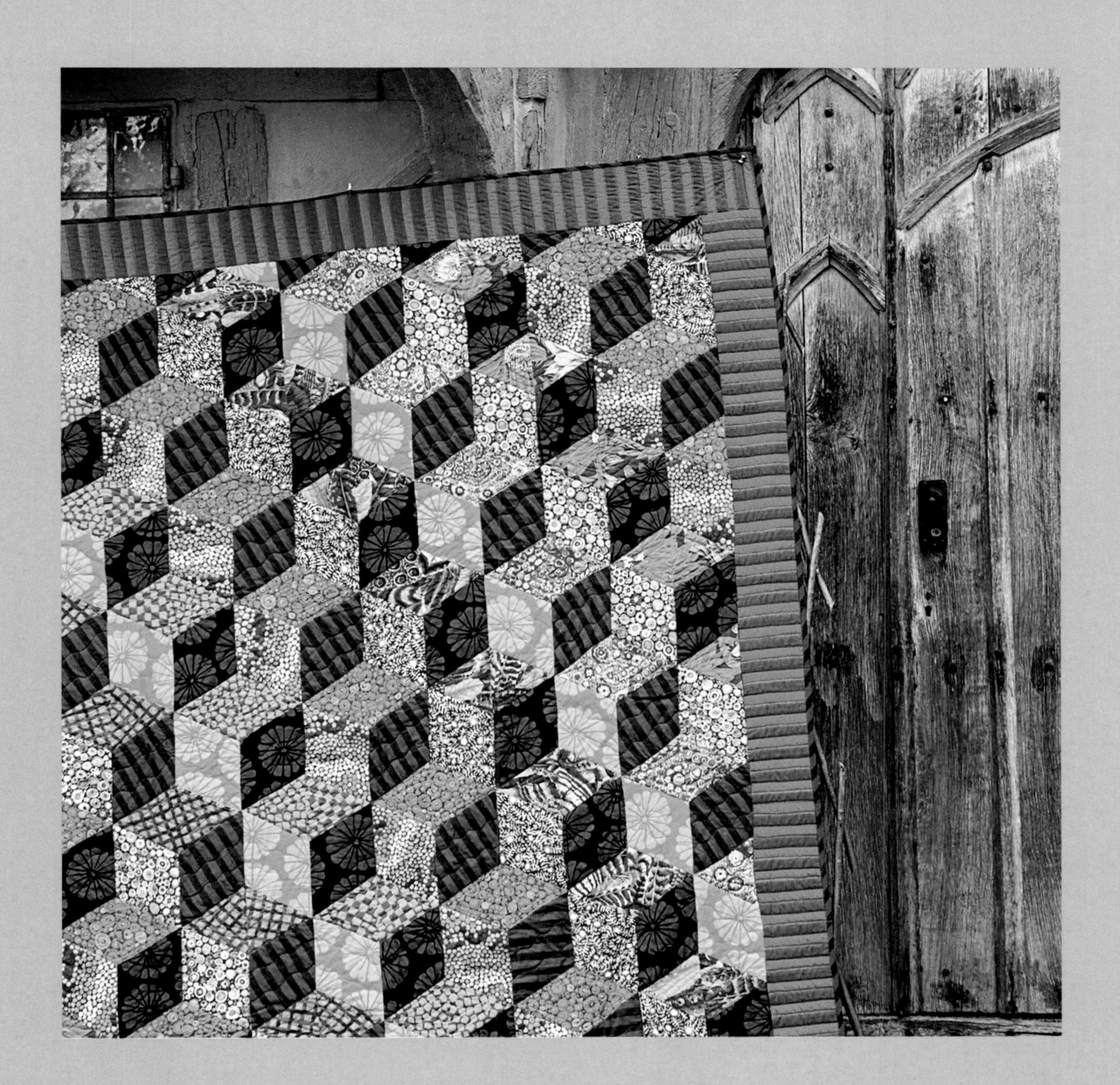

First published in the USA in 2021 by

The Taunton Press, Inc.
63 South Main Street
Newtown, CT 06470
email: tp@taunton.com

Reprinted 2022

Patchwork designs	Kaffe Fassett Liza Prior Lucy
Quilt making coordination	Heart Space Studios (UK) Liza Prior Lucy (US)
Technical editor	Bundle Backhouse
Designer Art direction/styling	Anne Wilson Kaffe Fassett
Location photography Additional photography Stills photography	Debbie Patterson Brandon Mably, pages 5, 7 (bottom) Steven Wooster
Quilt illustrations Map illustration	Heart Space Studios Héloïse Wooster
Publishing consultant	Susan Berry (Berry & Co)

Library of Congress Cataloging-in-Publication Data
in progress

ISBN 978-1-64155-150-2

Colour reproduction	Pixywalls Ltd, London

Printed in China

Page 1: My *Marquetry Blocks* quilt, one of my favourite quilt designs with its glowing 3-D quality.
Right: My *Dark Watermelons* quilt which makes a strong statement against the exquisite half-timbered houses of Lavenham in Suffolk.

Contents

introduction

When I was a youngster in California, my father moved us from our town house to a log cabin in the small coastal community of Big Sur. The house had real character with an enormous built-in table and storage chest in the main room. I loved living in a structure that constantly reminded us of the creative energy that built it.

Growing up in the fastest developing state in America, I was horrified to witness wonderful old buildings getting torn down or converted to slick soul-less modernity. This made me long for a place that would value its heritage of historic houses.

When I moved to England in my late 20s, I was often asked, 'How could you leave sunny California to come to dreary old England?' My answer was: to find a bit of the history I felt was being so systematically eliminated in California.

On a trip back to California, my sister gave me a copy of *The Pillars of the Earth* by Ken Follett. I was captivated by the imagination of builders in ancient times who conceived and constructed those magnificent gothic churches and buildings.

Imagine my delight when I first clapped eyes on the wondrous village of Lavenham in Suffolk to find so many houses each with such a creative signature and, best of all, in a stunning array of colours. As I explored the rest of the British Isles, finding many other architectural gems, I always kept coming back to the unique quality of Lavenham.

It was no surprise to read that the village went from being dazzlingly rich in the 15th century, as a centre for England's burgeoning wool trade, to becoming a lot less solvent when competitive sources outpriced them. But, in fact, this apparent disadvantage has helped to keep the inhabitants from overdeveloping their village and to preserve its unique architecture. So here we find, hundreds of years later, a wonderfully preserved place still bursting with characterful buildings, lovingly kept up by its appreciative community of residents. It is little wonder that the first Harry Potter film used this village as the birthplace of the 'boy wizard'.

Brandon and I, with our photographer Debbie Patterson, have done our best to show as many architectural details as we could on our shoot for this book. I hope you enjoy seeing how the soft colours of the buildings set off our quilts – many of them designed with these Tudor structures in mind.

Editor's note: Lavenham is situated in Suffolk, one of the counties of East Anglia in the UK (see map on page 144).

Trip around the Snowball

by Kaffe Fassett

This quilt structure was inspired by a deliciously scrappy Australian quilt. I enjoyed creating a new take on the classic snowball quilt. The golden colours of the Brassica backing fabric reflect the tawny shades of this ancient building.

Paperweight Checkerboard
by Kaffe Fassett

I designed this simple checkerboard quilt in silvery greys to go with the pale plaster and silvery weathered wood of one of Lavenham's beautiful half-timbered buildings.

Starry Night
by Kaffe Fassett

The bright stars of my *Starry Night* quilt seem to twinkle against the rich rusty pink hue of this handsome house.

Dark Watermelons
by Kaffe Fassett

The old hand-made bricks of this half-timbered house made a perfect setting for the rich smouldering tones of my *Dark Watermelons* quilt.

Peach Sunset
by Kaffe Fassett

I was recalling the warm pinks of some of Lavenham's loveliest houses when I designed this quilt. Gathering together every peach- and apricot-toned fabric in our collection made this quilt really glow.

Woodstock
by Liza Prior Lucy

Liza put together a lovely leafy-coloured group of our print fabrics for her *Woodstock* quilt. The way this beautiful old bridge reflects those tones sent shivers up my spine on our shoot.

Cottage Garden Flowers
by Kaffe Fassett

It was a joyous task to fussy cut all the bold blooms in our fabric collection to create this botanical bobby-dazzler of a quilt. Isn't this weathered Tudor building a perfect setting for those bright pastels?

Leafy Diamonds

by Kaffe Fassett

The soft yellow plaster of this half-timbered house makes my multi-green diamond quilt really shimmer.

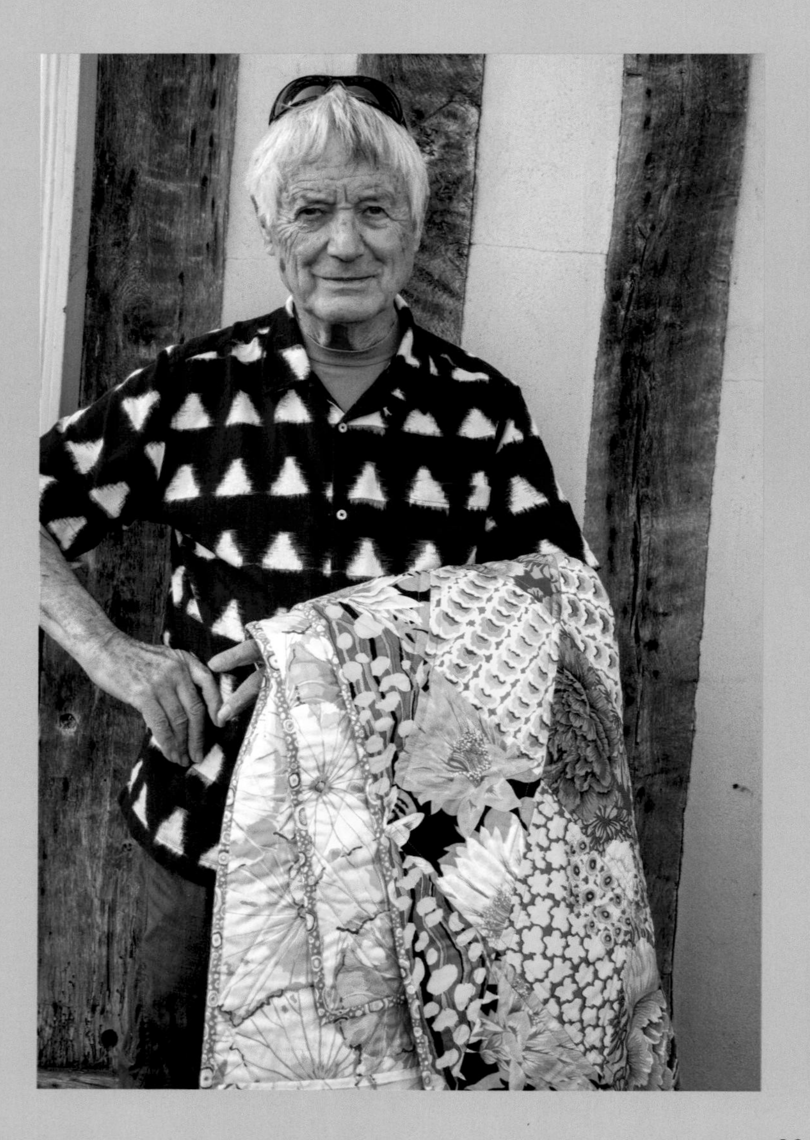

Dark Boxes
by Kaffe Fassett

Wanting a really dark quilt for this book, I needed a simple background to show off our darkest prints. The old barn door with its faded maroon wood makes it come to life, I feel.

Cotton Candy Pinwheels
by Kaffe Fassett

I've always loved pinwheels in patchwork, knitting and needlepoint. Here I've gathered all the spicy pinks, lavenders and cool pastels together to create a sunny jewel of a quilt. The glowing terracotta of the house with its brick mosaic wall really sets it off gorgeously.

Shards
by Kaffe Fassett

If I had to choose just one quilt, this delicacy would certainly be a contender. Brandon says the *Shards* quilt reminds him of butterflies' wings. The silvered wood and creamy white of this building really bring it to life.

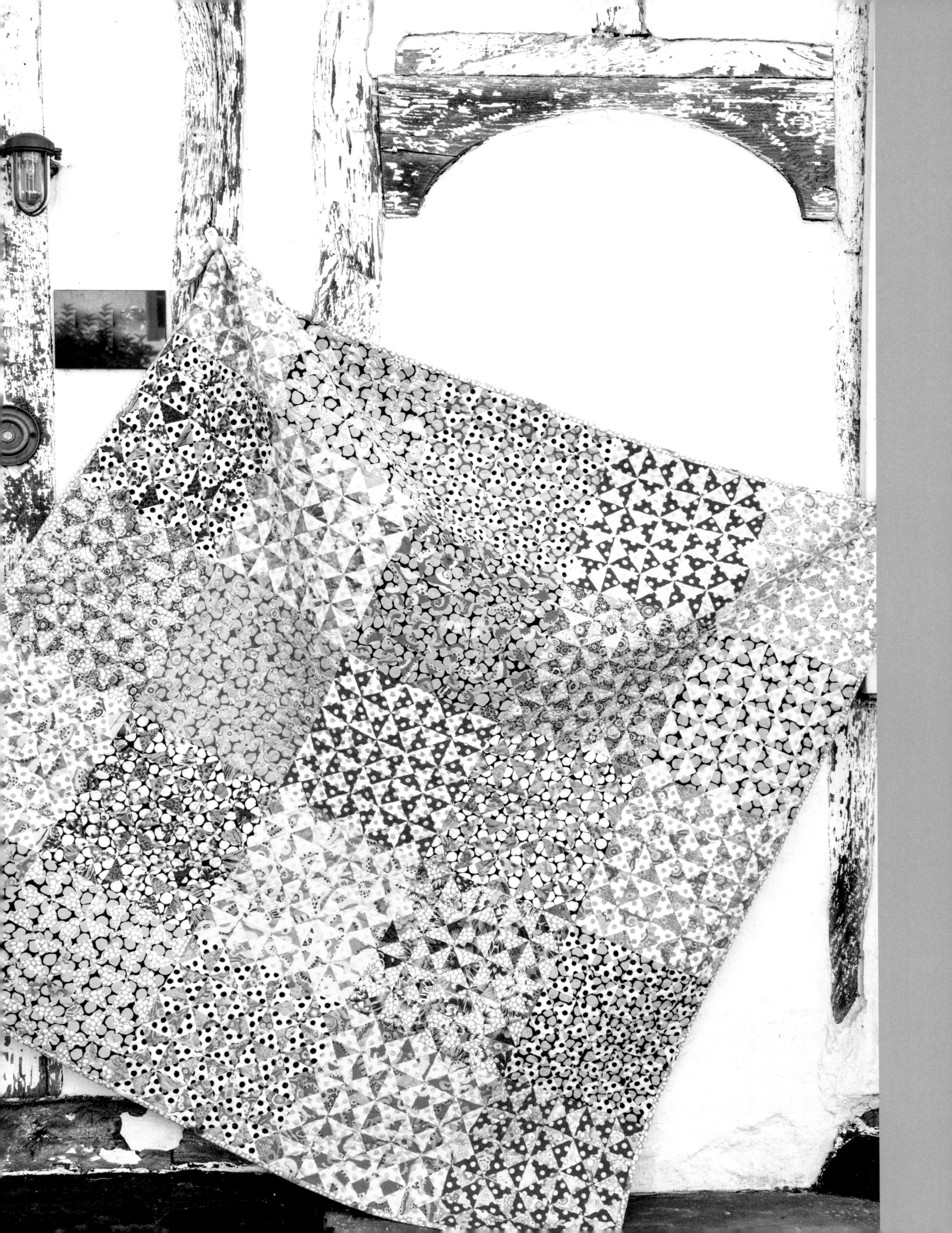

Ancient Glade
by Kaffe Fassett

We were thrilled to find these atmospheric old gates just outside Lavenham. What a perfect setting for the subtle green fabrics in the *Ancient Glade* quilt.

Bright Weave
by Liza Prior Lucy

Liza made quite a sunny splash with this recolouring of a quilt from our past books. I was stunned to find how well it sat against this Lavenham house. This street view (above) shows how exciting several of these half-timbered beauties look in a row.

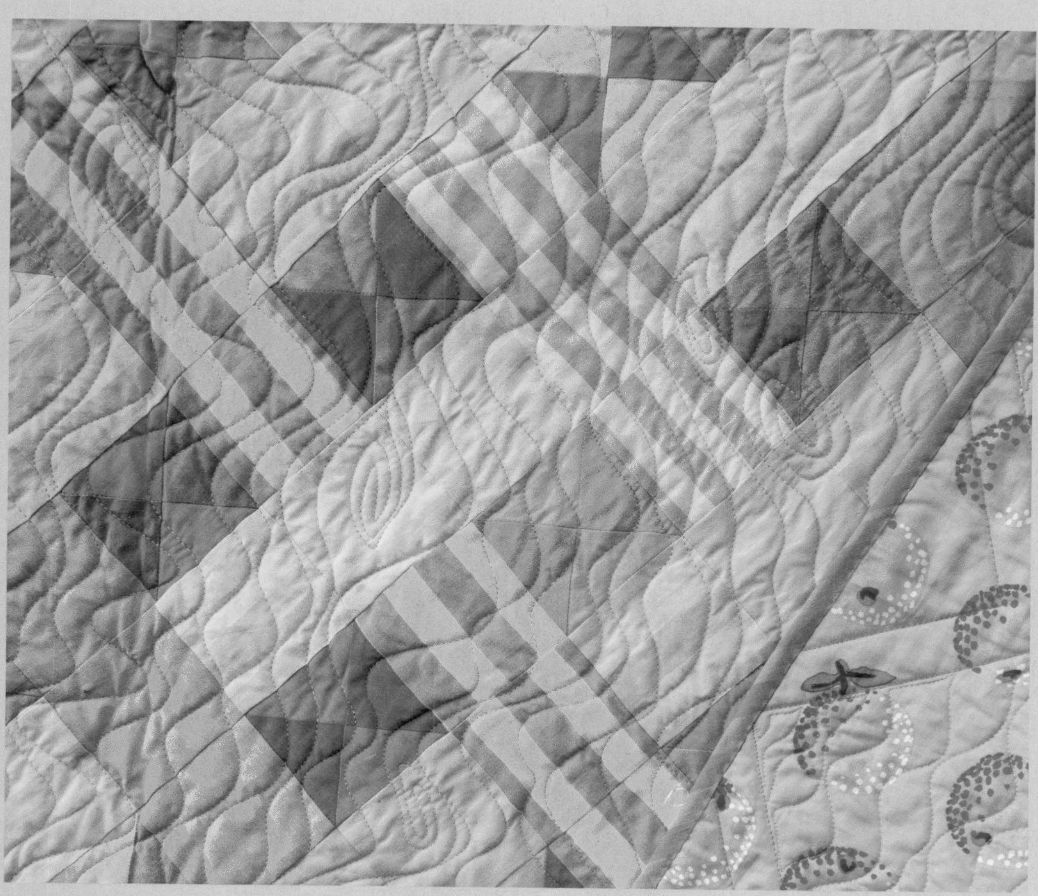

Marquetry Blocks
by Kaffe Fassett

Tumbling blocks is an irresistible layout that I return to often. Here I've upscaled it in bold autumn colours, knowing how great it would look against the deep gold of this Lavenham building. Even the pale green in the stained glass window is echoed in the quilt.

Blooming Columns
by Kaffe Fassett

The bold black and white half-timbered façade cried out for a strong quilt. Cutting dark blooms from our collection and placing them on these powerful contrasting stripes does the trick, I think. The wonderfully wonky lines of the house (below) are what make Lavenham so unique.

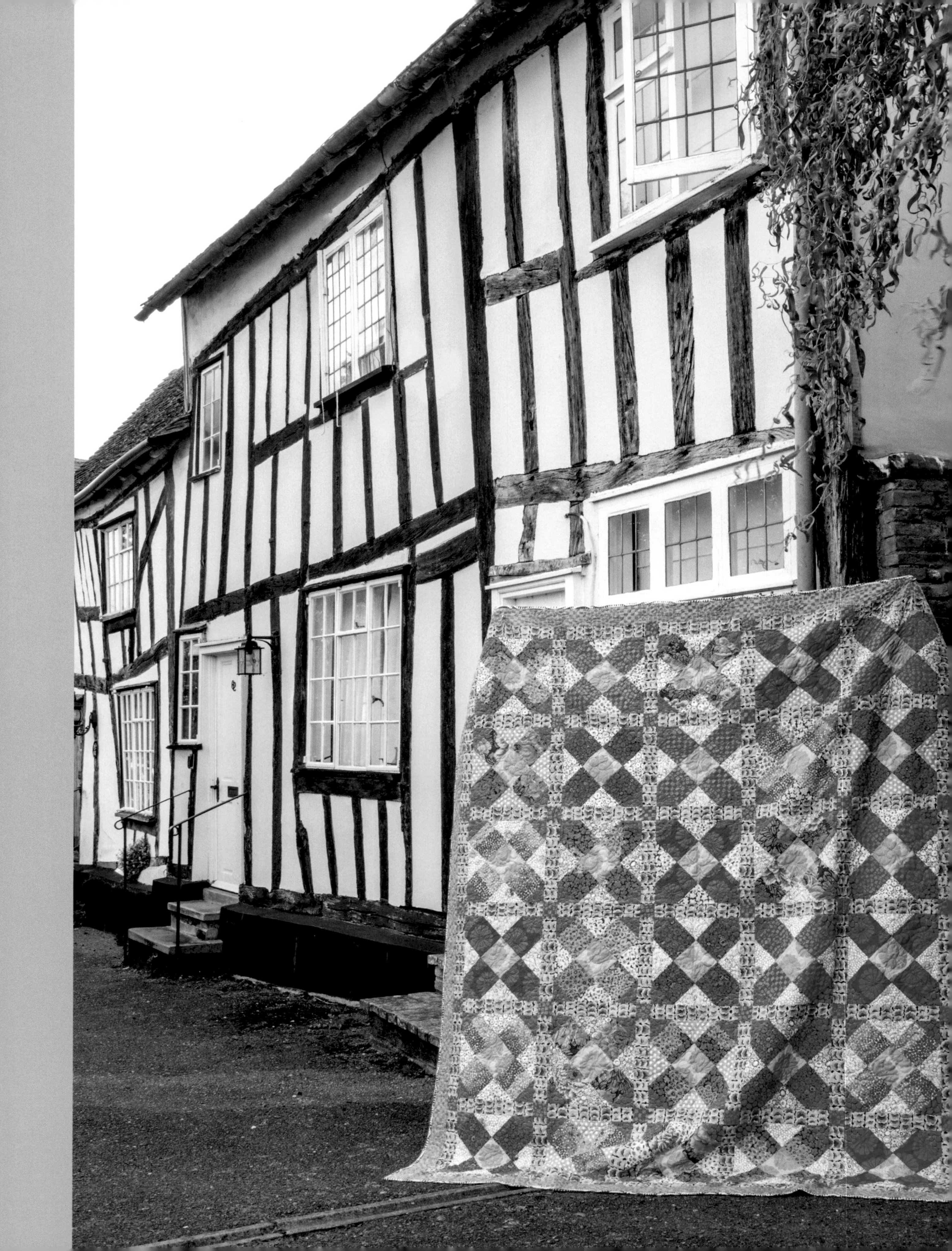

Opal Crosses
by Kaffe Fassett

What is it about the combination of blue and white that makes it so eternally fresh and attractive? This pale pink house sets these pastel blues off to a 'T'.

Mirror Columns
by Kaffe Fassett

It was good to make a simple columns quilt to showcase the blowsy nature of our current fabric prints, shown off here against the pale plaster and bleached wood of this spectacular house.

Tiddlywinks Rosy
by Liza Prior Lucy

This layout is one of the very first we played with in our hardback book, *Glorious Patchwork*. How this cobalt version of Liza's glows against the weathered barn!

Shaded Squares
by Kaffe Fassett

Our Shot Cottons and Woven Stripes were perfect to show off on this traditional pink house. I love the way the diagonals in the quilt are echoed by those diagonal bracing timbers.

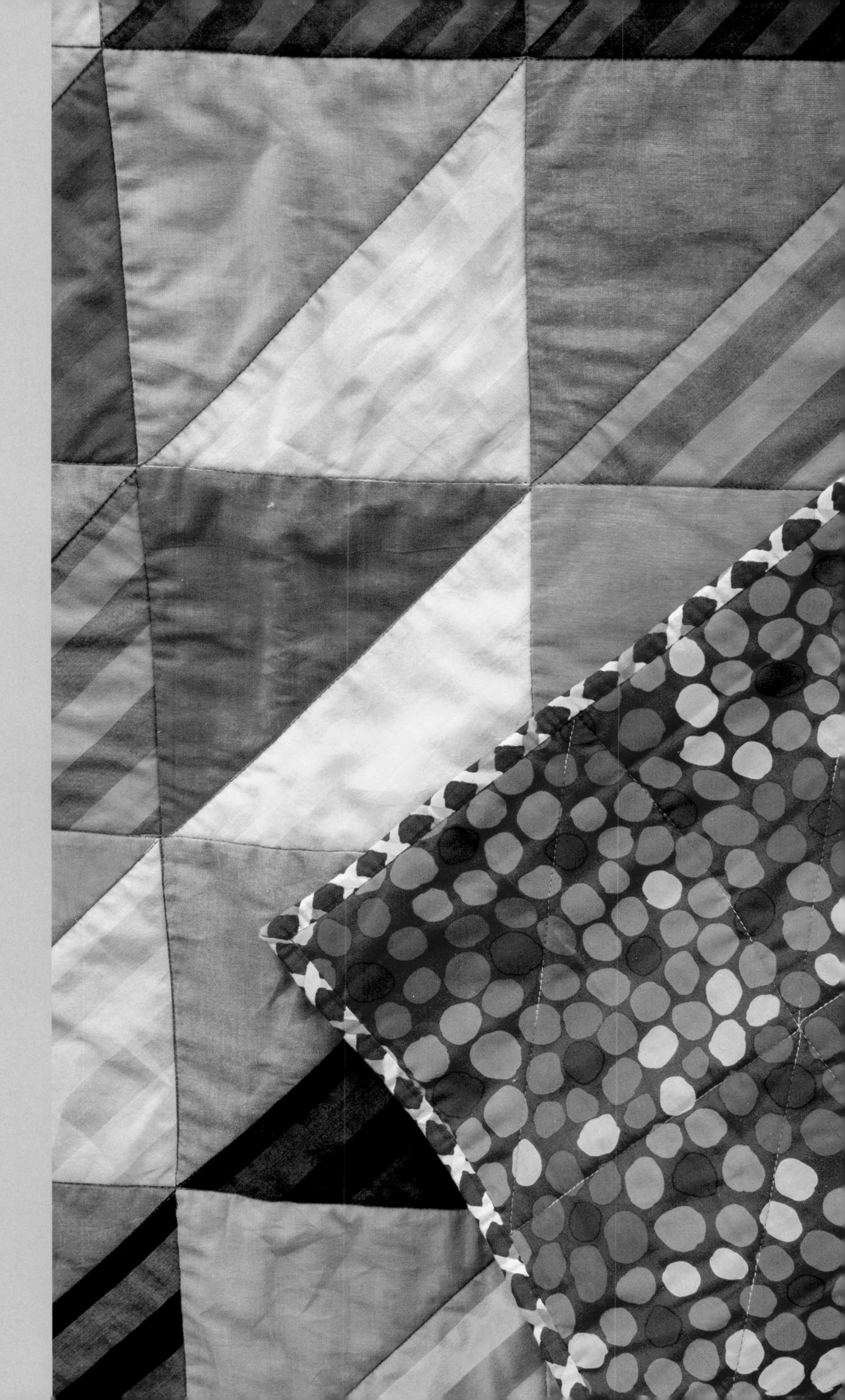

paperweight checkerboard *

Kaffe Fassett

This is a 'one patch' quilt, perfect for beginners, in which the entire top is made with same-size, softly contrasting squares.

SIZE OF FINISHED QUILT

55in x 65in (140cm x 165cm)

FABRICS

Fabrics have been calculated at a maximum width of 40in (102cm). They have been given a number – see Fabric Swatch Diagram for details.

Patchwork Fabrics

PAPERWEIGHT

Fabric 1	Grey	1¾yd (1.7m)

* see also Binding Fabric

Fabric 2	Pastel	⅜yd (40cm)

SPOT

Fabric 3	Sky	⅜yd (40cm)
Fabric 4	Silver	¼yd (25cm)
Fabric 5	Soft Blue	⅜yd (40cm)

MILLEFIORE

Fabric 6	Lilac	⅜yd (40cm)
Fabric 7	Grey	¼yd (25cm)
Fabric 8	Pink	¼yd (25cm)

GUINEA FLOWER

Fabric 9	Grey	¼yd (25cm)

BRASSICA

Fabric 10	Sky	⅜yd (40cm)

ABORIGINAL DOT

Fabric 11	Cream	⅜yd (40cm)

Backing and Binding Fabrics

AGATE

Fabric 12	Pink	3⅝yd (3.4m)

PAPERWEIGHT

Fabric 1	Grey	⅝yd (60cm)

* see also Patchwork Fabric

Batting

65in x 75in (165cm x 191cm)

PATCHES

Patches are 5in (12.7cm) finished squares, set in a checkerboard pattern of darker and paler squares in 13 rows of 11. Fabric 1 is used for all the darker squares.

CUTTING OUT

Fabric is cut across the width unless otherwise stated.

FABRIC SWATCH DIAGRAM

Patchwork Fabrics

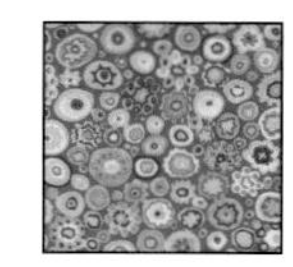

Fabric 1
PAPERWEIGHT
Grey
GP20GY

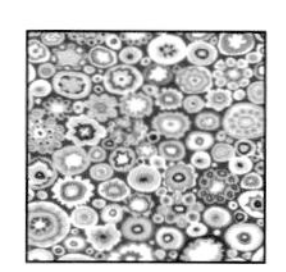

Fabric 2
PAPERWEIGHT
Pastel
GP20PT

Fabric 3
SPOT
Sky
GP70SK

Fabric 4
SPOT
Silver
GP70SV

Fabric 5
SPOT
Soft Blue
GP70SF

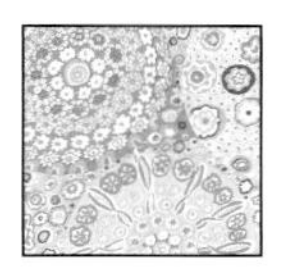

Fabric 6
MILLEFIORE
Lilac
GP92LI

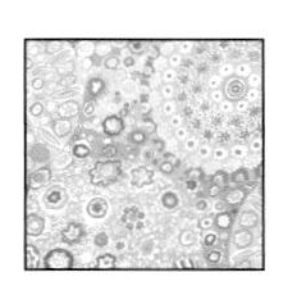

Fabric 7
MILLEFIORE
Grey
GP92GY

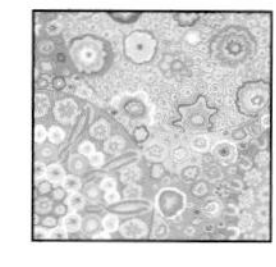

Fabric 8
MILLEFIORE
Pink
GP92PK

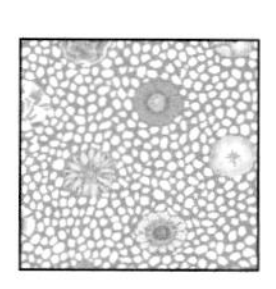

Fabric 9
GUINEA FLOWER
Grey
GP59GY

Fabric 10
BRASSICA
Sky
PJ051SK

Fabric 11
ABORIGINAL DOT
Cream
GP71CM

Backing and Binding Fabrics

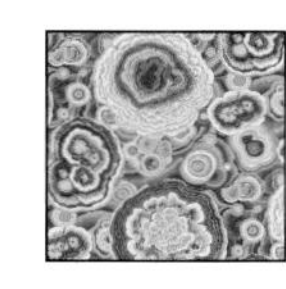

Fabric 12
AGATE
Pink
PJ106PK

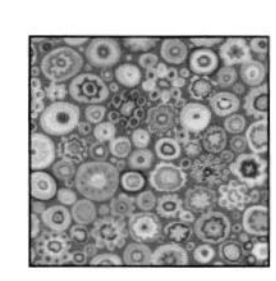

Fabric 1
PAPERWEIGHT
Grey
GP20GY

Squares

Cut strips 5½in (14cm) wide across the width and cross cut 5½in (14cm) squares. Each strip will yield 7 squares. Cut a total of 143 squares from fabrics as follows:
Fabric 1 (11 strips) 71 squares;
Fabric 2 (2 strips) 8 squares;
Fabric 3 (2 strips) 8 squares;
Fabric 4 (1 strip) 7 squares;
Fabric 5 (2 strips) 9 squares;
Fabric 6 (2 strips) 9 squares;
Fabric 7 (1 strip) 4 squares;
Fabric 8 (1 strip) 4 squares;
Fabric 9 (1 strip) 6 squares;
Fabric 10 (no strips) 8 squares avoiding the darkest areas;
Fabric 11 (2 strips) 9 squares.

Backing

Cut Fabric 12 in half to make 2 pieces 65in x 40in (165cm x 101.6cm).

Binding

From Fabric 1 cut 7 strips 2½in (6.4cm) wide. Remove selvedges and sew strips end to end with 45-degree seams (see page 141).

MAKING THE QUILT

Using a design wall will help to place patches in the required layout.

Use ¼in (6mm) seams throughout.

Lay out the blocks referring to the Quilt Assembly Diagram and the quilt photograph for fabric placement. Sew 11 squares together for each row. Press seams in the same direction in alternating rows – odd rows to the left, even rows to the right – to allow the seams to lie flat. Sew the 13 rows together, pinning to avoid stretching and taking care to match crossing seams as you sew.

FINISHING THE QUILT

Remove the selvedges from backing Fabric 12 and sew the 2 pieces together. Trim to make a piece 65in x 75in (165cm x 191cm).

Press the quilt top. Layer the quilt top, batting and backing, and baste together (see page 140).

Quilt as desired.

Trim the quilt edges and attach the binding (see page 141).

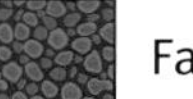 Fabric 1

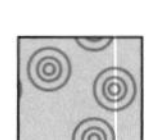 Fabric 7

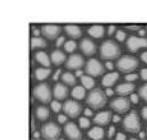 Fabric 2

 Fabric 8

 Fabric 3

 Fabric 9

 Fabric 4

 Fabric 10

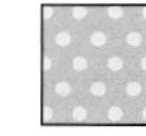 Fabric 5

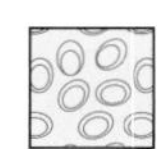 Fabric 11

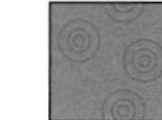 Fabric 6

QUILT ASSEMBLY DIAGRAM

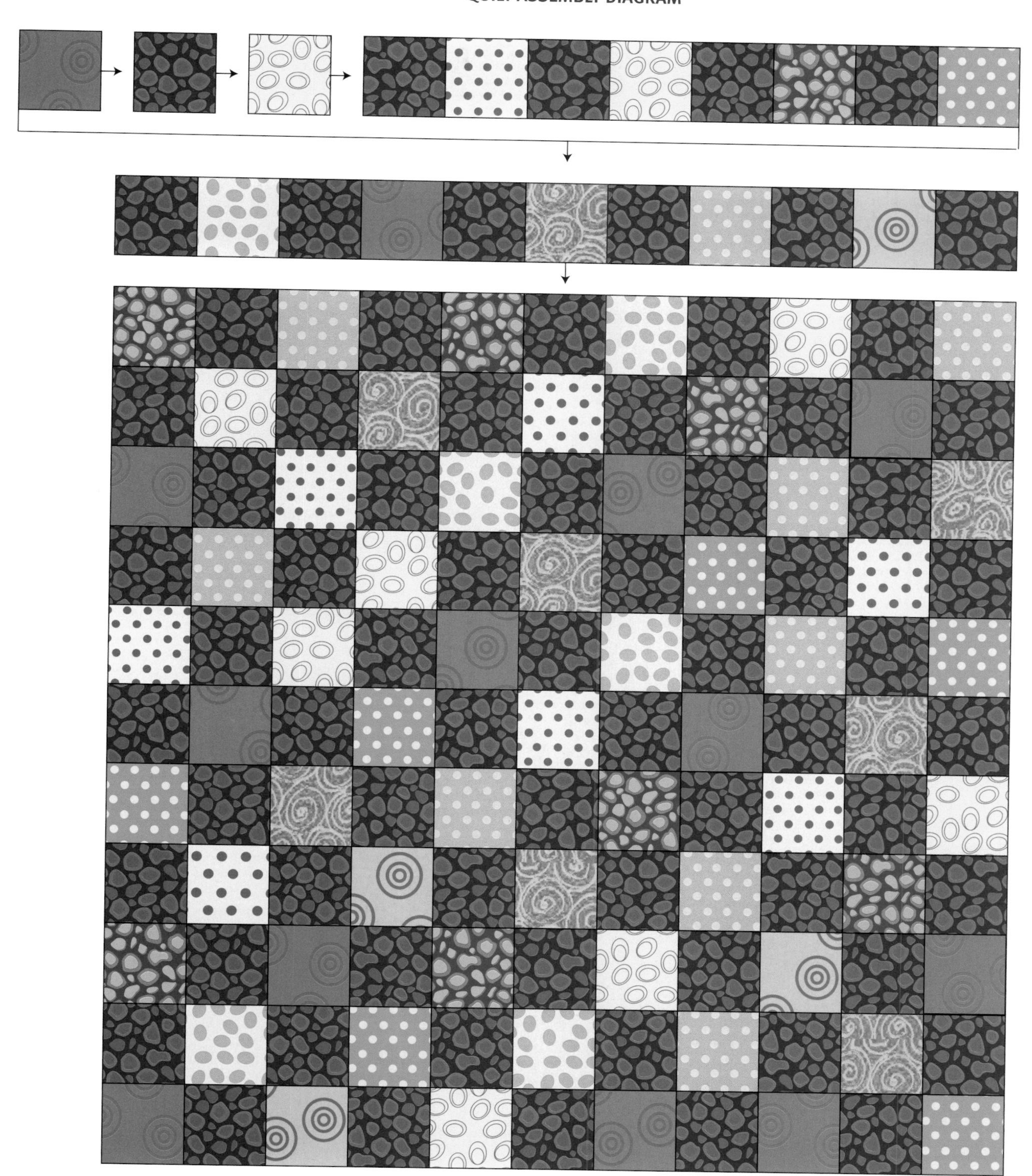

bright weave **

Liza Prior Lucy

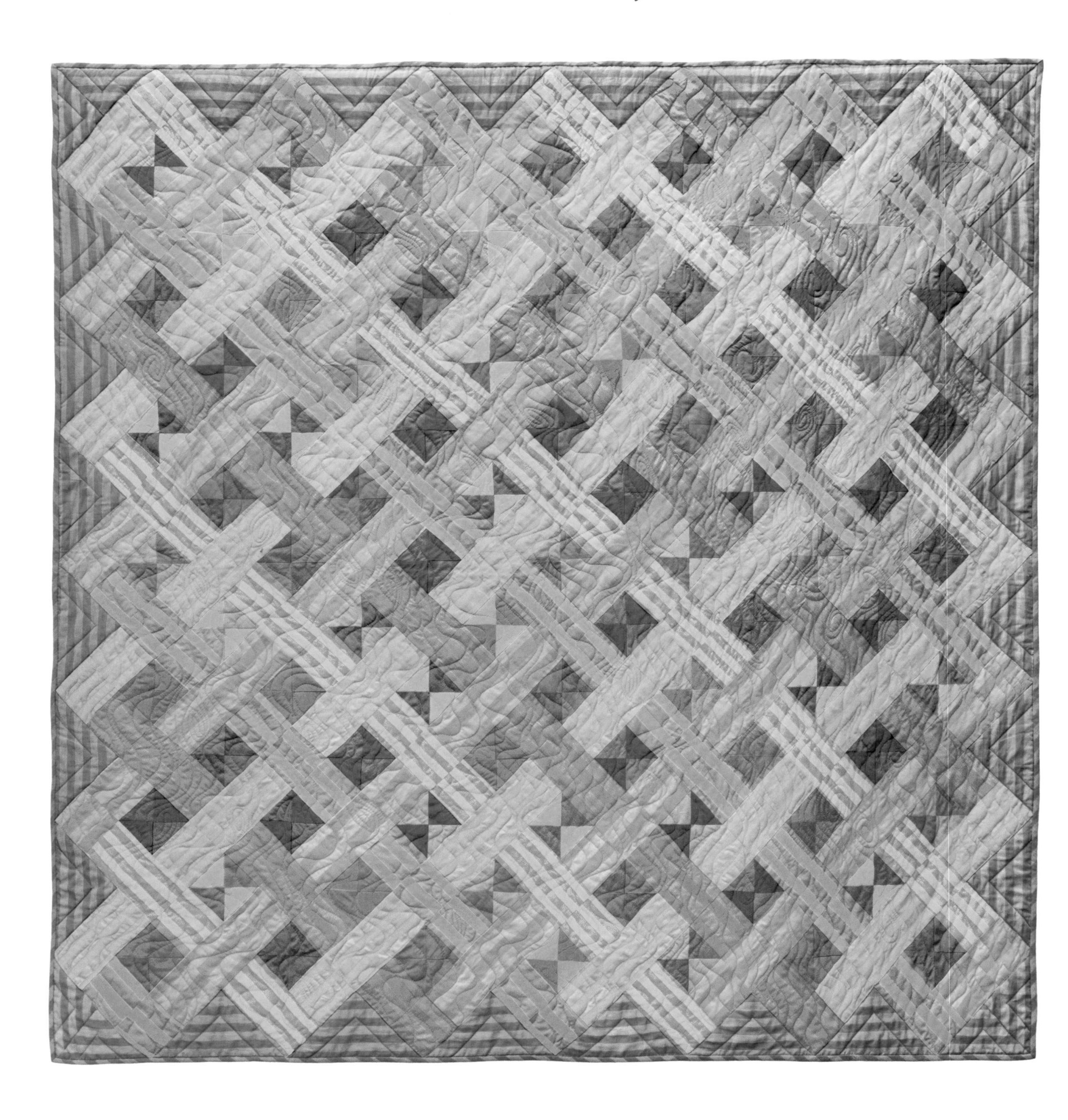

This is a variation of a pattern called African Weave that we first made in soft colours in *Passionate Patchwork*. This version features the newest bright-coloured Shot Cottons and Stripes woven in India.

FABRIC SWATCH DIAGRAM

Patchwork Fabrics

Fabric 1
WIDE STRIPE
Aloe
SS001AO

Fabric 2
WIDE STRIPE
Turmeric
SS001TU

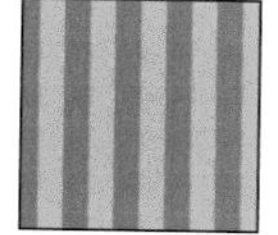

Fabric 3
WIDE STRIPE
Cantaloupe
SS001CA

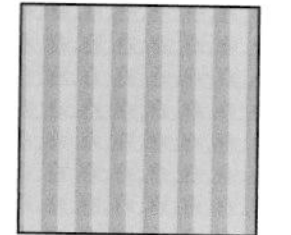

Fabric 4
NARROW STRIPE
Gooseberry
SS002GO

Fabric 5
NARROW STRIPE
Sulfur
SS002SU

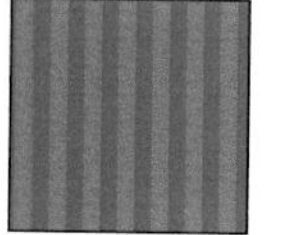

Fabric 6
NARROW STRIPE
Plaster
SS002PJ

Fabric 7
SHOT COTTON
Airforce
SC104AF

Fabric 8
SHOT COTTON
Khaki
SC107KH

Fabric 9
SHOT COTTON
Camellia
SC109CX

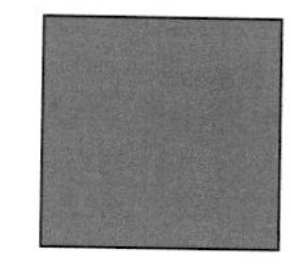

Fabric 10
SHOT COTTON
Pistachio
SC111PX

Fabric 11
SHOT COTTON
Sunflower
SC112SF

Fabric 12
SHOT COTTON
Lupin
SC113LU

Fabric 13
SHOT COTTON
Opal
SC114OP

Fabric 14
SHOT COTTON
Paprika
SC001PP

Backing and Binding Fabrics

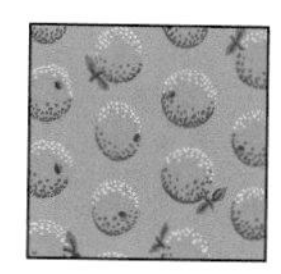

Fabric 15
ORANGES
Blue
GP177BL

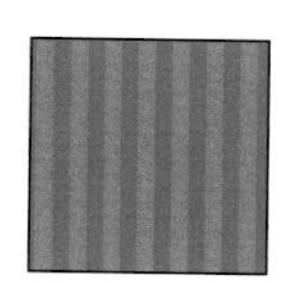

Fabric 6
NARROW STRIPE
Plaster
SS002PJ

SIZE OF FINISHED QUILT

64in x 64in (163cm x 163cm).

FABRICS

Fabrics have been calculated at a maximum width of 40in (102cm). They have been given a number – see Fabric Swatch Diagram for details.

Patchwork Fabrics

WIDE STRIPE

Fabric 1	Aloe	¾yd (70cm)
Fabric 2	Turmeric	⅝yd (60cm)
Fabric 3	Cantaloupe	⅝yd (60cm)

NARROW STRIPE

Fabric 4	Gooseberry	¾yd (70cm)
Fabric 5	Sulfur	⅝yd (60cm)
Fabric 6	Plaster	¾yd (70cm)

* see also Binding Fabric

SHOT COTTON

Fabric 7	Airforce	⅜yd (40cm)
Fabric 8	Khaki	⅜yd (40cm)
Fabric 9	Camellia	⅜yd (40cm)
Fabric 10	Pistachio	⅜yd (40cm)
Fabric 11	Sunflower	⅜yd (40cm)
Fabric 12	Lupin	⅜yd (40cm)
Fabric 13	Opal	⅜yd (40cm)
Fabric 14	Paprika	⅜yd (40cm)

Backing and Binding Fabrics

ORANGES

Fabric 15	Blue	4yd (3.7m)

NARROW STRIPE

Fabric 6	Plaster	⅝yd (60cm)

* see also Patchwork Fabric

Batting

72in x 72in (183cm x 183cm)

TEMPLATES

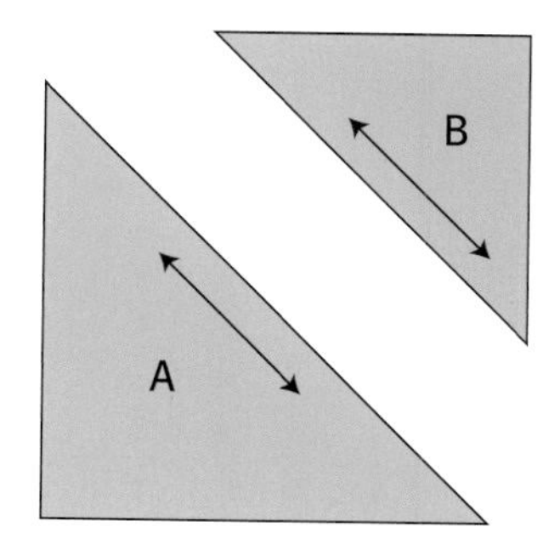

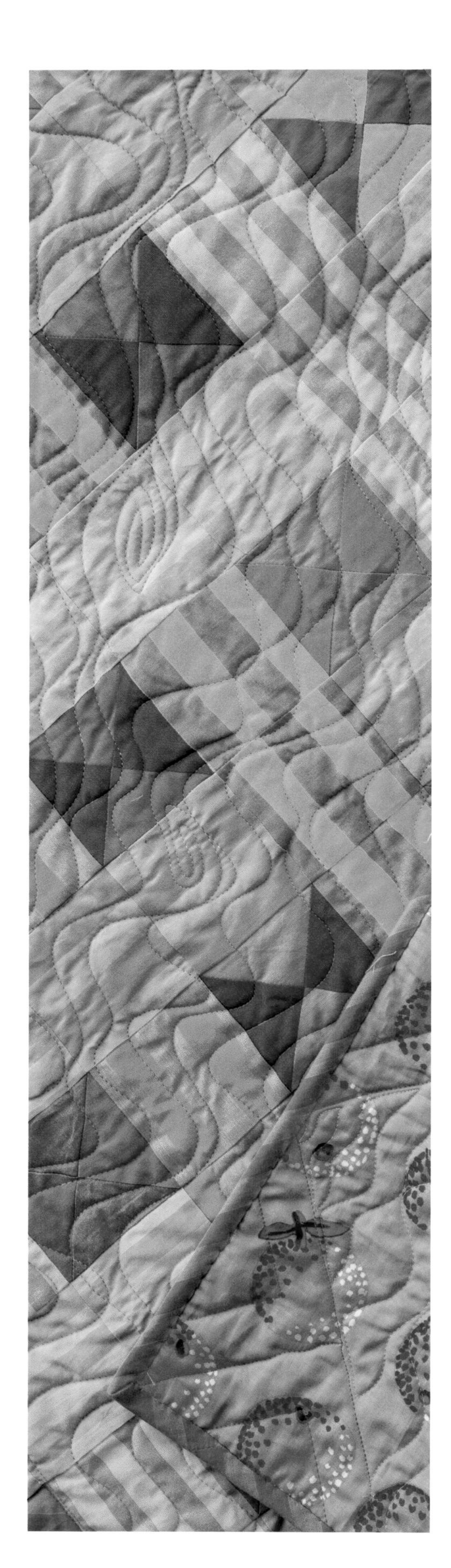

PATCHES

This quilt is constructed 'on point' with squares and hourglass blocks, surrounded by an edging of striped setting triangles. The squares are all cut from striped fabrics, arranged so as to appear to weave throughout. Do not try to line up the stripes – it looks much better if not – nor try to place each of the Shot Cotton colours exactly as in the original. Make sure the darker shades are in the upper right and lower left of the 'on point' squares.

CUTTING OUT

Fabric is cut across the width except for the setting triangles which are cut from lengthwise strips so that the stripes run parallel to the edge of the quilt.

Hourglass Patches

From each of Fabrics 7, 8, 9, 10, 11, 12, 13 and 14 cut 2 strips 4¼in (10.8cm) wide. Cross cut 11 squares 4¼in (10.8cm) from each fabric.
Total: 88 squares.

Striped Square Patches

For the woven striped patches, cut strips 3½in (8.9cm) wide and cross cut squares at 3½in (8.9cm). Cut strips and a total of 308 squares as follows:
Fabric 1 (7 strips) 77 squares;
Fabric 2 (5 strips) 50 squares;
Fabric 3 (5 strips) 52 squares;
Fabric 4 (7 strips) 77 squares;
Fabric 5 (5 strips) 52 squares.

Border Setting Triangles

From Fabric 6 cut 6 strips 4⅞in (12.4cm) wide **down the length** of the fabric, and cut triangles using either Template A (see page 135) or as follows:
Using the 45-degree angle mark on your rotary ruler and, referring to the Triangle Cutting Diagram, cut 24 Triangle A patches, 4 from each strip, rotating the template/ruler after each cut.
From the remaining Fabric 6 cut 2 strips 3⅞in (9.8cm) wide **down the length** of the fabric. Cut triangles using either Template B (see page 135) or as follows:
Using the 45-degree angle mark on your rotary ruler and referring to the Triangle Cutting Diagram, cut 8 Triangle B patches, rotating the template/ruler after each cut.

Backing

Cut Fabric 15 backing fabric in half.

TRIANGLE CUTTING DIAGRAM

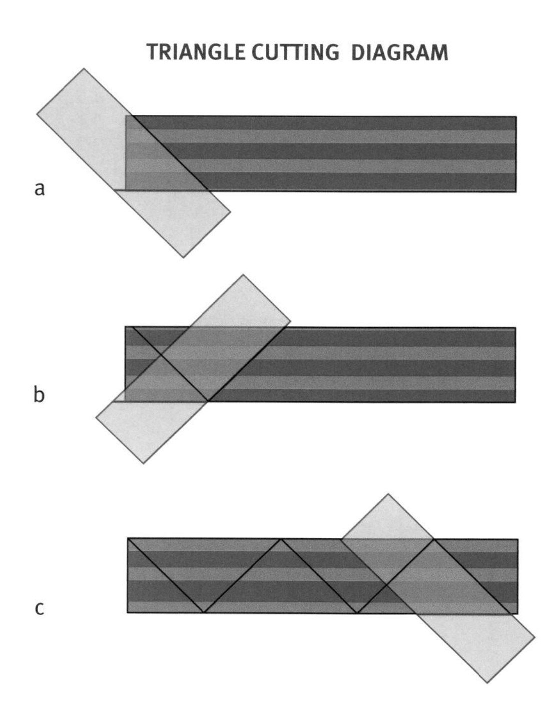

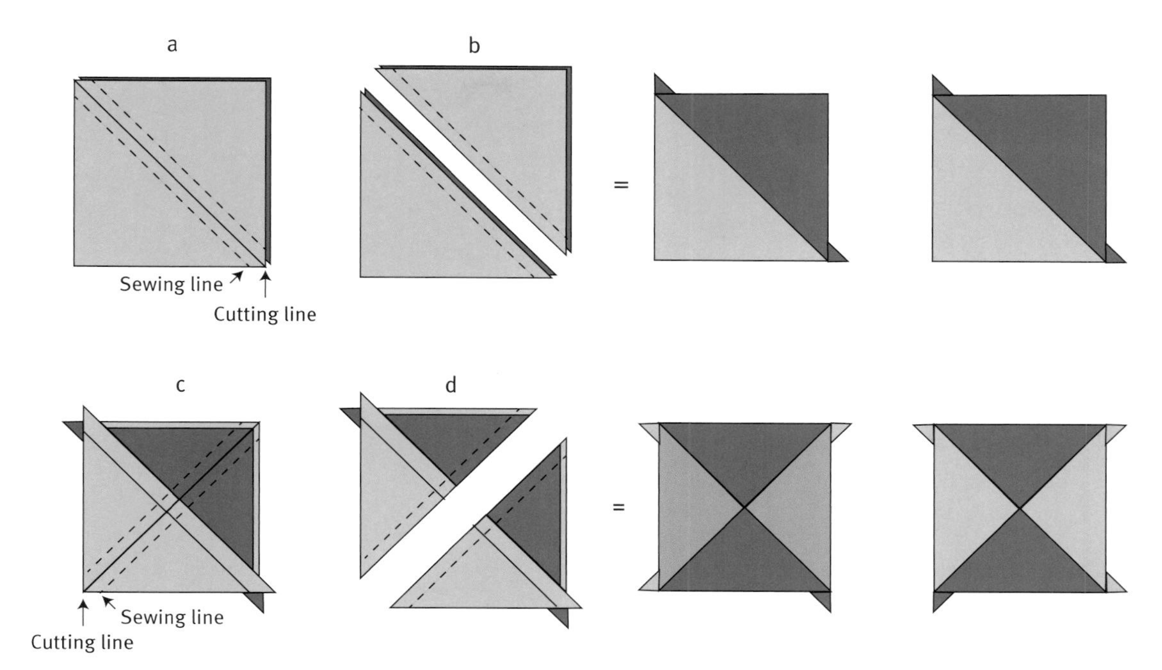

Binding

From Fabric 6 remove selvedges and cut 9 bias strips 2½in (6.4cm) wide, cutting diagonally at 45 degrees. Sew end to end with 45-degree seams (see page 141).

MAKING THE QUILT

Using a design wall will help to place patches in the required layout.
Use ¼in (6mm) seams throughout.

Making the Hourglass Patches

Each pair of contrasting 4¼in (10.8cm) squares will make 2 hourglass patches. Take 2 squares of contrasting fabrics, referring to the Quilt Assembly Diagram (overleaf) and quilt photograph for fabric choices. Place right sides together, matching the edges accurately, and mark a diagonal cutting line from corner to corner. Referring to the Patch Diagram, stitch the squares ¼in (6mm) each side of the cutting line (a).
Cut along the marked cutting line to separate the 2 pieced squares (b) and press the seam allowance on both squares towards the darker fabric.
Place the 2 pieced squares right sides together. matching the seam lines accurately, with the dark side of the upper square laid against the pale side of the lower square. Mark a diagonal cutting line from corner to corner at right angles to the previous sewing line. Stitch the squares ¼in (6mm) each side of the cutting line as before (c).
Cut along the marked cutting line to separate the 2 completed hourglass patches (d) and press the seam allowance to one side.
Make a total of 86 patches – you will need 85 of these.

ASSEMBLING THE QUILT

Lay out the blocks referring to the Quilt Assembly Diagram and quilt photograph. Be sure to place the darker tone of each hourglass patch in the upper right and lower left position. Add the side and corner setting triangles to the layout. Stand back to check the layout is correct. Sew the patches into diagonal rows as shown in the Quilt Assembly Diagram. Press seams in the same direction on alternate rows – odd rows to the left, even rows to the right– to allow seams to lie flat. Sew the rows together carefully matching crossing seams.

FINISHING THE QUILT

Sew the Fabric 15 backing pieces together and trim to form a piece 72in x 72in (183cm x 183cm).
Press the quilt top. Layer the quilt top, batting and backing, and baste together (see page 140).
Quilt as desired.
Trim the quilt edges and attach the binding (see page 141).

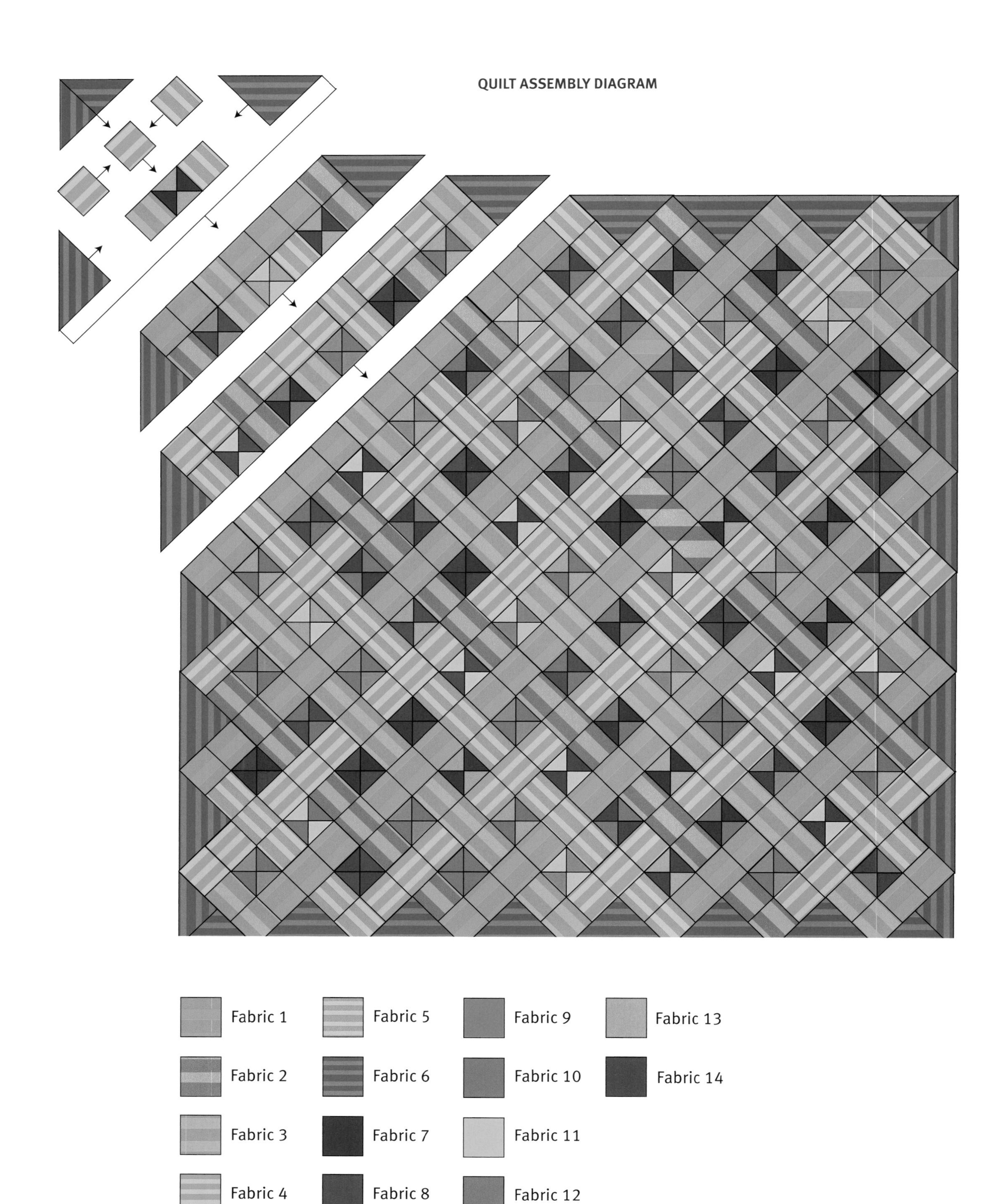
QUILT ASSEMBLY DIAGRAM
Fabric 1
Fabric 2
Fabric 3
Fabric 4
Fabric 5
Fabric 6
Fabric 7
Fabric 8
Fabric 9
Fabric 10
Fabric 11
Fabric 12
Fabric 13
Fabric 14

trip around the snowball **

Kaffe Fassett

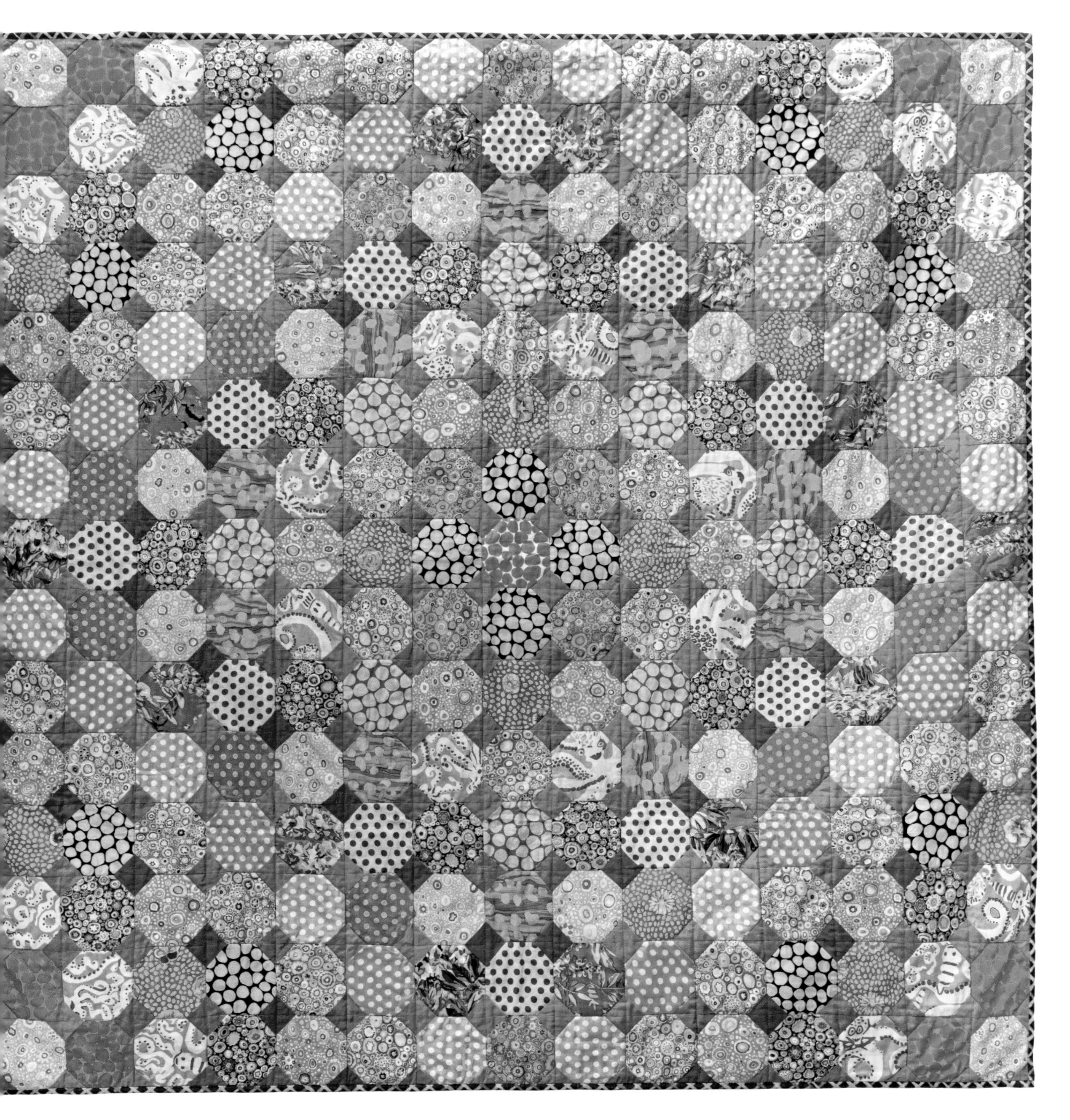

A series of concentric snowball blocks arranged in a diamond pattern showcases some of Kaffe's fabrics from the latest collections.

SIZE OF FINISHED QUILT
64in x 64in (163cm x 163cm)

FABRICS
Fabrics have been calculated at a maximum width of 40in (102cm). They have been given a number – see Fabric Swatch Diagram for details.

Patchwork Fabrics

JUMBLE		
Fabric 1	Cobalt	¼yd (25cm)
JUMBLE		
Fabric 2	Rose	⅜yd (40cm)
JUMBLE		
Fabric 3	Turquoise	¼yd (25cm)
JUMBLE		
Fabric 4	Magenta	¼yd (25cm)
PAPERWEIGHT		
Fabric 5	Pink	¼yd (25cm)
PAPERWEIGHT		
Fabric 6	Sludge	⅝yd (60cm)
PAPERWEIGHT		
Fabric 7	Pumpkin	½yd (50cm)
GUINEA FLOWER		
Fabric 8	Apricot	⅜yd (40cm)
ROMAN GLASS		
Fabric 9	Lavender	½yd (50cm)
ROMAN GLASS		
Fabric 10	Pink	⅜yd (40cm)
OCTOPUS		
Fabric 11	Turquoise	½yd (50cm)
STREAM		
Fabric 12	Orange	⅜yd (40cm)
SPOT		
Fabric 13	Mauve	⅜yd (40cm)
SPOT		
Fabric 14	Red	¼yd (25cm)
SPOT		
Fabric 15	Spring	⅜yd (40cm)
SPOT		
Fabric 16	Steel	⅜yd (40cm)
WISTERIA		
Fabric 17	Red	⅜yd (40cm)
SHOT COTTON		
Fabric 18	Pistachio	½yd (50cm)
SHOT COTTON		
Fabric 19	Lupin	⅝yd (60cm)
SHOT COTTON		
Fabric 20	Paprika	½yd (50cm)
SHOT COTTON		
Fabric 21	Blood Orange	½yd (50cm)
SHOT COTTON		
Fabric 22	Camellia	⅜yd (40cm)

FABRIC SWATCH DIAGRAM

Patchwork Fabrics

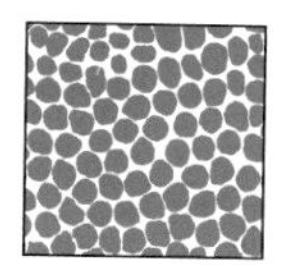

Fabric 1
JUMBLE
Cobalt
BM53CB

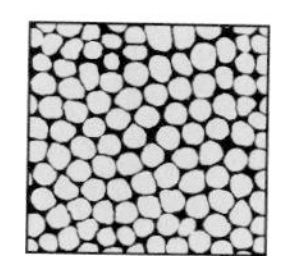

Fabric 2
JUMBLE
Rose
BM53RO

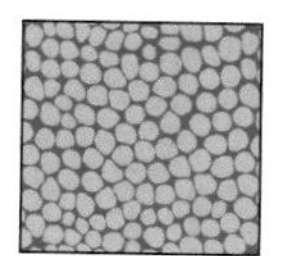

Fabric 3
JUMBLE
Turquoise
BM53TQ

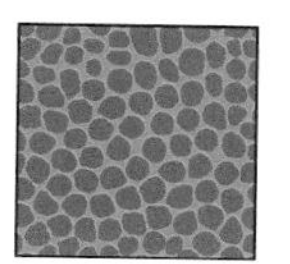

Fabric 4
JUMBLE
Magenta
BM53MG

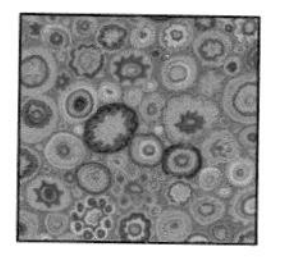

Fabric 5
PAPERWEIGHT
Pink
GP20PK

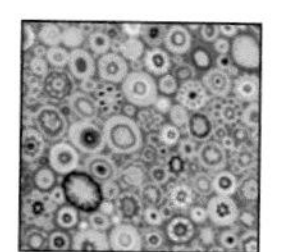

Fabric 6
PAPERWEIGHT
Sludge
GP20SL

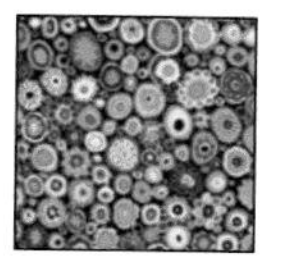

Fabric 7
PAPERWEIGHT
Pumpkin
GP20PN

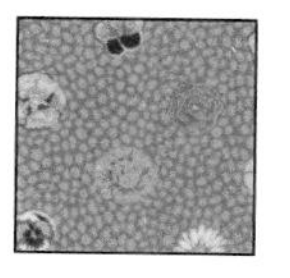

Fabric 8
GUINEA FLOWER
Apricot
GP51AP

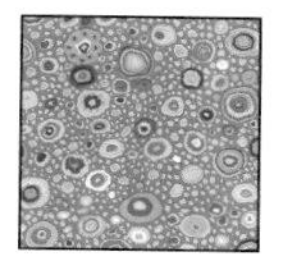

Fabric 9
ROMAN GLASS
Lavender
GP02LV

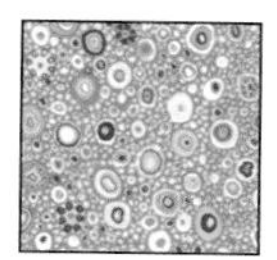

Fabric 10
ROMAN GLASS
Pink
GP01PK

Fabric 11
OCTOPUS
Turquoise
BM74TQ

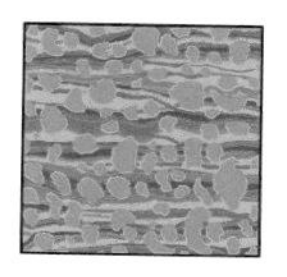

Fabric 12
STREAM
Orange
BM75OR

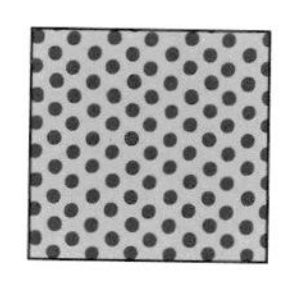

Fabric 13
SPOT
Mauve
GP70MV

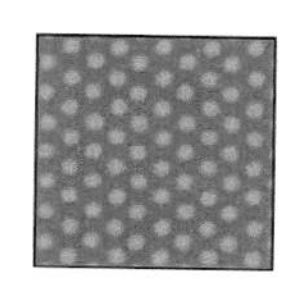

Fabric 14
SPOT
Red
GP70RD

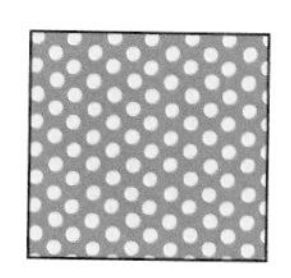

Fabric 15
SPOT
Spring
GP70SP

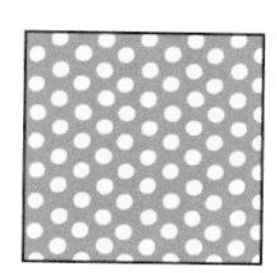

Fabric 16
SPOT
Steel
GP70ST

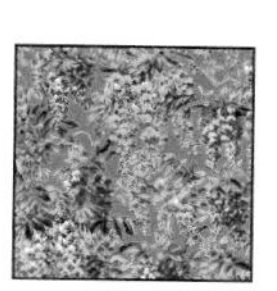

Fabric 17
WISTERIA
Red
PJ102RD

Fabric 18
SHOT COTTON
Pistachio
SCGP111

Fabric 19
SHOT COTTON
Lupin
SCGP113

Fabric 20
SHOT COTTON
Paprika
SCGP101

Fabric 21
SHOT COTTON
Blood Orange
SCGP110

Fabric 22
SHOT COTTON
Camellia
SCGP109

Backing and Binding Fabrics

Fabric 23
BRASSICA
Orange
PJ51OR

Fabric 24
MAD PLAID
Maroon
BM37MM

Backing and Binding Fabrics
BRASSICA
Fabric 23 Orange 4yd (3.7m)
MAD PLAID
Fabric 24 Maroon ⅝yd (60cm)

Batting
72in x 72in (183cm x 183cm)

PATCHES
Each snowball block is made with 1 large feature square 4¾in x 4¾in (12.1cm x 12.1cm) and 4 small corner squares 1¾in x 1¾in (4.5cm x 4.5cm).

CUTTING OUT
Fabric is cut across the width unless otherwise stated.

Large Feature Squares
Cut strips 4¾in (12.1cm) wide and cross cut squares 4¾in (12.1cm). Each strip will yield 8 squares.
Cut a total of 225 squares from fabrics as follows:
Fabric 1 (1 strip) 1 square;
Fabric 2 (2 strips) 12 squares;
Fabric 3 (1 strip) 8 squares;
Fabric 4 (1 strip) 8 squares;
Fabric 5 (1 strip) 8 squares;
Fabric 6 (4 strips) 30 squares;
Fabric 7 (3 strips) 18 squares;
Fabric 8 (2 strips) 14 squares;
Fabric 9 (3 strips) 18 squares;
Fabric 10 (2 strips) 16 squares;
Fabric 11 (3 strips) 20 squares;
Fabric 12 (2 strips) 10 squares;
Fabric 13 (2 strips) 12 squares;
Fabric 14 (1 strip) 8 squares;
Fabric 15 (2 strips) 12 squares;
Fabric 16 (2 strips) 16 squares;
Fabric 17 (2 strips) 14 squares.

Small Corner Squares
Cut strips 1¾in (4.5cm) wide and cross cut squares 1¾in (4.5cm). Each strip will yield 22 squares.
Cut a total of 900 squares from fabrics as follows:
Fabric 18 (9 strips) 180 squares;
Fabric 19 (11 strips) 240 squares;
Fabric 20 (9 strips) 192 squares;
Fabric 21 (8 strips) 176 squares;
Fabric 22 (6 strips) 112 squares.

BLOCK ASSEMBLY DIAGRAM

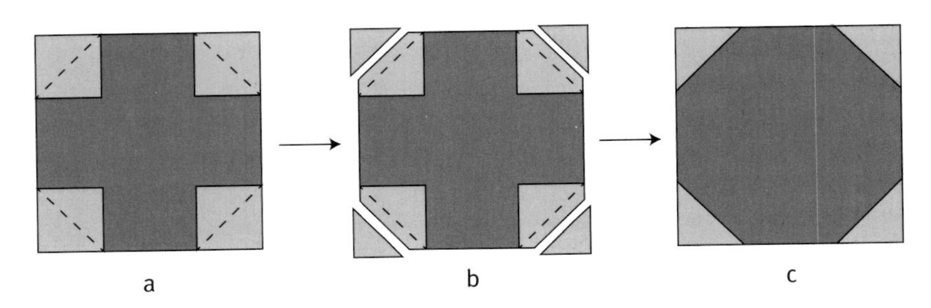

Backing
From Fabric 23 cut 1 piece 40in x 72in (101.6cm x 183cm) and 1 piece 32½in x 72in (82.6cm x 183cm).

Binding
From Fabric 24 cut 7 strips 2½in (6.4cm) wide. Remove selvedges and sew strips end to end with 45-degree seams (see page 141).

MAKING THE QUILT
Using a design wall will help to place patches in the required layout.
Use ¼in (6mm) seams throughout.
Arrange all the snowball blocks on the design wall, ensuring that the corner colours line up and match each other. There should be 4 corner triangles in the same colour meeting at each corner.

Snowball Blocks
Take one large feature square and 4 small corner squares. Following the sequence in the Block Assembly Diagram, place the 4 small corner squares right sides together onto each corner of the large feature square, matching the edges carefully. Stitch diagonally across the small squares as shown (a). Trim the corners to a ¼in (6mm) seam allowance (b). Press the seams towards the block centre (c). Make 225 blocks in total and return them to the design wall.

Quilt Assembly
Lay out the completed blocks on a design wall in 15 rows of 15 blocks, referring to the Quilt Assembly Diagram and the quilt photograph for block placement, and noting the symmetrical layout. Sew the blocks together into rows, pressing seams in the same direction on alternate rows – odd rows to the left, even rows to the right. This will allow the finished seams to lie flat. Pin, then sew the rows together, taking care to match crossing seams.

FINISHING THE QUILT
Sew the two Fabric 23 backing pieces together to form a piece 72in x 72in (183cm x 183cm).
Press the quilt top. Layer the quilt top, batting and backing, and baste together (see page 140).
Quilt as desired.
Trim the quilt edges and attach the binding (see page 141).

QUILT ASSEMBLY DIAGRAM

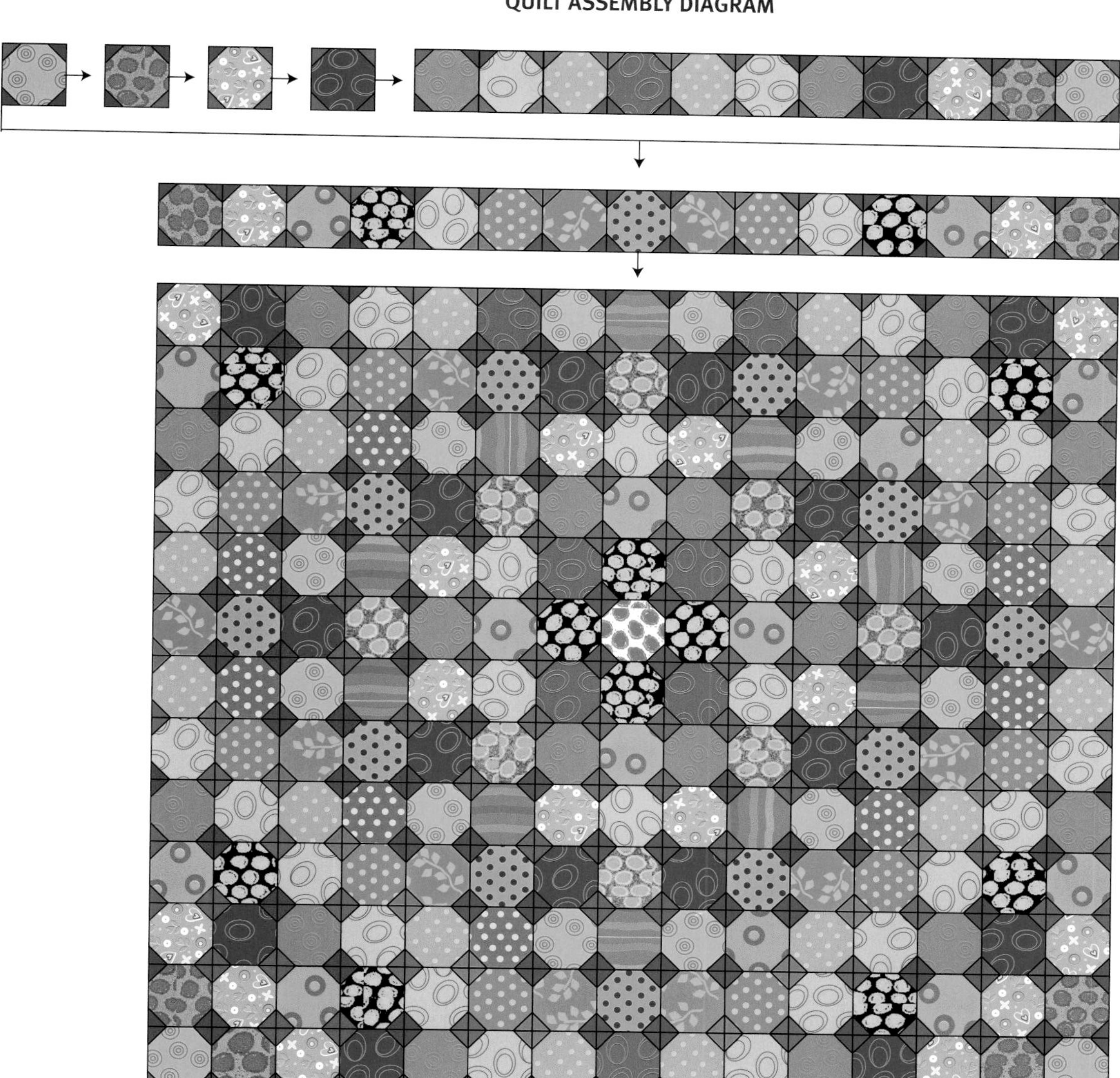

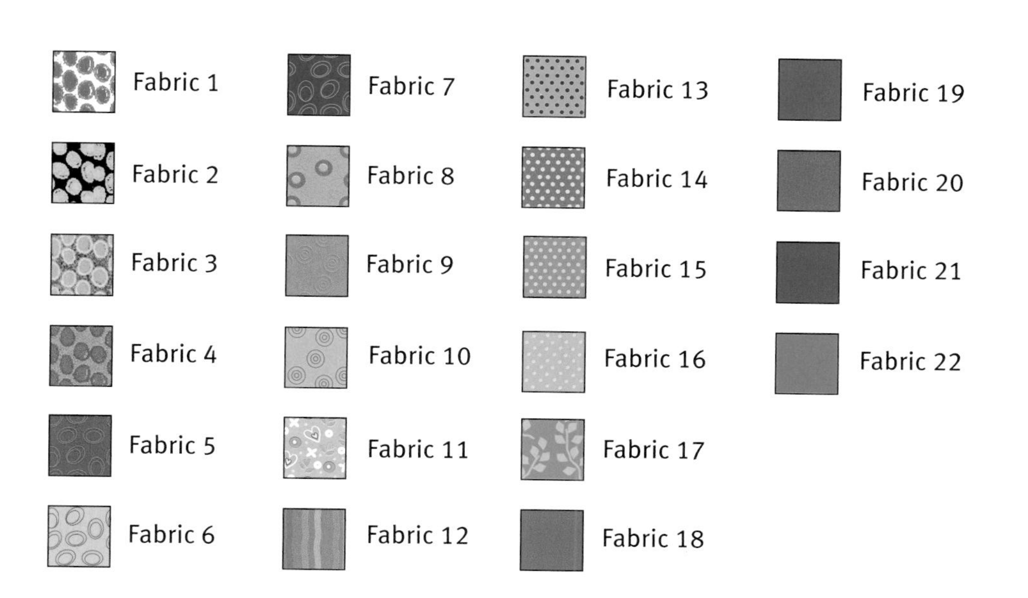

woodstock **

Liza Prior Lucy

This combination of star and snowball blocks creates an additional pieced, diagonal sashing effect. The large snowballs are perfect for featuring bold large-scale motifs.

SIZE OF FINISHED QUILT

72in x 90in (183cm x 229cm)

FABRICS

Fabrics have been calculated at a maximum width of 40in (102cm). They have been given a number – see Fabric Swatch Diagram for details.

Patchwork Fabrics

SNOWBALL CENTRES:

COLEUS

Fabric 1	Gold	¾yd (70cm)

FEATHERS

Fabric 2	Lime	⅝yd (60cm)

BROCADE PEONY

Fabric 3	Moss	1½yd (1.4m)

CACTUS FLOWER

Fabric 4	Contrast	1yd (95cm)

GREENS:

BUTTON MOSAIC

Fabric 5	Green	⅜yd (40cm)

JUMBLE

Fabric 6	Lime	⅜yd (40cm)

SPOT

Fabric 7	Pond	⅜yd (40cm)

GARLAND

Fabric 8	Green	⅜yd (40cm)

ORANGES:

PEBBLE MOSAIC

Fabric 9	Rust	⅝yd (60cm)

PAPERWEIGHT

Fabric 10	Red	⅝yd (60cm)

SPOT

Fabric 11	Orange	⅝yd (60cm)

BUTTON MOSAIC

Fabric 12	Orange	⅝yd (60cm)

PURPLES:

DAMASK FLOWER

Fabric 13	Purple	⅜yd (40cm)

PAPERWEIGHT

Fabric 14	Purple	⅜yd (40cm)

ABORIGINAL DOT

Fabric 15	Plum	⅜yd (40cm)

* see also Binding Fabric

BUTTON MOSAIC

Fabric 16	Purple	⅜yd (40cm)

FABRIC SWATCH DIAGRAM

Patchwork Fabrics

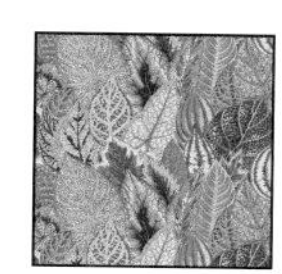

Fabric 1
COLEUS
Gold
PJ30GD

Fabric 2
FEATHERS
Lime
PJ55LM

Fabric 3
BROCADE PEONY
Moss
PJ62MS

Fabric 4
CACTUS FLOWER
Contrast
PJ96CN

Fabric 5
BUTTON MOSAIC
Green
GP182GN

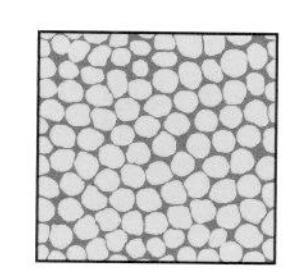

Fabric 6
JUMBLE
Lime
BM53LM

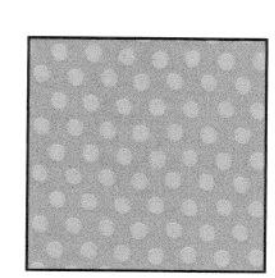

Fabric 7
SPOT
Pond
GP70PO

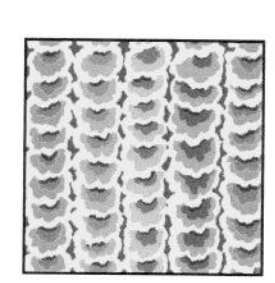

Fabric 8
GARLAND
Green
GP181GN

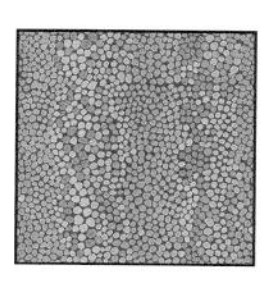

Fabric 9
PEBBLE MOSAIC
Rust
BM42RU

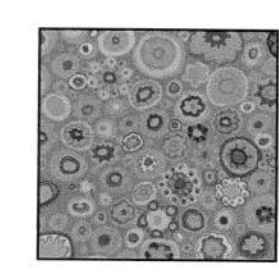

Fabric 10
PAPERWEIGHT
Red
GP20RD

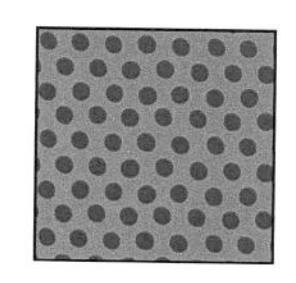

Fabric 11
SPOT
Orange
GP70OR

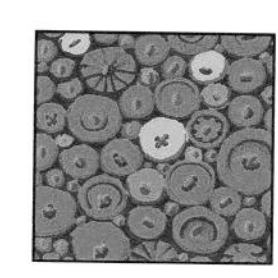

Fabric 12
BUTTON MOSAIC
Orange
GP182OR

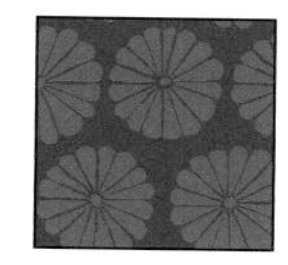

Fabric 13
DAMASK FLOWER
Purple
GP183PU

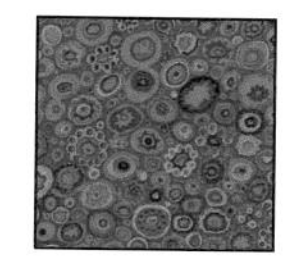

Fabric 14
PAPERWEIGHT
Purple
GP20PU

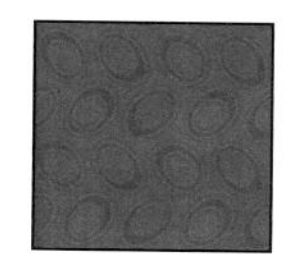

Fabric 15
ABORIGINAL DOT
Plum
GP71PL

Fabric 16
BUTTON MOSAIC
Purple
GP182PU

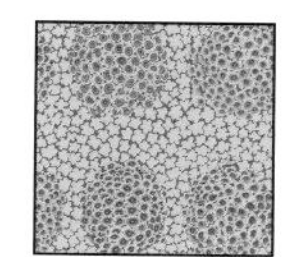

Fabric 17
HYDRANGEA
Green
GP180GN

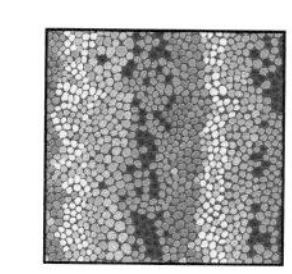

Fabric 18
PEBBLE MOSAIC
Jungle
BM42JU

Backing and Binding Fabrics

Fabric 19
LOTUS LEAF (wide)
Purple
QB007PU

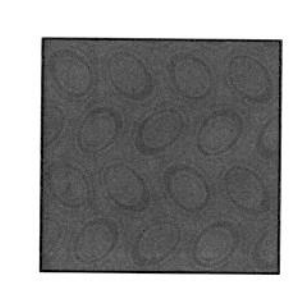

Fabric 15
ABORIGINAL DOT
Plum
GP71PL

STAR CENTRES:
HYDRANGEA
Fabric 17 Green 1½yd (1.4m)

BORDER:
PEBBLE MOSAIC
Fabric 18 Jungle 1¼yd (1.2m)

Backing and Binding Fabrics
LOTUS LEAF (wide)
Fabric 19 Purple 2¼yd (2.1m)
ABORIGINAL DOT
Fabric 15 Plum ¾yd (70cm)
* See also Patchwork Fabric

Batting
81in x 98in (206cm x 249cm)

BLOCKS
Woodstock is made of alternating star blocks and snowball blocks. They are set in 9 rows of 7 alternating blocks. There are 31 star blocks and 32 snowball blocks. All blocks are made up of squares and triangles in various sizes.

CUTTING OUT
Fabric is cut across the width except for Fabric 2 and Fabric 3 where the blossoms are fussy cut.

Star Blocks
The amounts below will yield enough to make 32 blocks. You will need 31.

Centre Squares
From Fabric 17 fussy cut 31 squares 5in x 5in (12.7cm x 12.7cm). Cut as many as possible from the blossom parts of the fabric and the remainder from the background fabric.

Green Corner Squares
From each of the green Fabrics 5, 6, 7 and 8 cut 3 strips 2¾in (7cm) wide and cross cut 31 squares 2¾in (7cm) from each fabric. Total: 124 squares.

Orange Triangles
From each of the orange Fabrics 9, 10, 11 and 12 cut 2 strips 5¾in (14.6cm) wide and cross cut 8 squares 5¾in (14.6cm) from each fabric. Cut each square diagonally from corner to corner twice to make 4 quarter-square triangles (QSTs) from each square. Total: 124 triangles.

Purple Star Triangles
From each of the purple Fabrics 13, 14, 15 and 16 cut 3 strips 3⅛in (7.9cm) wide and cross cut 31 squares 3⅛in (7.9cm) from each fabric. Cut each square diagonally from corner to corner once to make 2 half-square triangles (HSTs) from each square. Total: 248 triangles.

Snowball Blocks
Snowball Feature Squares: From each of Fabrics 1 and 2 cut 2 strips 9½in (24.1cm) wide and cross cut 8 squares 9½in (24.1cm) from each fabric.
From each of Fabrics 3 and 4 fussy cut 8 squares 9½in (24.1cm) from each fabric, centring a bloom in each square.
Snowball Corners: From the remaining orange Fabrics 9, 10, 11 and 12 cut 3 strips 2¾in (7cm) wide and cross cut 32 squares 2¾in (7cm) from each fabric.

Border
From Fabric 18 cut 8 strips 5in (12.7cm) wide. Remove the selvedges and sew together end to end, making a casual match at the seams. From the length, cut 2 pieces 81½in (207cm) long for the side borders and cut two pieces 63½in (161.3cm) for the top and bottom borders.
From the remaining Fabric 1 cut 1 strip 5in (12.7cm) wide and cross cut 4 squares 5in (12.7cm) for the border corner squares.

Backing
Trim Fabric 19 backing fabric to approx. 81in x 98in (206cm x 249cm).

Binding
From Fabric 15 cut 9 strips 2½in (6.4cm) wide. Remove selvedges and sew strips end to end with 45-degree seams (see page 141).

MAKING THE QUILT
Using a design wall will help to place patches in the required layout.
Use ¼in (6mm) seams throughout.

Making the Star Blocks
Note: These blocks are scrappy – it is not necessary to make each block exactly as in the original.
For each star block, take 8 purple star triangles, 4 green corner squares, 4 orange triangles and 1 Fabric 17 square. Referring to the Star Block Assembly Diagram, lay out the pieces, sew 2 purple triangles to each orange triangle (a) and press seams away from the purple triangles. Next sew the pieces into 3 rows (b) and again press seams away from the purple triangles. Sew the 3 rows together to complete the block (c).
Make a total of 31 blocks.

STAR BLOCK ASSEMBLY DIAGRAM

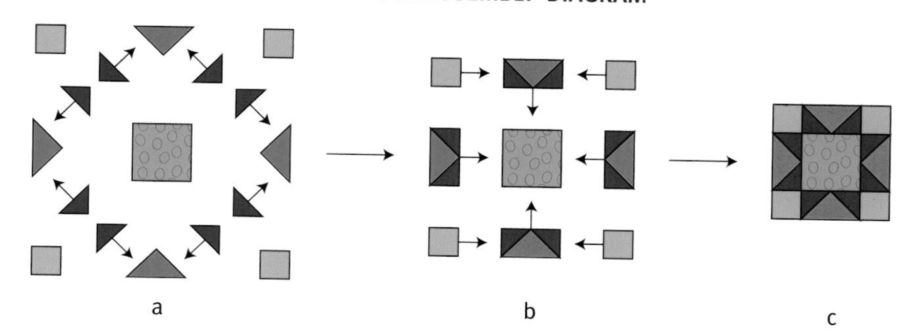

SNOWBALL BLOCK ASSEMBLY DIAGRAM

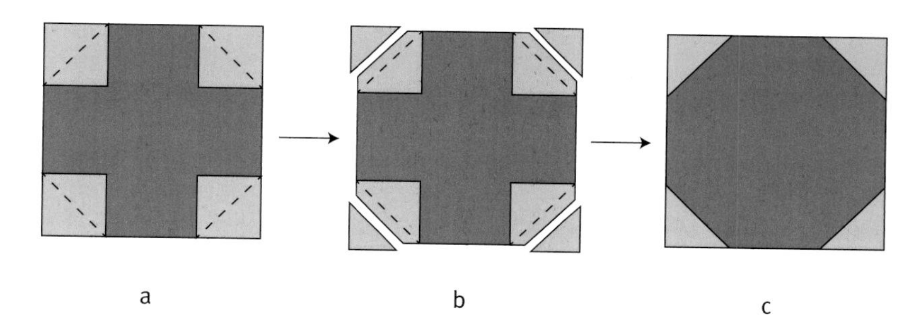

Making the Snowball Blocks
For each snowball block, take 1 large feature square and 4 orange corner squares. Following the sequence in the Snowball Block Assembly Diagram, place the 4 corner squares right sides together onto each corner of the large feature square, matching the edges carefully. Stitch diagonally across the small squares as shown (a). Trim the corners to a ¼in (6mm) seam allowance (b). Press the seams towards the block centre (c).
Make 8 snowballs from each of the 4 feature fabrics, varying the chosen corner squares, making a total of 32 blocks.

Centre
Lay out 9 rows of 7 alternating star and snowball blocks, referring to the Quilt Assembly Diagram (overleaf) and quilt photograph. Sew the blocks together one row at a time, pressing seams in the same direction on alternate rows – odd rows to the left, even rows to the right – to allow the finished seams to lie flat. Pin and sew the rows together, carefully matching crossing seams.

Border
Pin and sew the longer 81½in (207cm) Fabric 18 side borders to the quilt centre. Referring to the Quilt Assembly Diagram, sew Fabric 1 squares to each end of the 63½in (161.3cm) Fabric 18 top and bottom border pieces and press. Pin and sew the top and bottom borders to the centre to complete the quilt top.

FINISHING THE QUILT
Press the quilt top. Layer the quilt top, batting and backing, and baste together (see page 140).
Quilt as desired.
Trim the quilt edges and attach the binding (see page 141).

QUILT ASSEMBLY DIAGRAM

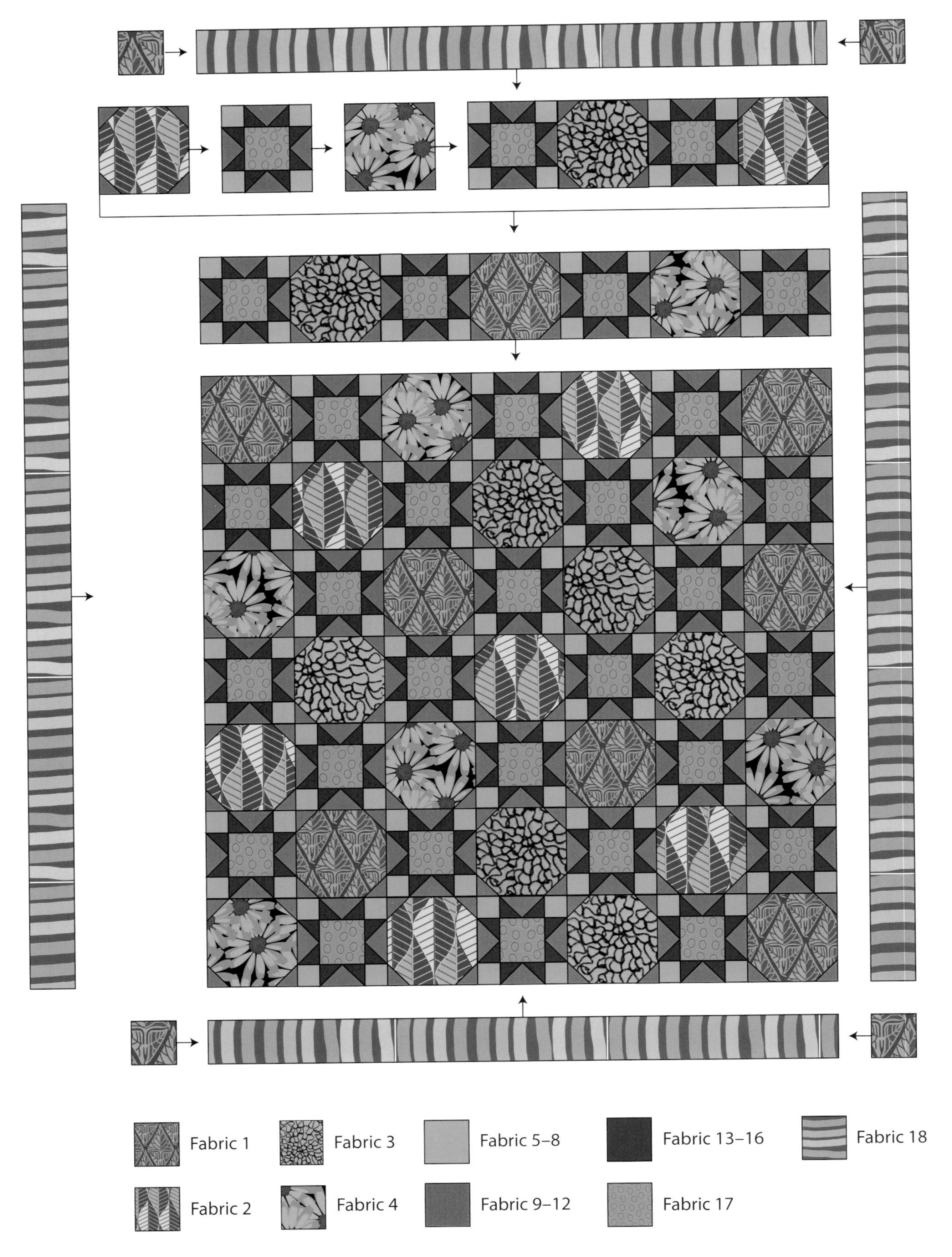

starry night ***

Kaffe Fassett

This quilt is a variation of *Green Star Bouquet* from *Kaffe Quilts Again*. In this version, the borders are different, but the centre is constructed as in the original, with feature fabric squares surrounded by 45-degree diamond star borders in Shot Cottons.

SIZE OF FINISHED QUILT

89in x 89in (226cm x 226cm)

FABRICS

Fabrics have been calculated at a maximum width of 40in (102cm). They have been given a number – see Fabric Swatch Diagram for details.

Patchwork Fabrics

Feature Squares

AGATE

Fabric 1	Ochre	⅜yd (40cm)
Fabric 2	Blue	⅜yd (40cm)

JAPANESE CHRYSANTHEMUM

Fabric 3	Antique	⅜yd (40cm)

BRASSICA

Fabric 4	Purple	⅜yd (40cm)

MILLEFIORE

Fabric 5	Dusty	⅜yd (40cm)

WATERMELONS

Fabric 6	Grey	⅜yd (40cm)
Fabric 7	Earth	⅜yd (40cm)

ANIMAL

Fabric 8	Sage	⅜yd (40cm)

LOTUS LEAF

Fabric 9	Vintage	⅜yd (40cm)

CACTUS FLOWER

Fabric 10	Black	⅜yd (40cm)

WISTERIA

Fabric 11	Black	⅜yd (40cm)

COLEUS

Fabric 12	Lavender	⅜yd (40cm)

DANCING DAHLIAS

Fabric 13	Blue	⅜yd (40cm)

Stars and Sashing

SHOT COTTON

Fabric 14	Pesto	⅜yd (40cm)
Fabric 15	Khaki	⅜yd (40cm)
Fabric 16	Plum	⅜yd (40cm)
Fabric 17	Blood Orange	⅜yd (40cm)
Fabric 18	Pistachio	⅜yd (40cm)
Fabric 19	Teal	⅜yd (40cm)
Fabric 20	Pimento	⅜yd (40cm)
Fabric 21	Harissa	⅜yd (40cm)
Fabric 22	Heliotrope	⅜yd (40cm)
Fabric 23	Lupin	⅜yd (40cm)
Fabric 24	Aubergine	¾yd (70cm)

* see also Binding Fabric

Fabric 25	Shadow	¾yd (70cm)

Borders

WIDE STRIPE

Fabric 26	Fjord	¾yd (70cm)

TURKISH DELIGHT

Fabric 27	Black	2½yd (2.3m)

Backing and Binding Fabrics

LOTUS LEAF WIDE

Fabric 28	Purple	2¾yd (2.6m)

SHOT COTTON

Fabric 24	Aubergine	¾yd (70cm)

* see also Patchwork Fabric

Batting

97in x 97in (246cm x 246cm)

TEMPLATES

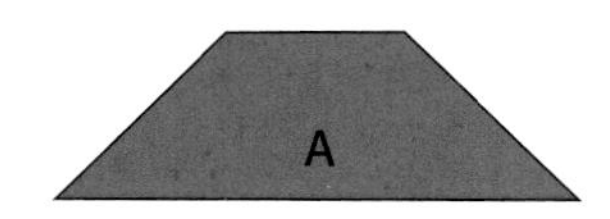

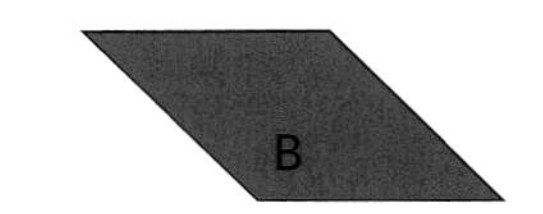

PATCHES

Feature squares are surrounded by borders made up of trapezoids and diamonds, cut from templates (see page 134), to form stars at the corners of each square. The quilt centre is formed of 5 rows of 5 blocks each.

CUTTING OUT

Fabric is cut across the width unless otherwise stated.

Feature Squares

From Fabric 8 cut 1 square 10in x 10in (25.4cm x 25.4cm).

From each of Fabrics 1, 2, 3, 4, 5, 6, 7, 9, 10, 11, 12 and 13 cut 2 squares 10in x 10in (25.4cm x 25.4cm).

Stars and Sashing

Trapezoid – Template A

From each of Fabrics 24 and 25 cut 8 strips 3in (7.6cm) wide across the width of the fabric. Using Template A, cut 50 trapezoid patches from each fabric. Each strip will yield 7 patches if the template is rotated 180 degrees after each cut.

Diamond – Template B

Cut 3 strips 3in (7.6cm) wide across the width of the fabric. Each strip will yield 9 diamond patches.

Using Template B:

From Fabric 14 and 15 cut 20 diamonds from each;

From Fabric 16, 17, 20 and 21 cut 19 diamonds from each;

From Fabric 18, 19, 22 and 23 cut 21 diamonds from each.

Total: 200 diamonds.

Inner Border

From Fabric 26 cut 8 strips 3in (7.6cm) wide. Remove selvedges and, matching the pattern, sew end to end. Cut 2 lengths 73in (185.4cm) for the side borders and 2 lengths 78in (198.1cm) for the top and bottom borders.

Outer Border

From Fabric 27 cut 4 strips 6in (15.2cm) wide **down the length** of the fabric. Trim 2 lengths to 89in (226cm) for the side borders and 2 lengths to 78in (198cm) for the top and bottom borders.

Backing

Trim Fabric 28 backing fabric to 97in x 97in (246cm x 246cm).

Binding

From Fabric 24 cut 10 strips 2½in (6.4cm) wide. Remove selvedges and sew end to end with 45-degree seams (see page 141).

MAKING THE QUILT

Using a design wall will help to place patches in the required layout.

Use ¼in (6mm) seams throughout.

Blocks

Referring to the Quilt Assembly Diagram overleaf and quilt photograph for fabric placement, lay out all the pieces to form the blocks and quilt centre.

Follow the Block Assembly Diagram to construct each block, taking care to position the corner star pieces correctly. Sew the 3 block border sections together on all 4 sides (a); sew opposite side border sections to the feature square (b);

FABRIC SWATCH DIAGRAM

Patchwork Fabrics

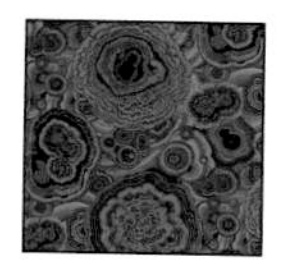

Fabric 1
AGATE
Ochre
PJ106OC

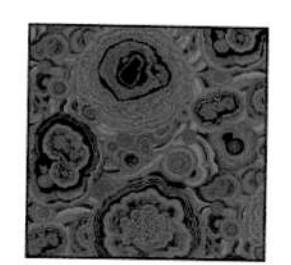

Fabric 2
AGATE
Blue
PJ106BL

Fabric 3
JAPANESE CHRYSANTHEMUM
Antique
PJ41AN

Fabric 4
BRASSICA
Purple
PJ51PU

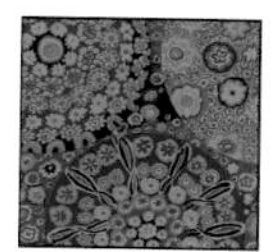

Fabric 5
MILLEFIORE
Dusty
GP92DY

Fabric 6
WATERMELONS
Grey
PJ103GY

Fabric 7
WATERMELONS
Earth
PJ103ER

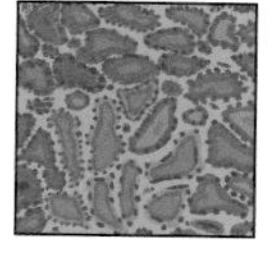

Fabric 8
ANIMAL
Sage
BM76SJ

Fabric 9
LOTUS LEAF
Vintage
GP29VN

Fabric 10
CACTUS FLOWER
Black
PJ96BK

Fabric 11
WISTERIA
Black
PJ102BK

Fabric 12
COLEUS
Lavender
PJ30LV

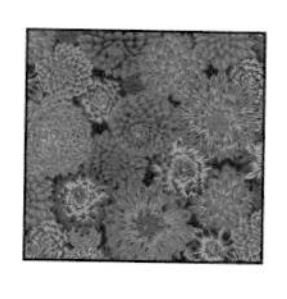

Fabric 13
DANCING DAHLIAS
Blue
PJ101BL

Fabric 14
SHOT COTTON
Pesto
SC118PD

Fabric 15
SHOT COTTON
Khaki
SC107KH

Fabric 16
SHOT COTTON
Plum
SC119PL

Fabric 17
SHOT COTTON
Blood Orange
SC110BO

Fabric 18
SHOT COTTON
Pistachio
SC111PX

Fabric 19
SHOT COTTON
Teal
SC105TE

Fabric 20
SHOT COTTON
Pimento
SC116PI

Fabric 21
SHOT COTTON
Harissa
SC115HA

Fabric 22
SHOT COTTON
Heliotrope
SC106HL

Fabric 23
SHOT COTTON
Lupin
SC113LU

Fabric 24
SHOT COTTON
Aubergine
SC117AB

Fabric 25
SHOT COTTON
Shadow
SC108SD

Fabric 26
WIDE STRIPE
Fjord
SS01FJ

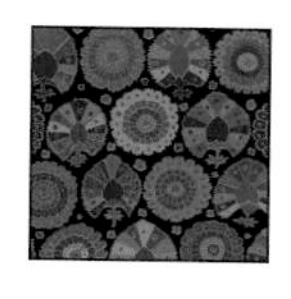

Fabric 27
TURKISH DELIGHT
Black
GP81BK

Backing and Binding Fabrics

Fabric 28
LOTUS LEAF WIDE
Purple
QB007PU

Fabric 24
SHOT COTTON
Aubergine
SC117AB

BLOCK ASSEMBLY DIAGRAM

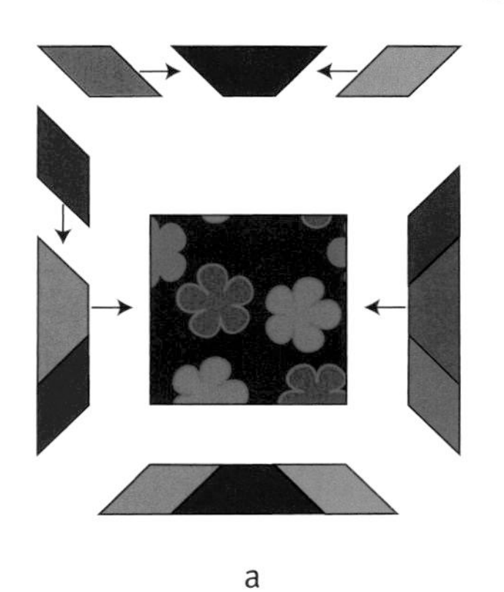

a

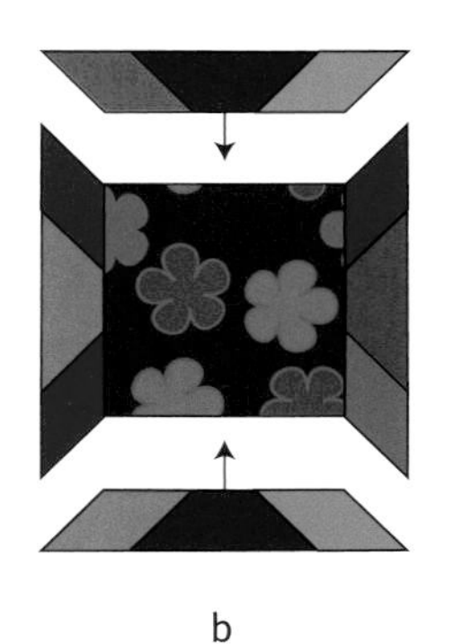

b

c

then sew the remaining 2 block borders to the block centre, using the inset seam method (see page 139).
Make 25 blocks.

Centre
Return the stitched blocks to the design wall and check the corners join correctly to form stars at each corner junction, referring to the Quilt Assembly Diagram for correct placement. Sew the blocks into 5 rows of 5 blocks, then sew the rows together, pressing seams in the same direction on alternate rows –odd rows to the left, even rows to the right – to allow the finished seams to lie flat.

Borders
Pin and sew the shorter inner border pieces to the quilt sides and press. Then pin and sew the longer inner border pieces to the top and bottom edges.
Pin and sew the shorter outer border pieces to the top and bottom and press. Then pin and sew the longer outer border pieces to the sides to complete the quilt top.

FINISHING THE QUILT

Press the quilt top and backing. Layer the quilt top, batting and backing and baste together (see page 140).
Quilt as desired.
Trim the quilt edges and attach the binding (see page 141).

Fabric 2
Fabric 16

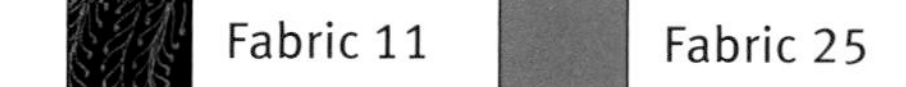

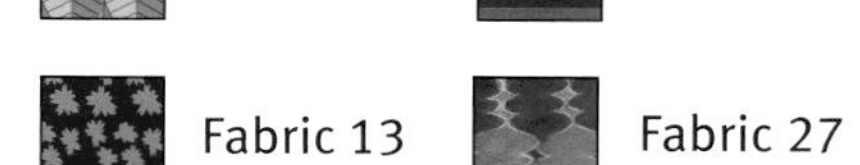

QUILT ASSEMBLY DIAGRAM

shards **

Kaffe Fassett

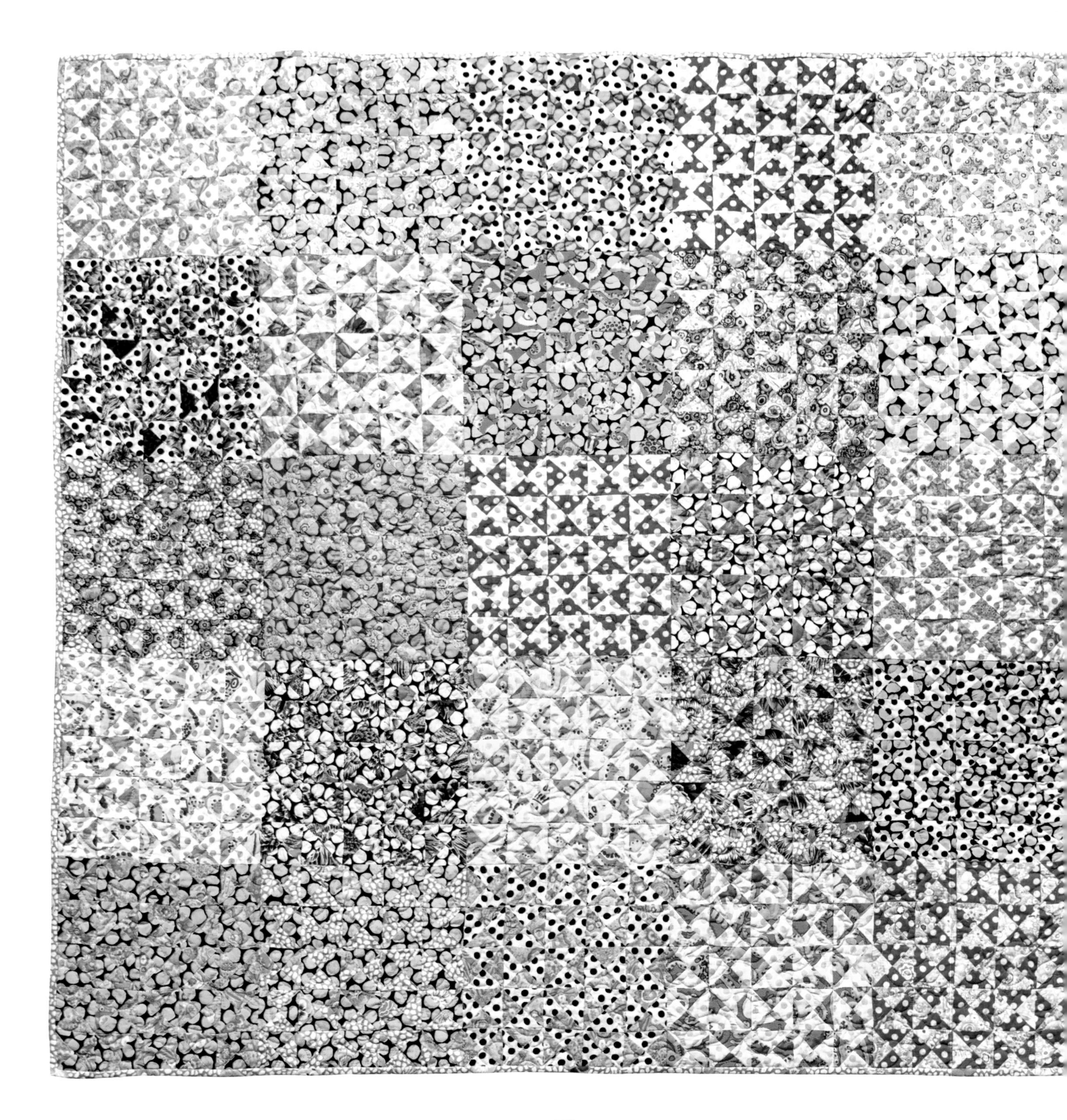

A traditional Broken Dishes design. This is the perfect quilt in which to use small-scale prints in a mixture of mid- and light tones.

SIZE OF FINISHED QUILT

56 3/4in x 56 3/4in (144cm x 144cm)

FABRICS

Fabrics have been calculated at a maximum width of 40in (102cm). They have been given a number – see Fabric Swatch Diagram for details.

PATCHWORK FABRICS

SPOT		
Fabric 1	Sky	5/8yd (60cm)
Fabric 2	Soft Blue	5/8yd (60cm)
Fabric 3	White	5/8yd (60cm)
Fabric 4	Grape	1/2yd (50cm)
PAPERWEIGHT		
Fabric 5	Grey	3/8yd (40cm)
Fabric 6	Lime	3/8yd (40cm)
MILLEFIORE		
Fabric 7	Mauve	5/8yd (60cm)
Fabric 8	Grey	1/2yd (50cm)
JUMBLE		
Fabric 9	Turquoise	3/8yd (40cm)
Fabric 10	White	3/8yd (40cm)
Fabric 11	Gold	3/8yd (40cm)
Fabric 12	Rose	5/8yd (60cm)
GUINEA FLOWER		
Fabric 13	Grey	1/2yd (50cm)
OCTOPUS		
Fabric 14	Turquoise	3/8yd (40cm)
Fabric 15	Orange	3/8yd (40cm)
DANCING DAHLIAS		
Fabric 16	Multi	1/2yd (50cm)
WISTERIA		
Fabric 17	Grey	3/8yd (40cm)

* see also Backing Fabric

Backing and Binding Fabrics

WISTERIA		
Fabric 17	Grey	3 5/8yd (3.35m)

* see also Patchwork Fabric

GUINEA FLOWER		
Fabric 18	White	5/8yd (60cm)

Batting

65in x 65in (165cm x 165cm)

FABRIC SWATCH DIAGRAM

Patchwork Fabrics

Fabric 1
SPOT
Sky
GP70SK

Fabric 2
SPOT
Soft Blue
GP70SF

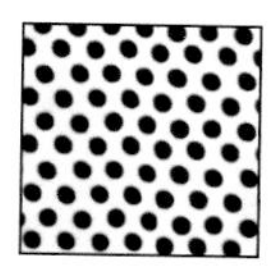

Fabric 3
SPOT
White
GP70WH

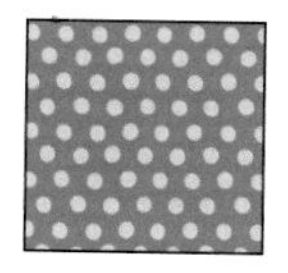

Fabric 4
SPOT
Grape
GP70GP

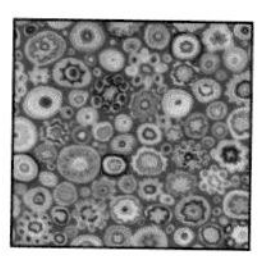

Fabric 5
PAPERWEIGHT
Grey
GP20GY

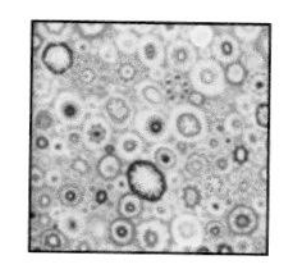

Fabric 6
PAPERWEIGHT
Lime
GP20LM

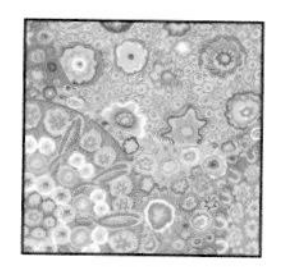

Fabric 7
MILLEFIORE
Mauve
GP92MV

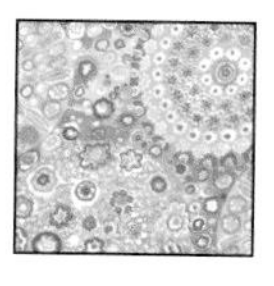

Fabric 8
MILLEFIORE
Grey
GP92GY

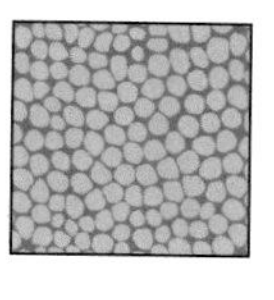

Fabric 9
JUMBLE
Turquoise
BM53TQ

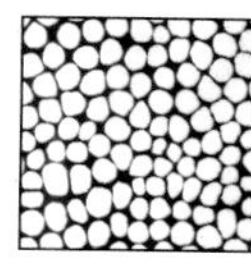

Fabric 10
JUMBLE
White
BM53WH

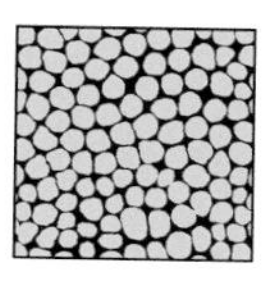

Fabric 11
JUMBLE
Gold
BM53GD

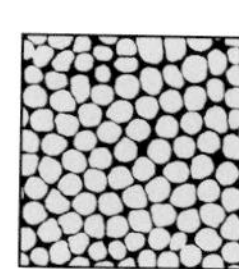

Fabric 12
JUMBLE
Rose
BM53RO

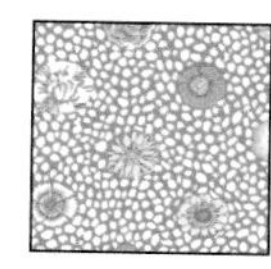

Fabric 13
GUINEA FLOWER
Grey
GP59GY

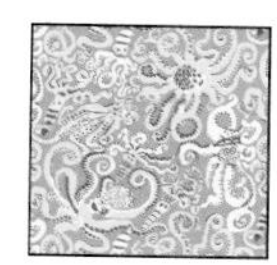

Fabric 14
OCTOPUS
Turquoise
BM74TQ

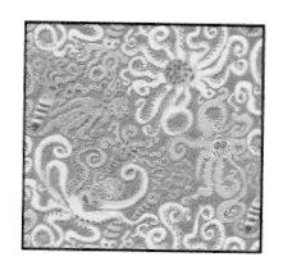

Fabric 15
OCTOPUS
Orange
BM74OR

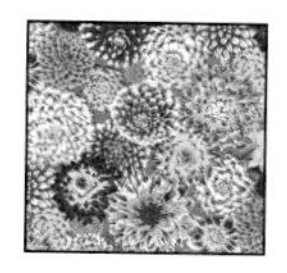

Fabric 16
DANCING DAHLIAS
Multi
PJ101MU

Fabric 17
WISTERIA
Grey
PJ102GY

Backing and Binding Fabrics

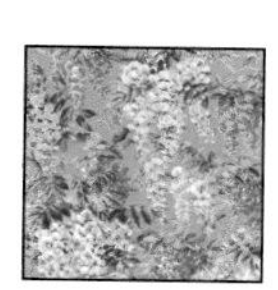

Fabric 17
WISTERIA
Grey
PJ102GY

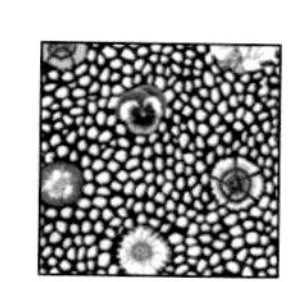

Fabric 18
GUINEA FLOWER
White
GP59WH

PATCHES

The quilt is made from 'hourglass' patches, each created with 2 contrasting squares of fabric cut 3½in (8.9cm) square. Finished hourglass patches are 2¼in (5.7cm) square. Patches are set in 5 rows of 5 patches to create 11¼in (28.6cm) finished square blocks.

CUTTING OUT

Fabric is cut across the width unless otherwise stated.

Blocks

Cut strips 3½in (8.9cm) wide across the width of the fabric and cross cut squares 3½in (8.9cm). Each strip will yield 11 squares. Each block requires 13 squares of one fabric and 13 squares of a contrasting fabric. From the following fabrics, cut strips and squares as follows:

Fabric 1 (6 strips) 65 squares;
Fabric 2 (6 strips) 65 squares;
Fabric 3 (5 strips) 52 squares;
Fabric 4 (4 strips) 39 squares;
Fabric 5 (3 strips) 26 squares;
Fabric 6 (3 strips) 26 squares;
Fabric 7 (5 strips) 52 squares;
Fabric 8 (4 strips) 39 squares;
Fabric 9 (3 strips) 26 squares;
Fabric 10 (3 strips) 26 squares;
Fabric 11 (3 strips) 26 squares;
Fabric 12 (5 strips) 52 squares;
Fabric 13 (4 strips) 39 squares;
Fabric 14 (3 strips) 26 squares;
Fabric 15 (3 strips) 26 squares;
Fabric 16 (4 strips) 39 squares;
Fabric 17 (3 strips) 26 squares.
Total: 650 squares.

Backing

From Fabric 12 backing fabric, cut 2 lengths 65in (165cm) long and remove selvedges.

Binding

From Fabric 1, cut 7 strips 2½in (6.4cm) wide. Remove selvedges and sew end to end with 45-degree seams (see page 141).

MAKING THE QUILT

Using a design wall will help to place patches in the required layout.
Use ¼in (6mm) seams throughout.

Hourglass Patches

Use 2 contrasting squares to make 2 hourglass patches. Referring to the Quilt Assembly Diagram (overleaf) and the quilt photograph for fabric choice, take 2 squares of contrasting fabrics. Place right sides together, matching the edges accurately, and mark a diagonal cutting line from corner to corner. Referring to the Patch Diagram, stitch the squares ¼in (6mm) each side of the cutting line (a).
Cut along the marked cutting line to separate the 2 pieced squares (b) and press the seam allowance towards the darker fabric.
Place the 2 pieced squares right sides together, matching the seam lines accurately, with the dark side of the upper square laid against the pale side of the lower square. Mark a diagonal cutting line accurately from corner to corner (at right angles to the previous sewing line). Stitch the squares ¼in (6mm) each side of the cutting line, as before (c).
Cut along the marked cutting line to separate the 2 completed hourglass patches (d). Press the seam allowance to one side.

ASSEMBLING THE BLOCKS

Each block is made up of 5 rows of 5 hourglass patches. Following the Block Assembly Diagram, position the 5 rows on the design wall, ensuring the dark triangles in one patch abut the pale triangles in the neighbouring patch, i.e. Patch 1 has dark triangles at the sides,

PATCH DIAGRAM

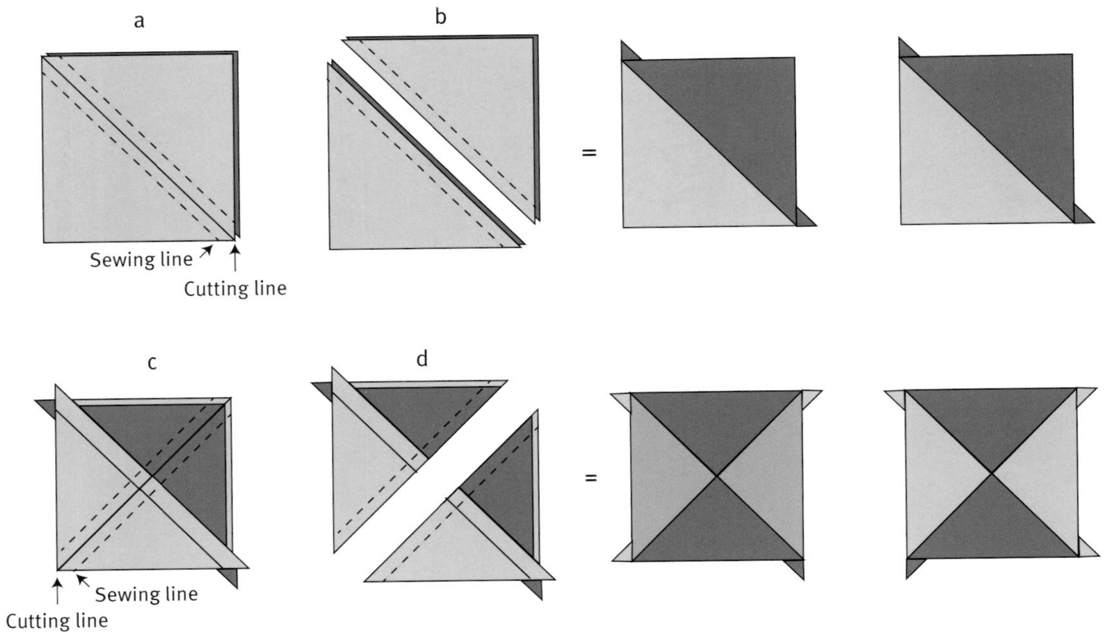

BLOCK ASSEMBLY DIAGRAM

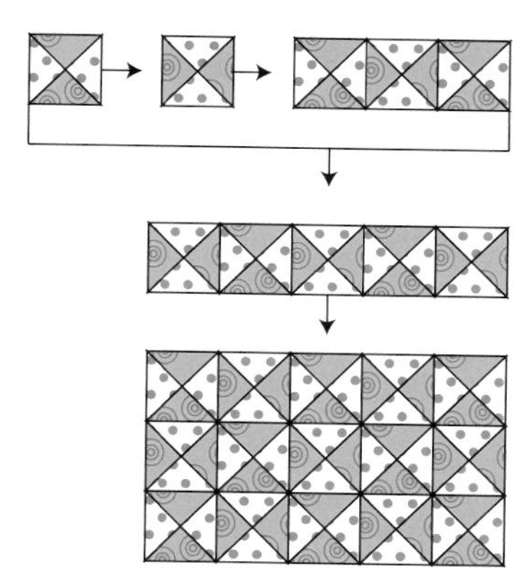

Patch 2 has dark triangles at the top and bottom, Patch 3 has dark triangles at the sides, and so on. Sew 5 patches together to form each row. Press the seams in the same direction on alternate rows – odd rows to the left, even rows to the right – to allow the seams to lie flat. Then sew the 5 rows together making sure that the same dark next to light sequence is followed.

ASSEMBLING THE QUILT

Lay out the 25 blocks on your design wall in 5 rows of 5 blocks, referring to the Quilt Assembly Diagram and the quilt photograph for placement. Rotate the blocks as necessary so that the hourglass patches sit dark next to light across all the blocks, in the same way as in the Block Assembly instructions.

Sew the blocks into 5 rows, taking care to match the crossing seams. Press seams in the same direction on alternate rows – odd rows to the left, even rows to the right – to allow the seams to lie flat. To complete the quilt top, pin, then sew the rows together, again taking care to match the crossing seams.

FINISHING THE QUILT

Sew the Fabric 17 backing pieces together. Trim to form a piece 65in x 65in (165cm x 165cm) square.

Press the quilt top. Layer the quilt top, batting and backing, and baste together (see page 140).

Quilt as desired.

Trim the quilt edges and attach the binding (see page 141).

QUILT ASSEMBLY DIAGRAM

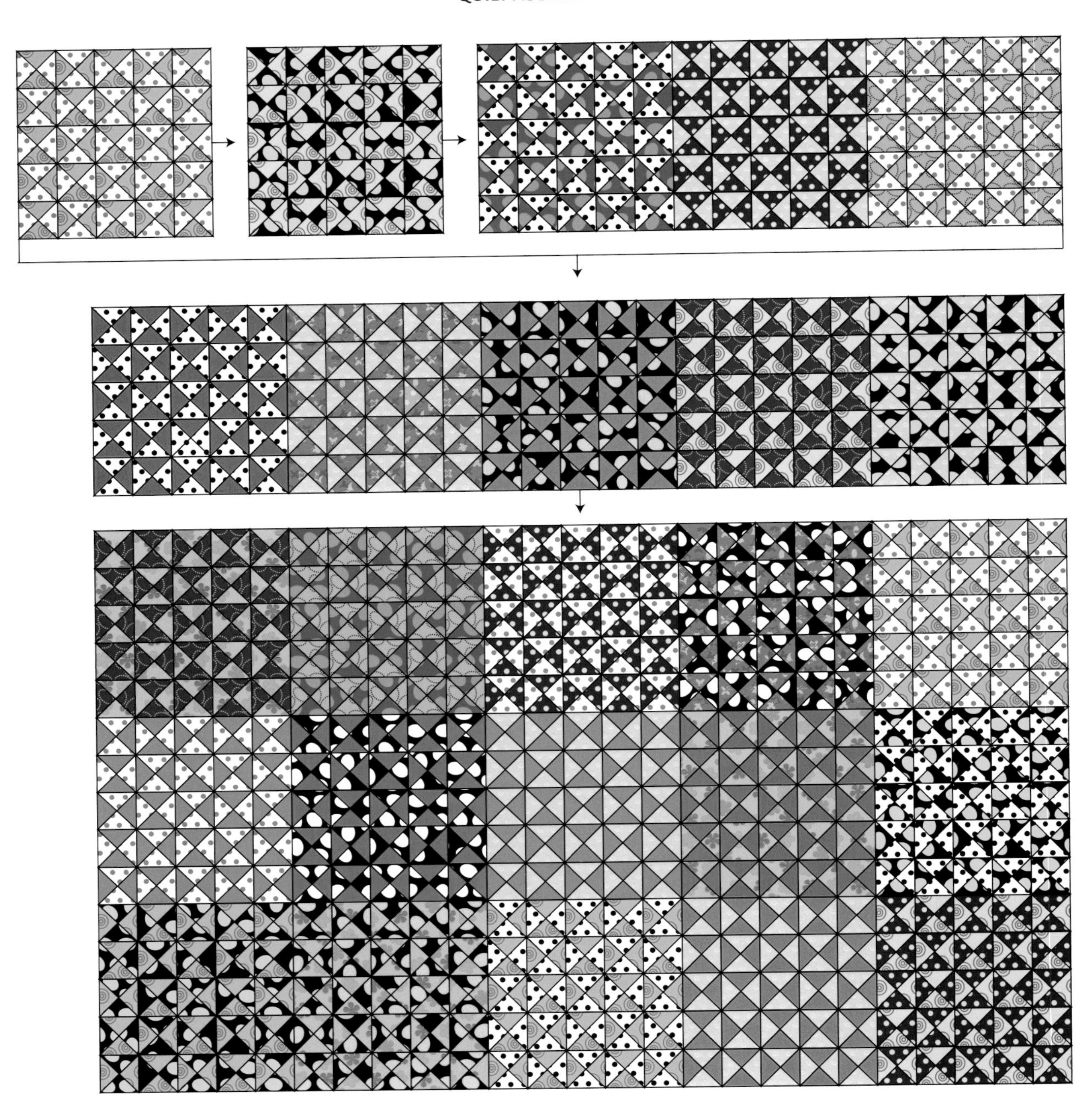

tiddlywinks rosy *

Liza Prior Lucy

The very first quilt Liza and I made for our first book was one in which large-scale prints alternated with 9-patch blocks, as they do here. A great quilt for beginners.

SIZE OF FINISHED QUILT
62in x 80in (157.5cm x 203.2cm)

FABRICS
Fabrics have been calculated at a maximum width of 40in (102cm). They have been given a number – see Fabric Swatch Diagram for details.

Patchwork Fabrics

TIDDLYWINKS
Fabric 1 Dark $1\frac{1}{8}$yd (1.1m)
MILLEFIORE
Fabric 2 Dusty $\frac{3}{8}$yd (40cm)
LUSCIOUS
Fabric 3 Black $\frac{3}{8}$yd (40cm)
CACTUS FLOWER
Fabric 4 Black $\frac{3}{8}$yd (40cm)
JAPANESE CHRYSANTHEMUM
Fabric 5 Antique $\frac{3}{8}$yd (40cm)
LOTUS LEAF
Fabric 6 Vintage $\frac{3}{8}$yd (40cm)
FEATHERS
Fabric 7 Autumn $\frac{3}{8}$yd (40cm)
MOSS FLOWER
Fabric 8 Blue $\frac{1}{4}$yd (25cm)
BUTTON MOSAIC
Fabric 9 Purple $\frac{1}{4}$yd (25cm)
* see also Binding Fabric
SPOT
Fabric 10 Bottle $\frac{1}{4}$yd (25cm)
Fabric 11 Indigo $\frac{1}{4}$yd (25cm)
Fabric 12 Plum $\frac{1}{4}$yd (25cm)
Fabric 13 Violet $\frac{1}{8}$yd (15cm)
ABORIGINAL DOT
Fabric 14 Periwinkle $\frac{3}{8}$yd (40cm)
Fabric 15 Plum $\frac{3}{8}$yd (40cm)
GARLANDS
Fabric 16 Dark $2\frac{1}{4}$yd (2.1m)

Backing and Binding Fabrics

MILLEFIORE (wide)
Fabric 17 Blue 2yd (1.9m)
BUTTON MOSAIC
FABRIC 9 Purple $\frac{5}{8}$yd (60cm)
* see also Patchwork Fabric

Batting
70in x 88in (178cm x 224cm)

FABRIC SWATCH DIAGRAM

Patchwork Fabrics

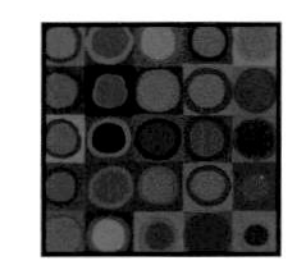
Fabric 1
TIDDLYWINKS
Dark
GP171DK

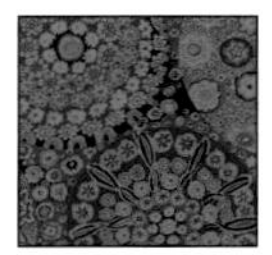
Fabric 2
MILLEFIORE
Dusty
GP92DY

Fabric 3
LUSCIOUS
Black
PJ11BK

Fabric 4
CACTUS FLOWER
Black
PJ96BK

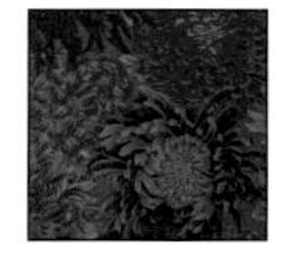
Fabric 5
JAPANESE CHRYSANTHEMUM
Antique
PJ41AN

Fabric 6
LOTUS LEAF
Vintage
GP29VN

Fabric 7
FEATHERS
Autumn
PJ55AU

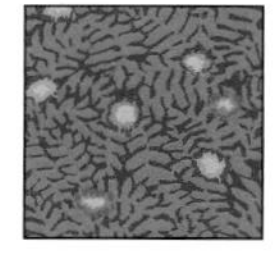
Fabric 8
MOSS FLOWER
Blue
GP184BL

Fabric 9
BUTTON MOSAIC
Purple
GP182PU

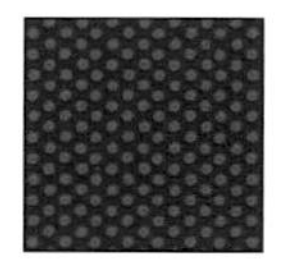
Fabric 10
SPOT
Bottle
GP70BT

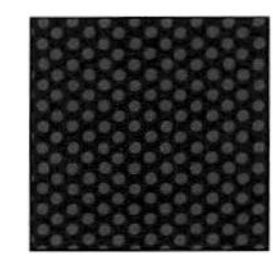
Fabric 11
SPOT
Indigo
GP70IN

Fabric 12
SPOT
Plum
GP70PL

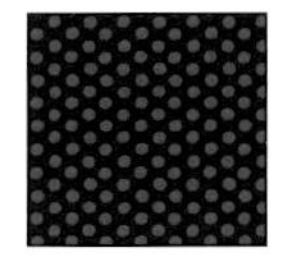
Fabric 13
SPOT
Violet
GP70VI

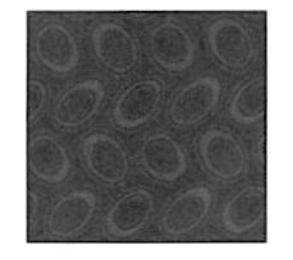
Fabric 14
ABORIGINAL DOT
Periwinkle
GP71PE

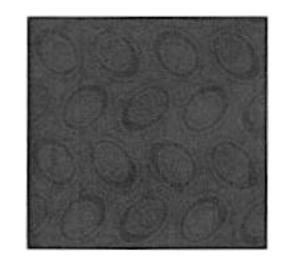
Fabric 15
ABORIGINAL DOT
Plum
GP71PL

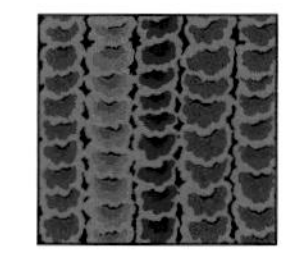
Fabric 16
GARLANDS
Dark
GP181DK

Backing and Binding Fabrics

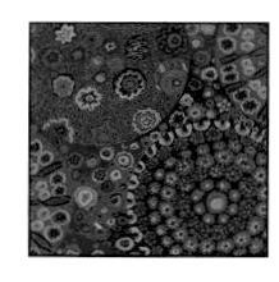
Fabric 17
MILLEFIORE (wide)
Blue
QB006BL

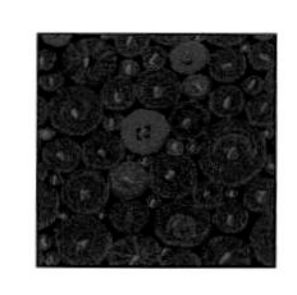
Fabric 9
BUTTON MOSAIC
Purple
GP182PU

PATCHES
Large feature squares are 9in (22.9cm) square finished, alternating with 9-patch blocks made up of 3in (7.6cm) squares finished in smaller-scale prints.

CUTTING OUT
The Fabric 16 border is cut down the length of the fabric. All other fabrics are cut across the width of the fabric.

Large Feature Squares
From Fabrics 2, 3, 4, 5, 6 and 7 cut 3 squares each 9½in x 9½in (24.1cm x 24.1cm). There is enough of each of these fabrics to allow a little movement in cutting to make the most of the larger-scale patterns.

9-Patch Blocks and Inner Border
Do not try to fussy cut Fabric 1. Cut all the smaller-scale fabrics from strips 3½in (8.9cm) wide. Each strip will yield 11 squares. Cut strips and a total of 229 squares from fabrics as follows:
Fabric 1 (10 strips) 105 squares;
Fabric 8 (2 strips) 12 squares;
Fabric 9 (2 strips) 12 squares;
Fabric 10 (2 strips) 12 squares;
Fabric 11 (2 strips) 12 squares;
Fabric 12 (2 strips) 12 squares;
Fabric 13 (1 strip) 8 squares;
Fabric 14 (3 strips) 32 squares;
Fabric 15 (3 strips) 24 squares.

Outer Border
From Fabric 16 fussy cut 4 strips 5¾in (14.6cm) wide **down the length** of the fabric so that all 4 strips have the same garland colours. Cut 2 lengths 74¾in (189.9cm) long for the side borders and 2 lengths 56¾in (144.2cm) long for the top and bottom.

Backing
Trim Fabric 17 backing fabric to approx. 70in x 88in (178cm x 224cm).

Binding
From Fabric 9 cut 8 strips 2½in (6.4cm) wide. Remove selvedges and sew end to end with 45-degree seams (see page 141).

MAKING THE QUILT
Using a design wall will help to place patches in the required layout.
Use ¼in (6mm) seams throughout.

9-Patch Blocks
Take 5 squares of Fabric 1 for each block plus 4 squares of another small-scale print fabric. Make 3 blocks using each of Fabric 8, 9, 10, 11 and 12. Make 2 blocks using Fabric 13.
Total: 17 blocks.
Lay out each block and, referring to the Block Assembly Diagram, sew the patches together in 3 rows of 3 patches. Press, then sew the 3 rows together to complete the block.

Centre
On a design wall, lay out the blocks alternating the 9-patch blocks with the large-scale feature squares, following the Quilt Assembly Diagram (overleaf) and quilt photograph. Sew the blocks together into 7 rows. Press seams, then pin and sew the rows together, taking care to match crossing seams.

Inner Border
Make inner borders squares from Fabrics 1, 14 and 15. Piece 21 squares for each side border and 17 squares for each of the top and bottom borders. Follow the Quilt Assembly Diagram and quilt photograph for the sequence. Pin and sew the side inner borders to the quilt centre. Press seams, then pin and sew the top and bottom inner borders to the quilt centre.

BLOCK ASSEMBLY DIAGRAM

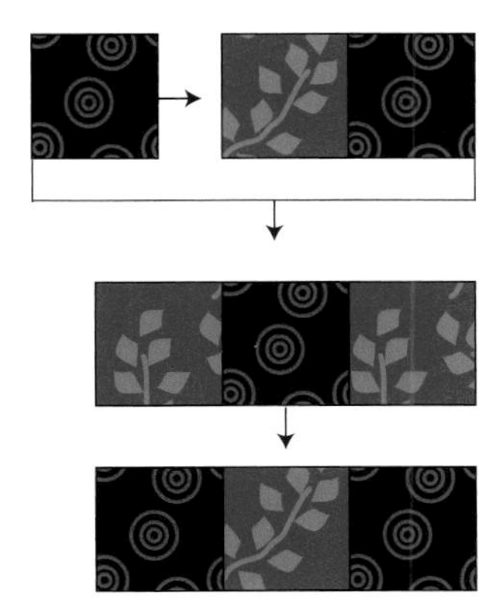

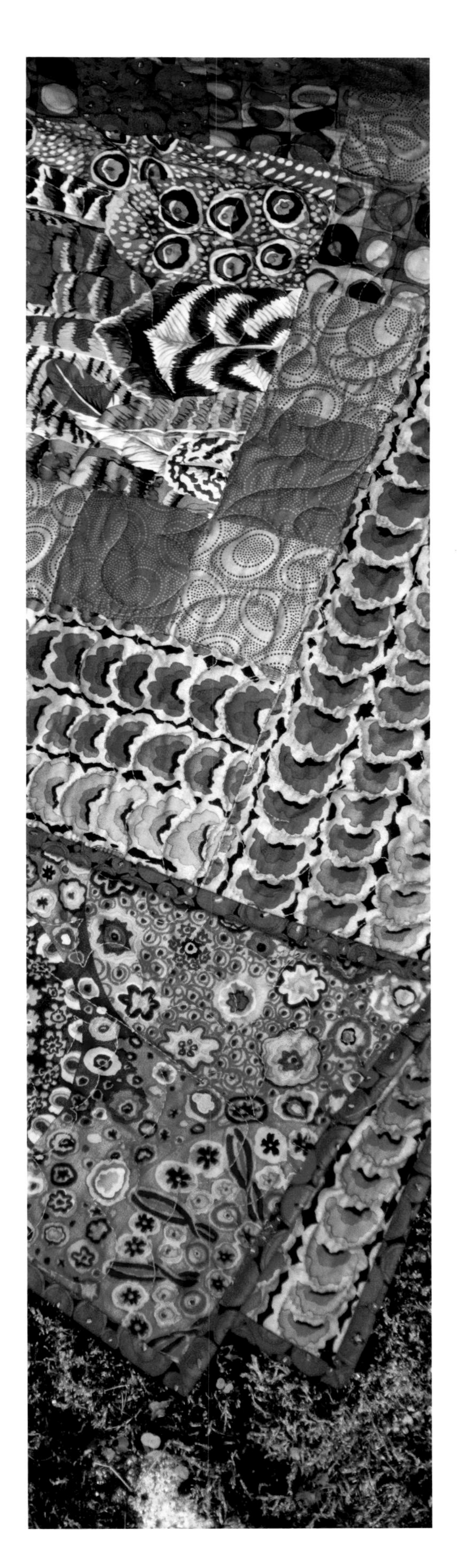

QUILT ASSEMBLY DIAGRAM

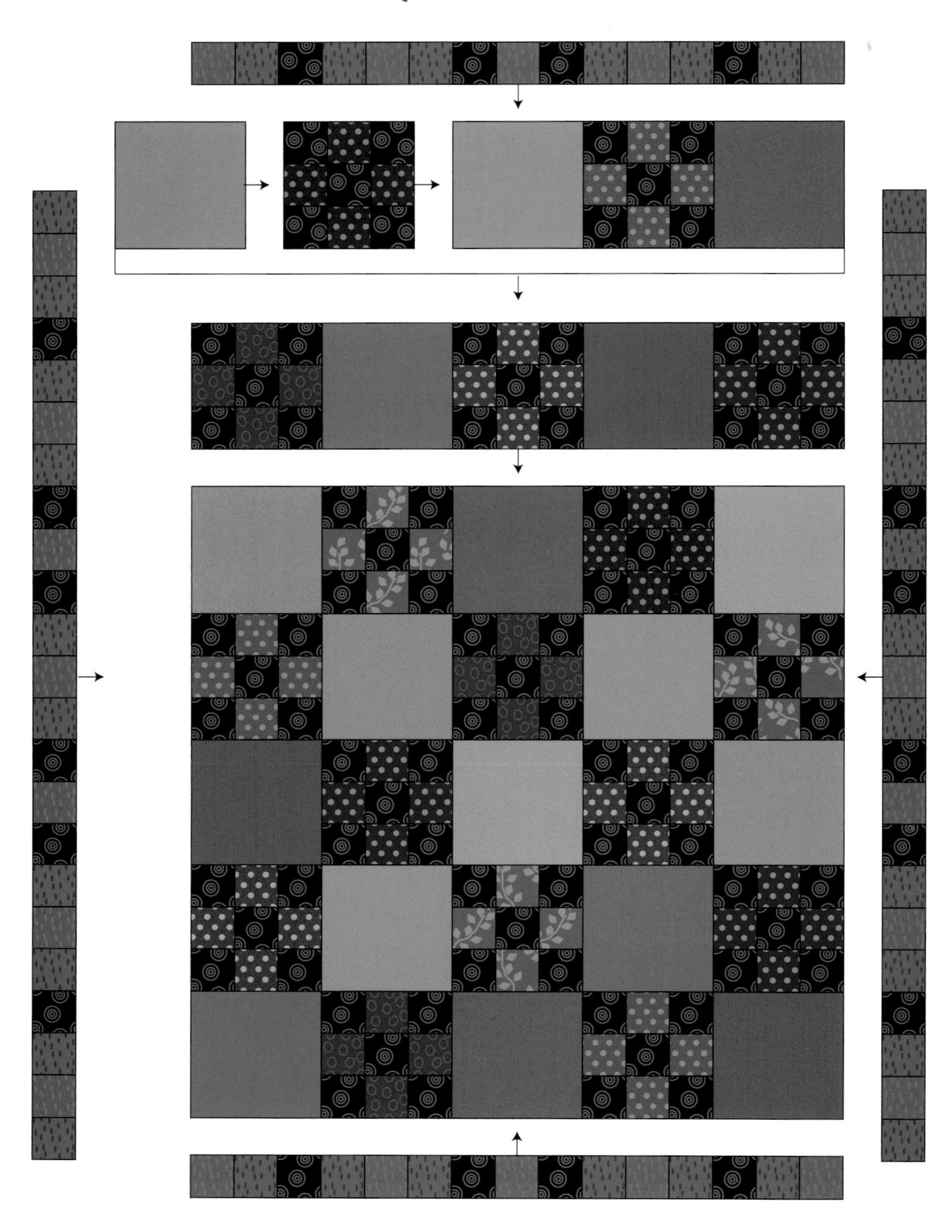

Outer Border

Fabric 16 is cut directionally and correct placement will ensure the same colour lies all the way around the inside edge of the border.

Attach the top border strip using a partial seam. Referring to the Outer Border Diagram, pin and sew the top border (1), leaving 5½in (14cm) of it extending from the right-hand side of the quilt top. Press the seam. Next pin and sew the left-hand side border (2) and press, then pin and sew the bottom border (3) and press. Next, pin the right-hand border (4) to the quilt centre, leaving the loose end of the top border open. Complete by returning to the top border and sewing the remaining partial seam (5) of the top border to the right-hand border.

FINISHING THE QUILT

Press the quilt top. Layer the quilt top, batting and backing, and baste together (see page 140).

Quilt as desired.

Trim the quilt edges and attach the binding (see page 141).

OUTER BORDER DIAGRAM

1

5

2

4

3

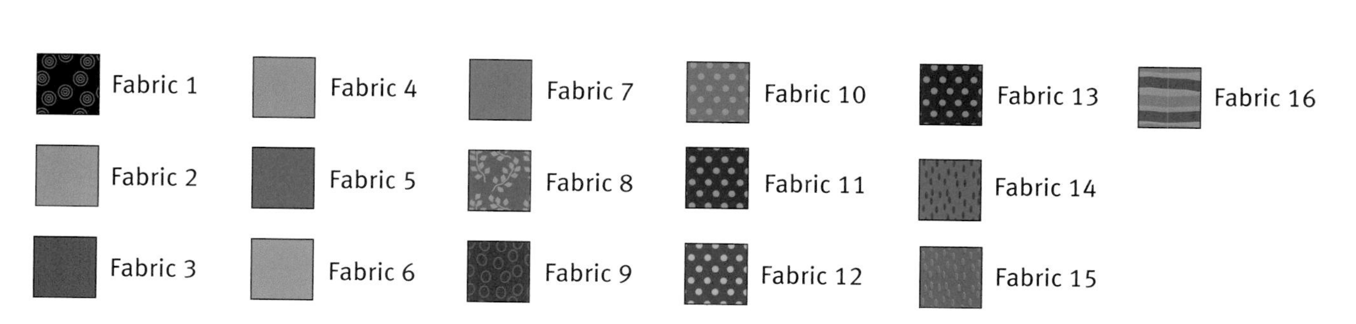

opal crosses **

Kaffe Fassett

In this elegant quilt in cool shades, the 'cross' blocks are separated with sashing strips in my Garlands blue fabric.

SIZE OF FINISHED QUILT
78½in x 92½in (199.4cm x 235cm)

FABRICS
Fabrics have been calculated at a maximum width of 40in (102cm). They have been given a number – see Fabric Swatch Diagram for details.

Patchwork Fabrics
LIGHTS:

MOSS FLOWER
Fabric 1 White ¼yd (25cm)
HYDRANGEA
Fabric 2 Grey ¼yd (25cm)
GUINEA FLOWER
Fabric 3 Grey ¼yd (25cm)
BUTTON MOSAIC
Fabric 4 White ¼yd (25cm)
PAPERWEIGHT
Fabric 5 Pastel ¼yd (25cm)
SPOT
Fabric 6 Steel ¼yd (25cm)

DARKS:

CHIPS
Fabric 7 Aqua ¾yd (70cm)
PEONY BROCADE
Fabric 8 Cool ½yd (50cm)
PEBBLE MOSAIC
Fabric 9 Ice ½yd (50cm)
HYDRANGEA
Fabric 10 Blue ½yd (50cm)
DAMASK FLOWER
Fabric 11 Blue ½yd (50cm)
BUTTON MOSAIC
Fabric 12 Blue ½yd (50cm)
JUMBLE
Fabric 13 Royal ¾yd (70cm)
DAMASK FLOWER
Fabric 14 Lilac ¾yd (70cm)
GARLANDS
Fabric 15 Blue 1⅞yd (1.8m)
CHIPS
Fabric 16 Fog 1yd (95cm)

Backing and Binding Fabrics
MILLEFIORE (wide)
Fabric 17 Pastel 2½yd (2.3m)
SHARK'S TEETH
Fabric 18 Cobalt ¾yd (70cm)

FABRIC SWATCH DIAGRAM

Patchwork Fabrics

LIGHTS

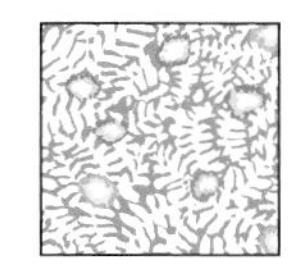

Fabric 1
MOSS FLOWER
White
GP184WH

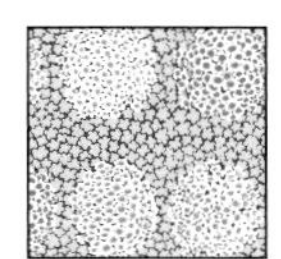

Fabric 2
HYDRANGEA
Grey
GP180GY

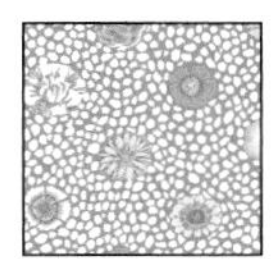

Fabric 3
GUINEA FLOWER
Grey
GP59GY

Fabric 4
BUTTON MOSAIC
White
GP182WH

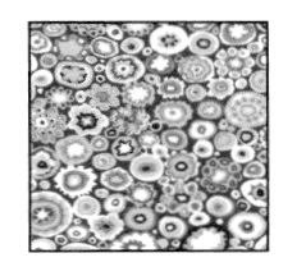

Fabric 5
PAPERWEIGHT
Pastel
GP20PT

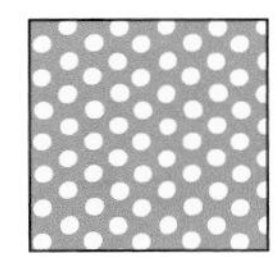

Fabric 6
SPOT
Steel
GP70ST

DARKS

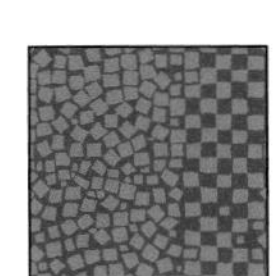

Fabric 7
CHIPS
Aqua
BM73AQ

Fabric 8
PEONY BROCADE
Cool
PJ62CL

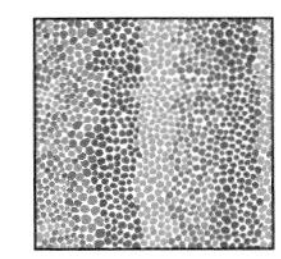

Fabric 9
PEBBLE MOSAIC
Ice
BM42IC

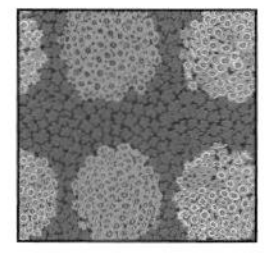

Fabric 10
HYDRANGEA
Blue
GP180BL

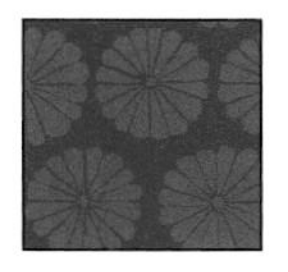

Fabric 11
DAMASK FLOWER
Blue
GP183BL

Fabric 12
BUTTON MOSAIC
Blue
GP182BL

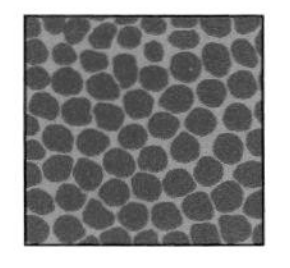

Fabric 13
JUMBLE
Royal
BM53RY

Fabric 14
DAMASK FLOWER
Lilac
GP183LI

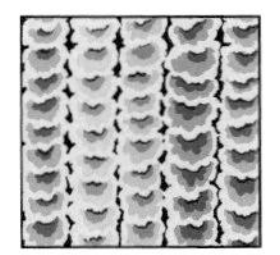

Fabric 15
GARLANDS
Blue
GP181BL

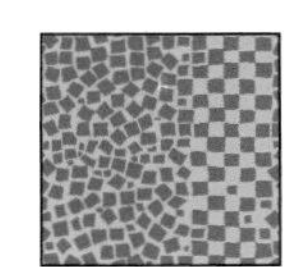

Fabric 16
CHIPS
Fog
BM73FG

Backing and Binding Fabrics

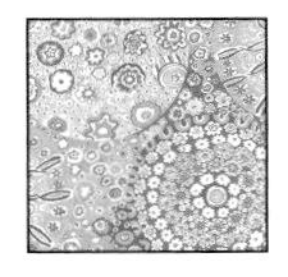

Fabric 17
MILLEFIORE (wide)
Pastel
QB06PT

Fabric 18
SHARK'S TEETH
Cobalt
BM60CB

Batting
87in x 101in (221cm x 257cm)

PATCHES

The blocks are made from 3 patch shapes: a square, a half-square triangle and a quarter-square triangle. All patches are cut from strips and pieced to form 30 blocks 12in (30.5cm) finished. Blocks, connected with sashing strips, form 6 rows of 5 blocks each. The quilt is finished with a border and corner squares.

CUTTING OUT

Fabric is cut across the width unless otherwise stated.

Block Corners
From Fabric 13 cut 6 strips $3\frac{7}{8}$in (9.8cm) wide and cross cut squares $3\frac{7}{8}$in (9.8cm). Cut each square diagonally from corner to corner to make 2 half-square triangles. Each strip will yield 10 squares – 20 triangles. Cut a total of 120 triangles.

Block Centres and Border Corner Squares
From Fabric 14 cut 4 strips $4\frac{3}{4}$in (12.1cm) wide and cross cut squares $4\frac{3}{4}$in (12.1cm). Each strip will yield 8 squares. Cut a total of 30 squares.
From the remaining Fabric 14 cut a strip $3\frac{1}{2}$in (8.9cm) wide and cross cut 4 squares $3\frac{1}{2}$in (8.9cm) for the border corner squares.

Light Background Triangles
From each of the 6 LIGHT fabrics (Fabrics 1, 2, 3, 4, 5 and 6) cut a strip $7\frac{1}{4}$in (18.4cm) wide. Cross cut 5 squares $7\frac{1}{4}$in (18.4cm) from each strip, then cut each square diagonally from corner to corner both ways to make 4 quarter-square triangles from each square; 5 squares (yielding 20 triangles) are needed from each fabric.

Dark Crosses
From each of the 6 DARK fabrics (Fabrics 7, 8, 9, 10, 11 and 12) cut 3 strips $4\frac{3}{4}$in (12.1cm) wide. Cross cut squares $4\frac{3}{4}$in (12.1cm). Each strip will yield 8 squares. Cut 20 squares from each fabric.

Sashing
From Fabric 15 cut 24 strips $2\frac{1}{2}$in (6.4cm) wide. From each strip cut 3 sashing strips $2\frac{1}{2}$in x $12\frac{1}{2}$in (6.4cm x 31.8cm). Cut 71 sashing strips.

Sashing Corner Squares
From the remaining Fabric 7 cut 3 strips $2\frac{1}{2}$in (6.4cm) wide. Cross cut squares $2\frac{1}{2}$in (6.4cm). Each strip will yield 16 squares. Cut a total of 42 squares.

Border
From Fabric 16 cut 9 strips $3\frac{1}{2}$in (8.9cm) wide. Remove the selvedges and casually match the pattern end to end. Sew together and press seams open. Cut 2 lengths $86\frac{1}{2}$in (219.7cm) for the side borders. Cut 2 lengths $72\frac{1}{2}$in (184.2cm) for the top and bottom borders.

Backing
Trim Fabric 17 backing fabric to approximately 87in x 101in (221cm x 257cm).

Binding
From Fabric 18 cut 9 strips $2\frac{1}{2}$in (6.4cm) wide. Remove selvedges and sew strips end to end with 45-degree seams (see page 141).

MAKING THE QUILT

Using a design wall will help to place patches in the required layout.
Use $\frac{1}{4}$in (6mm) seams throughout.

Blocks
For each block use 1 Fabric 14 square, 4 Fabric 13 half-square triangles, 4 squares from one of the DARK Fabrics (7, 8, 9, 10, 11 or 12) and 4 quarter-square triangles from one of the LIGHT Fabrics (1, 2, 3, 4, 5 or 6). You need not make each block as in the original. Each Light and Dark fabric will be used to make 5 blocks.
Referring to the Block Assembly Diagram, lay out each block. Sew together in diagonal rows (a). Press seams, then sew rows together to complete the block (b). Make 30 blocks.

ASSEMBLING THE QUILT

Arrange the blocks in 6 rows of 5 and alternate with sashing strips between each block and at each row end.
Referring to the Quilt Assembly Diagram, sew each row (6 in total) of 6 sashing strips and 5 blocks together. Press all seams towards the sashing strips.
Sew together 7 horizontal sashing units each made up of 6 sashing corner squares and 5 sashing strips. Press seams towards the sashing strips.
Return the block rows and sashing units to the design wall.
Referring to the Quilt Assembly Diagram, pin and sew the sashing units and block rows together, taking care to match crossing seams so the sashing corner squares sit neatly between the block corners.

Border
Pin and sew the longer Fabric 16 borders to each side. Sew a Fabric 14 $3\frac{1}{2}$in (8.9cm) square to each end of both shorter Fabric 16 borders. Pin, then sew to the top and bottom to complete the quilt top.

FINISHING THE QUILT

Press the quilt top. Layer the quilt top, batting and backing, and baste together (see page 140).
Quilt as desired.
Trim the quilt edges and attach the binding (see page 141).

BLOCK ASSEMBLY DIAGRAM

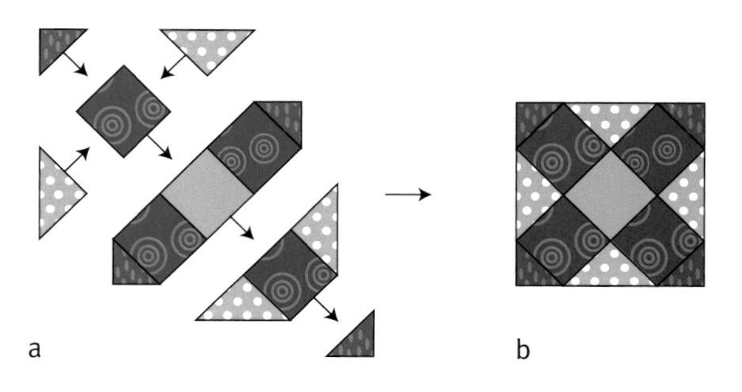

QUILT ASSEMBLY DIAGRAM

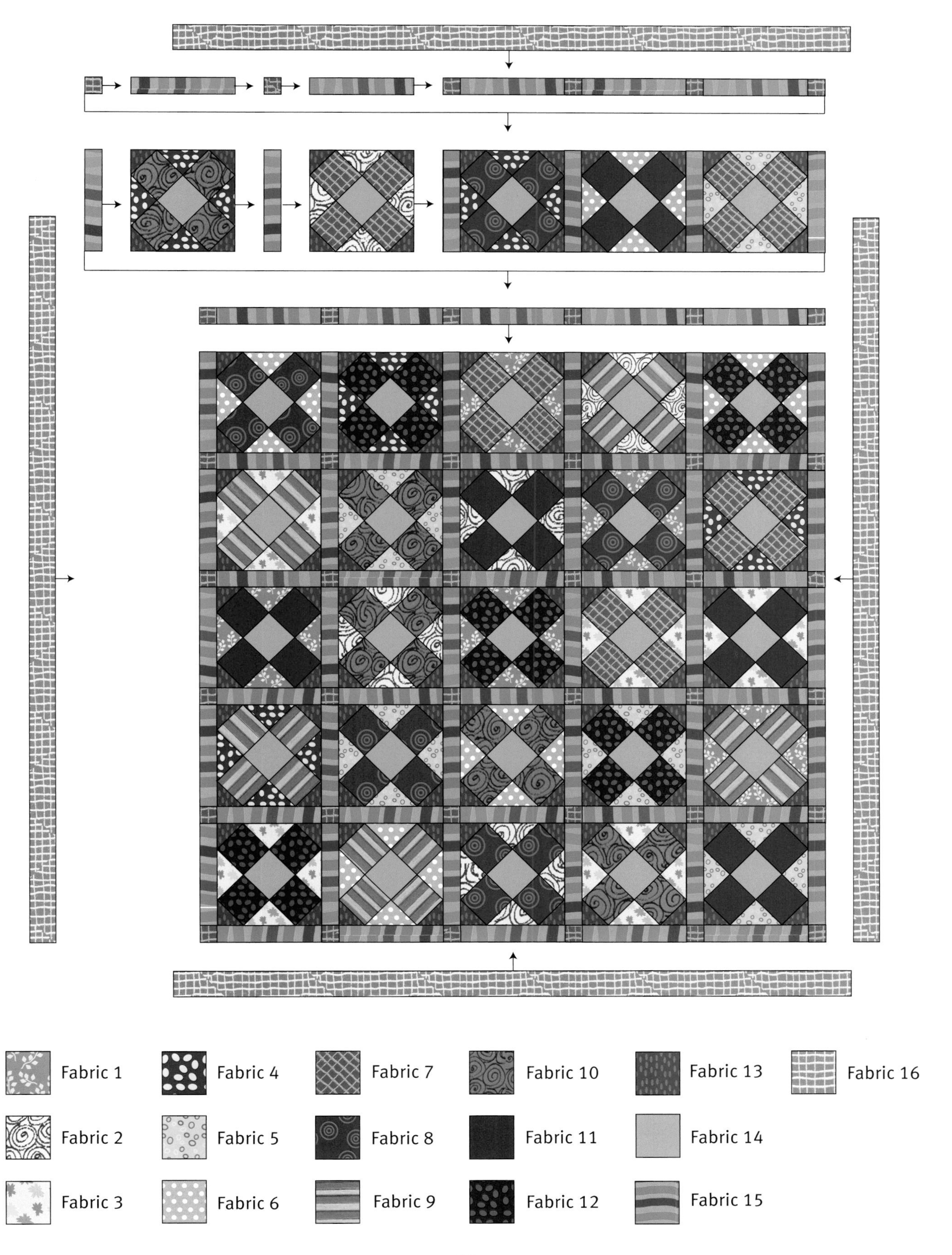

marquetry blocks **

Kaffe Fassett

Undoubtedly tumbling blocks is one of my favourite quilt designs, as it offers such a wonderful opportunity to create a 3-D effect using delicate tonal differences. In this version, the design has the quality of marquetry, hence my name for it.

FABRIC SWATCH DIAGRAM

Patchwork Fabrics

Fabric 1
NARROW STRIPE
Cocoa
SS002CH

Fabric 2
DAMASK FLOWER
Brown
GP183BR

Fabric 3
DAMASK FLOWER
Orange
GP183OR

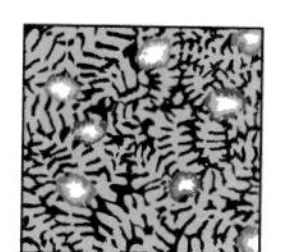

Fabric 4
MOSS FLOWER
Ochre
GP184OC

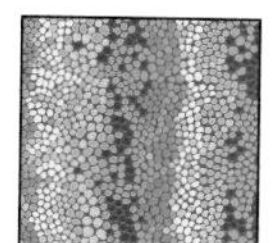

Fabric 5
PEBBLE MOSAIC
Jungle
BM42JU

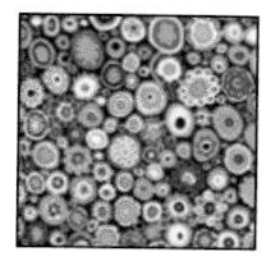

Fabric 6
PAPERWEIGHT
Pumpkin
GP20PN

Fabric 7
BUTTON MOSAIC
Orange
GP182OR

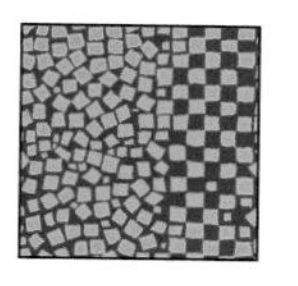

Fabric 8
CHIPS
Pine
BM73PY

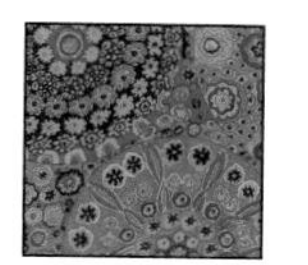

Fabric 9
MILLEFIORE
Antique
GP92AN

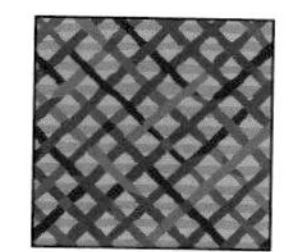

Fabric 10
MAD PLAID
Rust
GM37RU

Fabric 11
CACTUS FLOWER
Brown
PJ96BR

Fabric 12
FEATHERS
Summer
PJ55SU

Fabric 13
WIDE STRIPE
Chestnut
SS001CX

Backing and Binding Fabrics

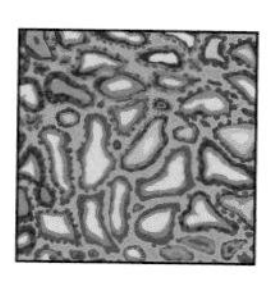

Fabric 14
ANIMAL
Orange
BM76OR

Fabric 1
NARROW STRIPE
Cocoa
SS002CH

SIZE OF FINISHED QUILT

63in x 84in (160cm x 213cm)

FABRICS

Fabrics have been calculated at a maximum width of 40in (102cm). They have been given a number – see Fabric Swatch Diagram for details.

Patchwork Fabrics

NARROW STRIPE

Fabric 1	Cocoa	¾yd (70cm)

* see also Binding Fabric

DAMASK FLOWER

Fabric 2	Brown	¾yd (70cm)
Fabric 3	Orange	½yd (50cm)

MOSS FLOWER

Fabric 4	Ochre	⅜yd (40cm)

PEBBLE MOSAIC

Fabric 5	Jungle	½yd (50cm)

PAPERWEIGHT

Fabric 6	Pumpkin	⅜yd (40cm)

BUTTON MOSAIC

Fabric 7	Orange	½yd (50cm)

CHIPS

Fabric 8	Pine	⅜yd (40cm)

MILLEFIORE

Fabric 9	Antique	⅜yd (40cm)

MAD PLAID

Fabric 10	Rust	⅜yd (40cm)

CACTUS FLOWER

Fabric 11	Brown	⅜yd (40cm)

FEATHERS

Fabric 12	Summer	½yd (50cm)

WIDE STRIPE

Fabric 13	Chestnut	1⅛yd (1.1m)

Backing and Binding Fabrics

ANIMAL

Fabric 14	Orange	5¼yd (4.9m)

NARROW STRIPE

Fabric 1	Cocoa	¾yd (70cm)

* see also Patchwork Fabric

Batting

71in x 92in (180cm x 234cm)

TEMPLATES

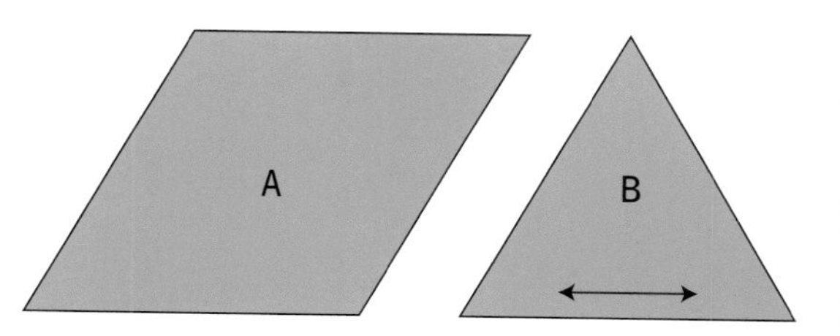

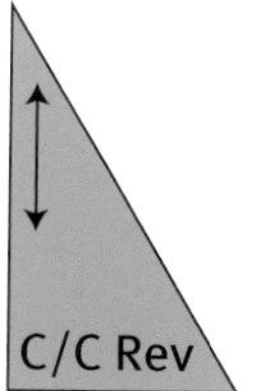

PATCHES

This easy-to-make version of the classic tumbling blocks pattern is made by splitting the top face of each tumbling block into 2 triangles (half diamonds). This makes it possible to piece the quilt in columns and avoids having to sew diamonds together with inset seams. Patches are 60-degree diamonds, half diamonds and quarter diamonds. They are cut from strips cut across the fabric width using the templates on pages 136 and 137.

CUTTING OUT

Fabrics are cut across the width unless otherwise stated.

Block Sides – Diamond A

Cut strips 5in (12.7cm) wide across the width of the fabric. Each strip will yield 6 diamonds. Cut strips and 108 diamonds from fabrics as follows:
Fabric 1 (5 strips) 27 diamonds;
Fabric 2 (5 strips) 27 diamonds;
Fabric 3 (3 strips) 15 diamonds;
Fabric 4 (2 strips) 12 diamonds;
Fabric 5 (3 strips) 16 diamonds;
Fabric 6 (2 strips) 11 diamonds.

Block Tops – Half Diamond B

Cut strips 5¼in (13.3cm) across the width of the fabric. Each strip will yield 11 triangles, rotating the template 180 degrees after each cut.
Cut strips and 108 half diamonds from fabrics as follows:
Fabric 7 (3 strips) 32 half diamonds;
Fabric 8 (2 strips) 18 half diamonds;
Fabric 9 (2 strips) 13 half diamonds;
Fabric 10 (2 strips) 13 half diamonds;
Fabric 11 (2 strips) 14 half diamonds;
Fabric 12 (3 strips) 18 half diamonds.

Partial Blocks – Quarter Diamonds C and C reverse

From the remaining pieces of fabric, cut 12 quarter diamonds and 12 reverse quarter diamonds as follows, ensuring the template grain-line arrow runs along the fabric strip:
Fabric 1 3 quarter diamonds;
Fabric 2 3 quarter diamonds;
Fabric 3 1 reverse quarter diamond;
Fabric 4 2 reverse quarter diamonds;
Fabric 5 2 reverse quarter diamonds;
Fabric 6 1 reverse quarter diamond;
Fabric 7 2 quarter diamonds, 2 reverse quarter diamonds;
Fabric 8 2 quarter diamonds, 2 reverse quarter diamonds;
Fabric 10 1 quarter diamond, 1 reverse quarter diamond;
Fabric 11 1 quarter diamond, 1 reverse quarter diamond.

Border

From Fabric 13 cut 7 strips 5½in (14cm) wide. Remove the selvedges and, matching the pattern, sew end to end. Cut 2 lengths 74in (188cm) for the quilt sides and 2 lengths 63in (160cm) for the quilt top and bottom.

Backing

From Fabric 14 cut 2 pieces 92in (234cm) long. Remove selvedges and sew together (the seam wil run vertically down the quilt). Trim to 71in x 92in (180cm x 234cm).

Binding

From Fabric 1 remove selvedges and cut 10 bias strips 2½in (6.4cm) wide, cutting diagonally at 45 degrees. Sew end to end with 45-degree seams (see page 141).

MAKING THE QUILT

Using a design wall will help to place patches in the required layout.
Use ¼in (6mm) seams throughout.

Centre

Referring to the Quilt Assembly Diagram and quilt photograph, lay out the patches to form diagonal rows of tumbling blocks. Check you have correctly placed the tumbling block sides – Diamond A, with dark sides on the right and lighter sides on the left. Position the block top half-diamond B pieces and fill in around the top and bottom edges with partial-block quarter-diamond C pieces.
Check your layout, then sew the patches together into 12 vertical columns, referring to the Quilt Assembly Diagram. Sew the columns together, taking care to match the crossing seams and the diamond points.

QUILT ASSEMBLY DIAGRAM

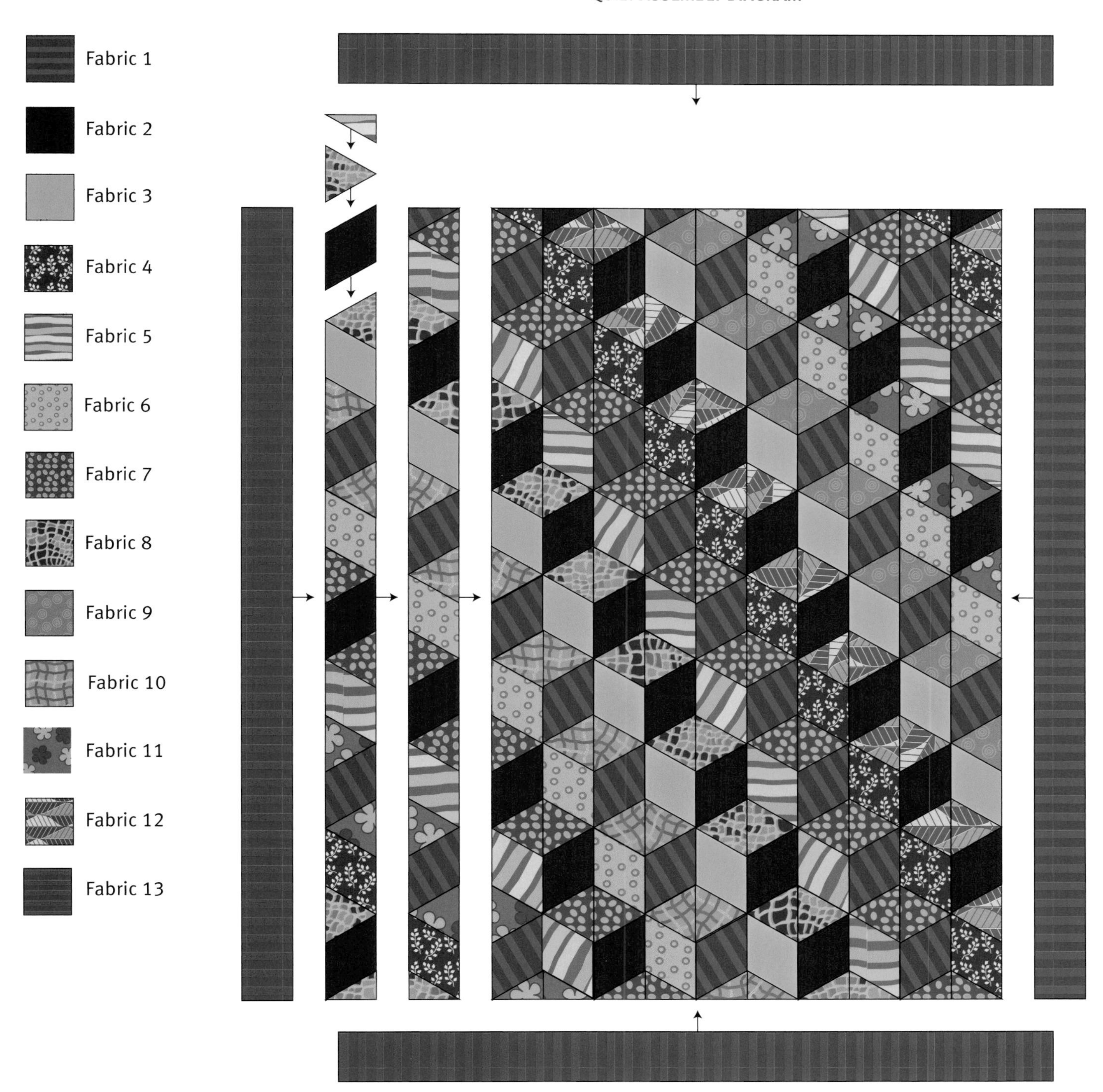

Borders

Pin the two longer borders to the sides of the quilt centre to prevent stretching, then sew. Press, then pin and sew the shorter borders to the top and bottom to complete the quilt top.

FINISHING THE QUILT

Press the quilt top. Layer the quilt top, batting and backing, and baste together (see page 140).

Quilt as desired.

Trim the quilt edges and attach the binding (see page 141).

cottage garden flowers **

Kaffe Fassett

Fussy-cut flowers in octagonal snowball blocks from brilliant flowery fabrics are set off by a wide border in Octopus fabric.

SIZE OF FINISHED QUILT
50$\frac{1}{2}$in x 62$\frac{1}{2}$in (129cm x 159cm)

FABRICS
Fabrics have been calculated at a maximum width of 40in (102cm). They have been given a number – see Fabric Swatch Diagram for details.

Patchwork Fabrics

AMARYLLIS

Fabric 1	Natural	$\frac{3}{8}$yd (40cm)
Fabric 2	Red	$\frac{3}{8}$yd (40cm)

BEARDED IRIS

Fabric 3	Cool	$\frac{3}{8}$yd (40cm)
Fabric 4	Ochre	$\frac{3}{8}$yd (40cm)

DANCING DAHLIAS

Fabric 5	Multi	$\frac{5}{8}$yd (60cm)
Fabric 6	Red	$\frac{3}{8}$yd (40cm)

CACTUS FLOWER

Fabric 7	Yellow	$\frac{3}{8}$yd (40cm)
Fabric 8	Multi	$\frac{3}{4}$yd (70cm)

COLEUS

Fabric 9	Green	$\frac{3}{8}$yd (40cm)

* see also Backing Fabric

WATERMELONS

Fabric 10	Green	$\frac{3}{8}$yd (40cm)

LOTUS LEAF

Fabric 11	Citrus	$\frac{3}{8}$yd (40cm)

ENCHANTED

Fabric 12	Green	$\frac{3}{8}$yd (40cm)
Fabric 13	Rust	$\frac{1}{2}$yd (50cm)

BRASSICA

Fabric 14	Pastel	$\frac{1}{2}$yd (50cm)

ABORIGINAL DOT

Fabric 15	Turquoise	1yd (95cm)

OCTOPUS

Fabric 16	Orange	1$\frac{5}{8}$yd (1.5m)

Backing and Binding Fabrics

COLEUS

Fabric 9	Green	3$\frac{3}{8}$yd (3.2m)

* see also Patchwork Fabric

SPOT

Fabric 17	White	$\frac{1}{2}$yd (50cm)

Batting
58$\frac{1}{2}$in x 70$\frac{1}{2}$in (149cm x 179cm)

FABRIC SWATCH DIAGRAM

Patchwork Fabrics

Fabric 1
AMARYLLIS
Natural
PJ104NL

Fabric 2
AMARYLLIS
Red
PJ104RD

Fabric 3
BEARDED IRIS
Cool
PJ105CL

Fabric 4
BEARDED IRIS
Ochre
PJ105OC

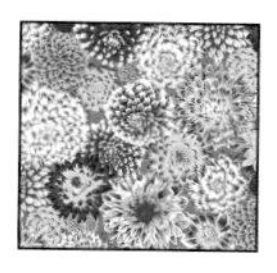
Fabric 5
DANCING DAHLIAS
Multi
PJ101MU

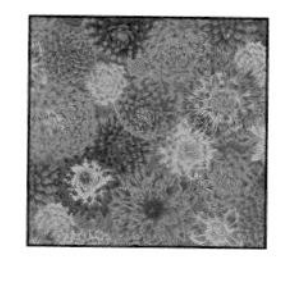
Fabric 6
DANCING DAHLIAS
Red
PJ101RD

Fabric 7
CACTUS FLOWER
Yellow
PJ96YE

Fabric 8
CACTUS FLOWER
Multi
PJ96MU

Fabric 9
COLEUS
Green
PJ30GN

Fabric 10
WATERMELONS
Green
PJ103GN

Fabric 11
LOTUS LEAF
Citrus
GP29CT

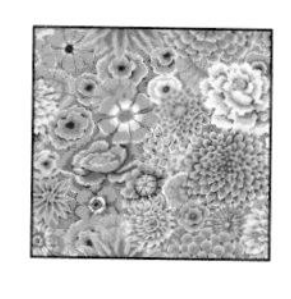
Fabric 12
ENCHANTED
Green
GP172GN

Fabric 13
ENCHANTED
Rust
GP172RU

Fabric 14
BRASSICA
Pastel
PJ51PT

Fabric 15
ABORIGINAL DOT
Turquoise
GP71TQ

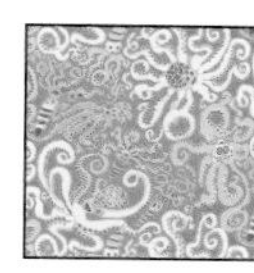
Fabric 16
OCTOPUS
Orange
BM74OR

Backing and Binding Fabrics

Fabric 9
COLEUS
Green
PJ30GN

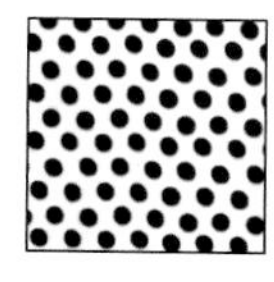
Fabric 17
SPOT
White
GP70WH

PATCHES

The quilt is made up with traditional octagonal snowball blocks. They are made the easy way using a large square of fussy-cut flowers, and 4 small squares of a contrasting fabric for each block. The small squares are stitched diagonally to each corner of the large square and trimmed and pressed to create each square block.

CUTTING OUT

Fabric is cut across the width unless otherwise stated.

Large Flower Squares

The large flower squares are fussy cut. You do not have to choose the ones shown in the quilt. Pick your own favourites if you prefer.

Fussy cut a total of 63 squares 6½in x 6½in (16.5cm x 16.5cm) from fabrics as follows:

Fabric 1 4 squares;
Fabric 2 3 squares;
Fabric 3 4 squares;
Fabric 4 3 squares;
Fabric 5 8 squares;
Fabric 6 3 squares;
Fabric 7 4 squares;
Fabric 8 10 squares;
Fabric 9 4 squares;
Fabric 10 2 squares;
Fabric 11 3 squares;
Fabric 12 4 squares;
Fabric 13 6 squares;
Fabric 14 5 squares.

Small Corner Squares

From Fabric 15 cut 15 strips 2¼in (5.7cm) wide and cross cut squares at 2¼in (5.7cm). Each strip will yield 17 squares. Cut a total of 252 squares.

Border

From Fabric 16 cut 4 strips 4½in (11.4cm) wide down the length of the fabric. Trim 2 strips to 54in (138.4cm) for the side borders and 2 strips to 50in (128.3cm) for the top and bottom borders.

Backing

From Fabric 16 cut 1 piece of fabric 40in x 58½in (101.6cm x 148.6cm) and 1 piece 31in x 58½in (78.7cm x 148.6cm).

BLOCK ASSEMBLY DIAGRAM

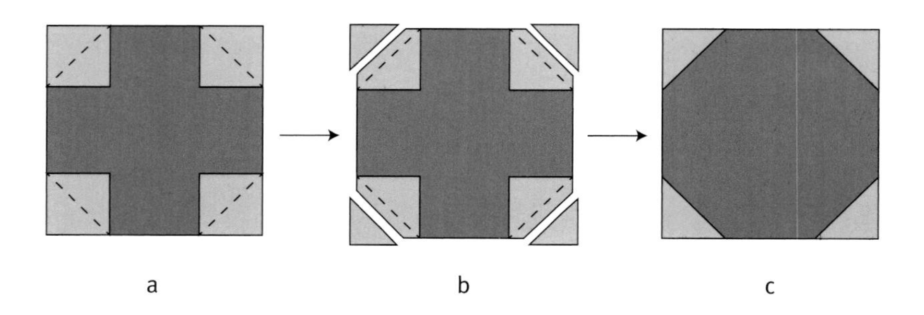

Binding

From Fabric 17 cut 6 strips 2½in (6.4cm) wide. Remove selvedges and sew strips end to end with 45-degree seams (see page 141).

MAKING THE QUILT

Using a design wall will help to place patches in the required layout.

Use ¼in (6mm) seams throughout.

Snowball Blocks

Take one large flower square and 4 small corner squares for each block. Following the sequence in the Block Assembly Diagram, place the 4 small squares right sides together on each corner of the large flower square, matching the edges carefully. Stitch diagonally across the small squares as shown (a) and trim the corners to a ¼in (6mm) seam allowance (b). Press the corners towards the centre (c). Make 63 blocks in total and return them to the design wall.

Quilt Centre

Lay out the blocks in 9 rows of 7, referring to the Quilt Assembly Diagram and the quilt photograph. Sew 1 row at a time, pressing the seams in the same direction on alternate rows – odd rows to the left, even rows to the right. This will allow the finished seams to lie flat. Pin, then sew, the 9 rows together, carefully matching crossing seams.

Border

Pin the side borders to the quilt centre (to prevent stretching) and sew, then press the seams. Pin and sew the top and bottom borders to the quilt centre and press to complete the top.

FINISHING THE QUILT

Sew the Fabric 9 backing pieces together to form a piece 58½in x 70½in (149cm x 179cm).

Press the quilt top. Layer the quilt top, batting and backing, and baste together (see page 140).

Quilt as desired.

Trim the quilt edges and attach the binding (see page 141).

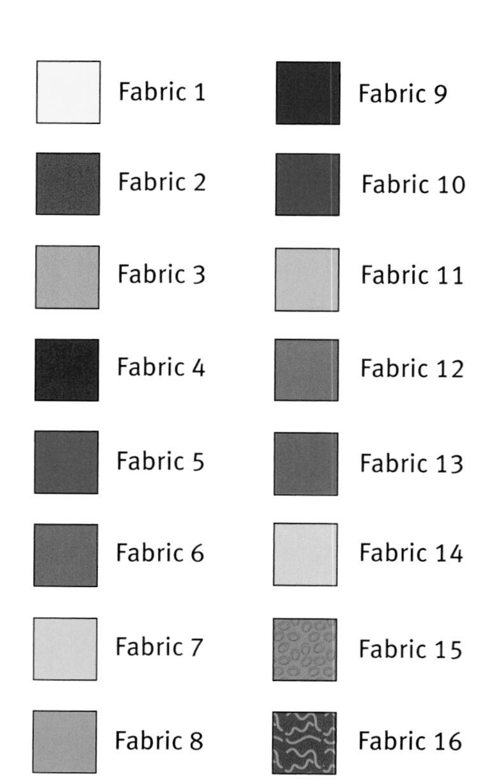

QUILT ASSEMBLY DIAGRAM

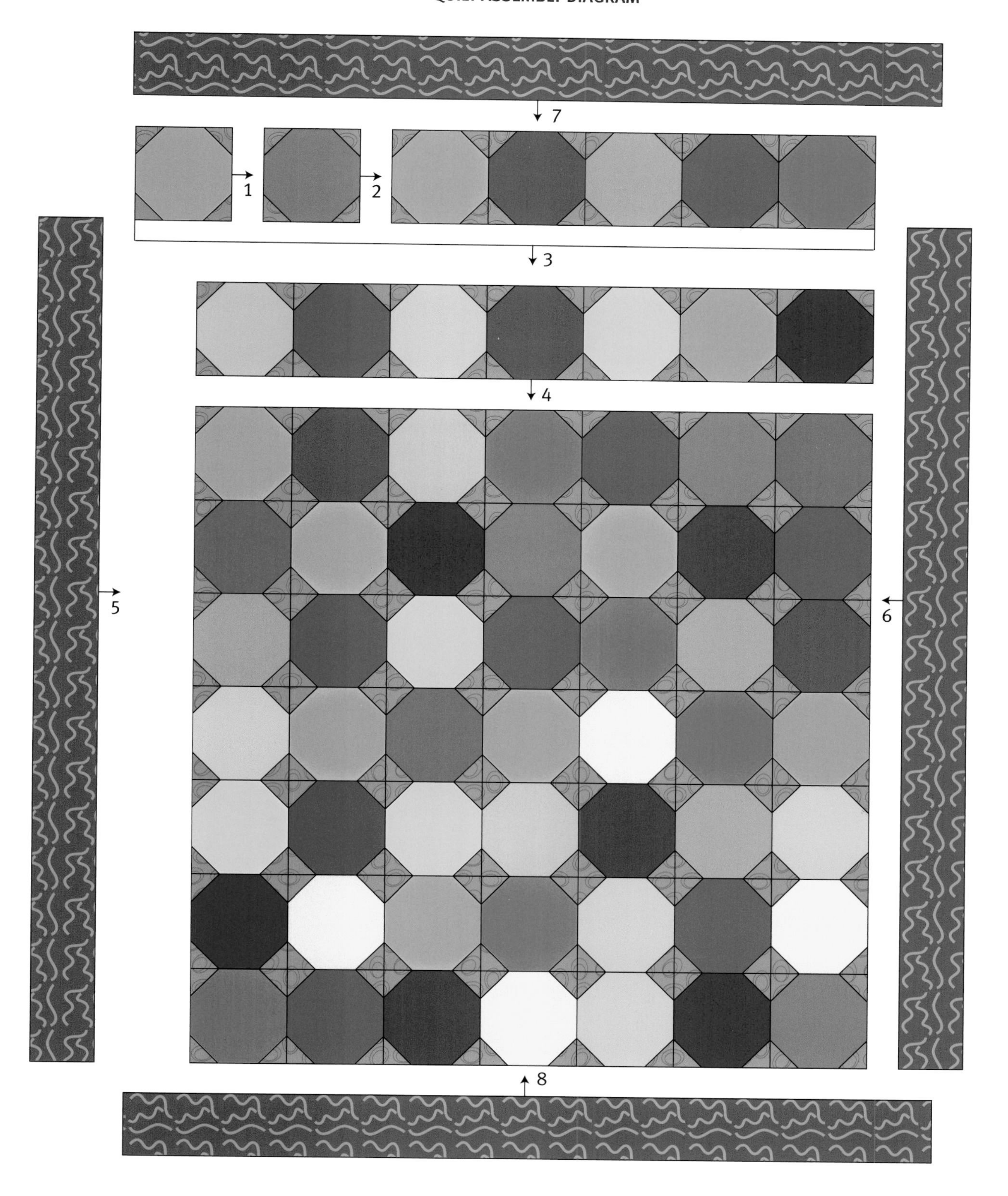

ancient glade **

Kaffe Fassett

Deep, rich glowing greens create a sumptuous quilt using triangles arranged to form a large on-point square pattern.

SIZE OF FINISHED QUILT

$81\frac{1}{2}$in x $68\frac{1}{2}$in (207cm x 174cm)

FABRICS

Fabrics have been calculated at a maximum width of 40in (102cm) . They have been given a number – see Fabric Swatch Diagram for details.

Patchwork Fabrics

AMARYLLIS
Fabric 1 Green $\frac{1}{4}$yd (25cm)
ROMAN GLASS
Fabric 2 Emerald $\frac{1}{2}$yd (50cm)
* see also Binding Fabric
WATERMELONS
Fabric 3 Grey $\frac{1}{2}$yd (50cm)
ANIMAL
Fabric 4 Sage 2yd (1.9m)
AGATE
Fabric 5 Green $\frac{7}{8}$yd (85cm)
PAPERWEIGHT
Fabric 6 Algae $\frac{3}{4}$yd (70cm)
WISTERIA
Fabric 7 Teal $\frac{1}{2}$yd (50cm)
JUMBLE
Fabric 8 Moss $\frac{1}{2}$yd (50cm)
MAD PLAID
Fabric 9 Contrast $\frac{5}{8}$yd (60cm)

Backing and Binding Fabrics

JUPITER
Fabric 10 Malachite 5yd (4.65m)
ROMAN GLASS
Fabric 2 Emerald $\frac{5}{8}$yd (60cm)
* see also Patchwork Fabric

Batting

90in x 77in (229cm x 196cm)

PATCHES

A half-square triangle shape, cut from squares, from strips cut across the width of the fabric. Triangles are arranged to create a large on-point square pattern, sewn together in pairs to form squares and set in 10 rows of 8 squares to form the centre of the quilt.

FABRIC SWATCH DIAGRAM

Patchwork Fabrics

Fabric 1
AMARYLLIS
Green
PJ104GN

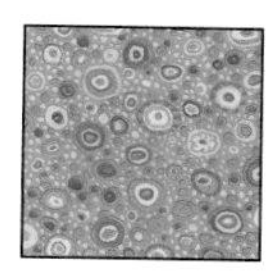

Fabric 2
ROMAN GLASS
Emerald
GP01EM

Fabric 3
WATERMELONS
Grey
PJ103GY

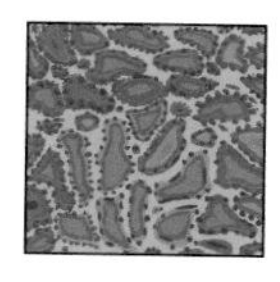

Fabric 4
ANIMAL
Sage
BM76SJ

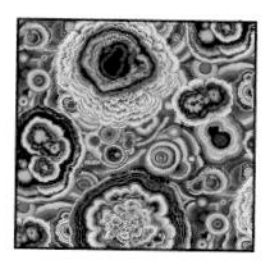

Fabric 5
AGATE
Green
PJ106GN

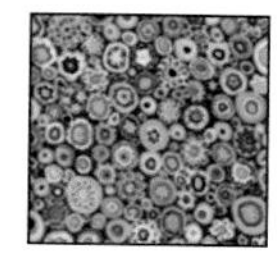

Fabric 6
PAPERWEIGHT
Algae
GP20AG

Fabric 7
WISTERIA
Teal
PJ102TE

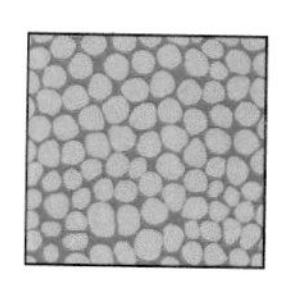

Fabric 8
JUMBLE
Moss
BM53MS

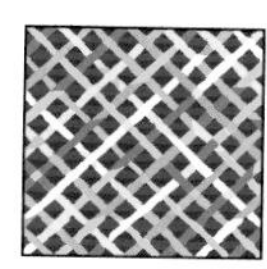

Fabric 9
MAD PLAID
Contrast
BM37CN

Backing and Binding Fabrics

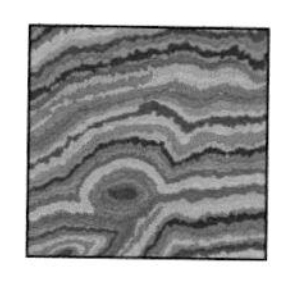

Fabric 10
JUPITER
Malachite
GP131MA

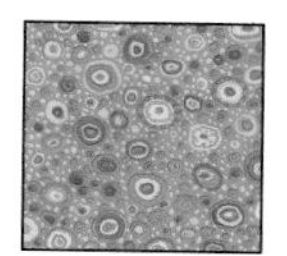

Fabric 2
ROMAN GLASS
Emerald
GP01EM

CUTTING OUT

Fabric is cut across the width of the fabric unless otherwise stated. When required strips are longer than 40in (102cm), remove selvedges and join strips end to end for required length.
Use $\frac{1}{4}$in (6mm) seams throughout.

Centre

Cut strips $7\frac{3}{8}$in (18.7cm) wide and cross cut squares at $7\frac{3}{8}$in (18.7cm). Cut each square once diagonally to make 2 triangles. Each strip will yield 5 squares, 10 triangles per strip. Cut a total of 80 squares to yield 160 triangles from fabrics as follows:
Fabric 1 (1 strip) 8 triangles;
Fabric 2 (2 strips) 12 triangles;
Fabric 3 (2 strips) 20 triangles;
Fabric 4 (3 strips) 28 triangles;
Fabric 5 (4 strips) 32 triangles;
Fabric 6 (3 strips) 28 triangles;
Fabric 7 (2 strips) 20 triangles;
Fabric 8 (2 strips) 12 triangles.

Border 1

From Fabric 4 cut 7 strips $6\frac{1}{2}$in (16.5cm) wide. Remove selvedges and sew together end to end. Press seams open.

Border 2

From Fabric 9 cut 8 strips $2\frac{1}{2}$in (6.4cm) wide. Remove selvedges and sew together end to end. Press seams open.

Backing

From Fabric 10 backing fabric cut 2 pieces 90in x 40in (228.6cm x 102cm).

Binding

From Fabric 2 cut 8 strips $2\frac{1}{2}$in (6.4cm) wide. Remove selvedges and sew strips end to end with 45-degree seams (see page 141).

MAKING THE QUILT
Using a design wall will help to place patches in the required layout. Use ¼in (6mm) seams throughout.

Centre
Lay out the triangles as shown in the quilt photograph and the Quilt Assembly Diagram. Sew the pairs of triangles together along the long diagonal edge to form the square blocks. (Take care not to stretch the triangles when sewing as they have bias edges.) Gently press seams flat without stretching them.
Return each square to the design wall. Check the layout is correctly formed of 80 square blocks (10 rows of 8) then sew the blocks together in rows, pressing seams in the same direction on alternate rows – odd rows to the left, even rows to the right – to allow the finished seams to lie flat. Sew the 10 rows together, carefully matching crossing seams, and press the quilt centre.

Border 1
From the Fabric 4 border fabric cut 2 pieces 65½in (166.4cm) for the side borders. Pin and sew to each side, and press seams open. Then cut 2 pieces 64½in (163.8cm) for the top and bottom borders. Pin and sew to the top and bottom, and press seams.

Border 2
From the Fabric 9 border fabric cut 2 pieces 77½in (196.9cm) for the side borders. Pin and sew to each side and press seams open. Cut 2 pieces 68½in (174cm) for the top and bottom borders. Pin and sew to the top and bottom to complete the quilt top.

FINISHING THE QUILT
Sew the Fabric 2 backing pieces together along the long edge and trim to form a piece 90in x 77in (229cm x 196cm).
Press the quilt top. Layer the quilt top, batting and backing, and baste together (see page 140).
Quilt as desired.
Trim the quilt edges make and attach the binding (see page 141).

QUILT ASSEMBLY DIAGRAM

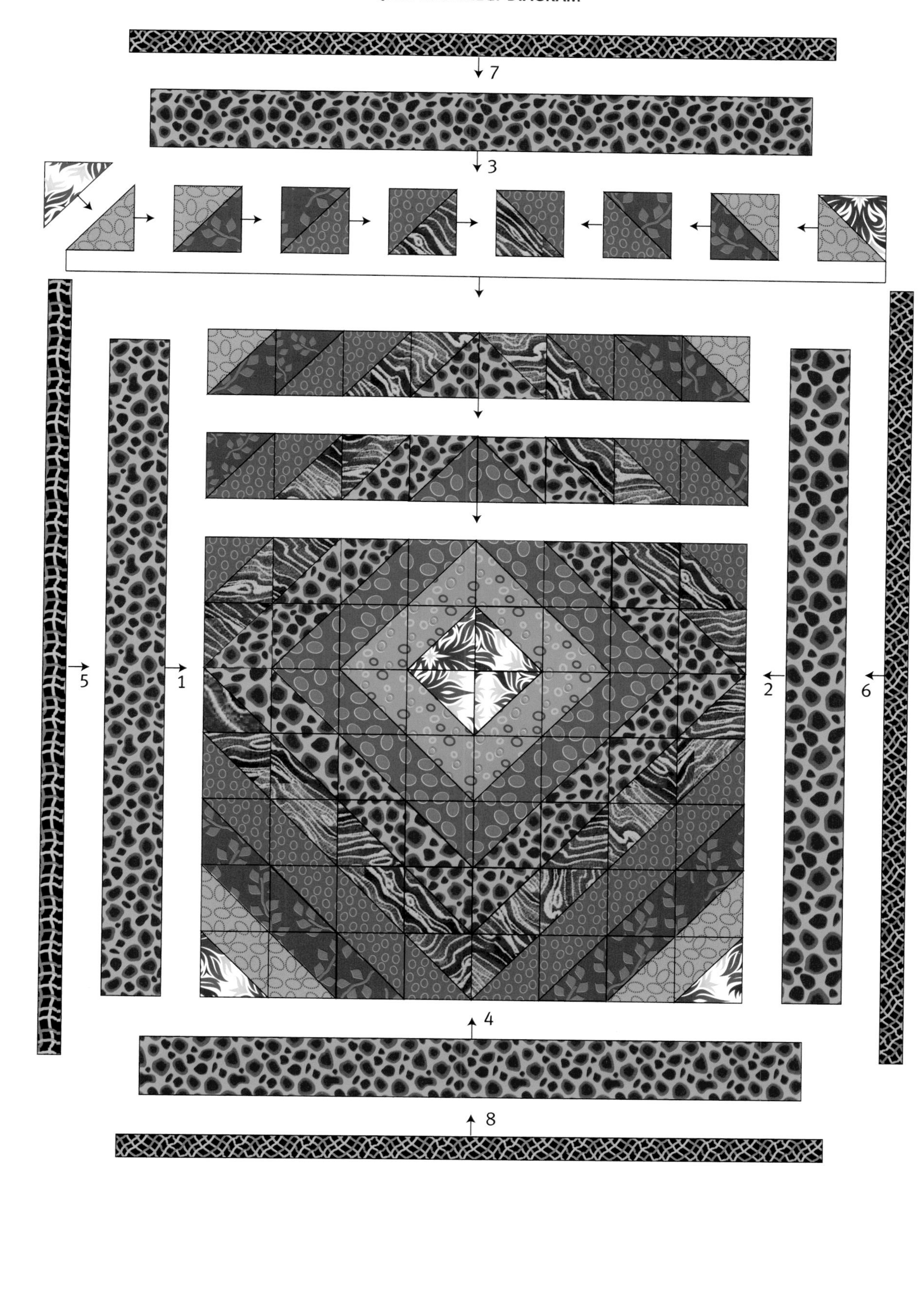

Fabric 1

Fabric 2

Fabric 3

Fabric 4

Fabric 5

Fabric6

Fabric 7

Fabric 8

Fabric 9

blooming columns **

Kaffe Fassett

This bold contrasting striped quilt with brilliant Japanese Chrysanthemum fabric blooms will require experience of machine appliqué techniques to achieve the best results.

SIZE OF FINISHED QUILT

67½in x 52½in (171.5cm x 133.4cm)

FABRICS

Fabrics have been calculated at a maximum width of 40in (102cm). They have been given a number – see Fabric Swatch Diagram for details.

Patchwork Fabrics

SPOT
Fabric 1 Duck Egg 1⅛yd (1.1m)
ABORIGINAL DOT
Fabric 2 Orchid 1⅜yd (1.3m)
JAPANESE CHRYSANTHEMUM
Fabric 3 Autumn 1yd (95cm)
Fabric 4 Scarlet 1yd (95cm)
SHOT COTTON
Fabric 5 Paprika ⅞yd (85cm)

Backing and Binding Fabrics

GUINEA FLOWER
Fabric 6 White 3½yd (3.3m)
JUMBLE
Fabric 7 Black ⅝yd (60cm)

Batting

76 in x 61in (193cm x 155cm)

Double-sided fusible webbing

1½yd x 1yd (137.2cm x 91.5cm)

PATCHES

The background is made up of 11 alternating strips, 6 dark and 5 light. Fussy-cut flower patches are fused and machine embroidered onto the background. A simple contrasting border completes the quilt.

CUTTING OUT

Fabric is cut across the width of the fabric unless otherwise stated. When required strips are longer than 40in (102cm) – the width of the fabric – join strips end to end to obtain the required length. Use a ¼in (6mm) seam and press seams open.

Centre

From Fabric 1 cut 8 strips 4½in (11.4 cm) wide.
From Fabric 2 cut 10 strips 4½in (11.4 cm) wide.

Appliqué Flowers

Using the quilt photograph as a guide, apply a piece of fusible webbing (following the manufacturer's instructions) to the wrong side of each chosen flower, making sure it extends at least ½in (1.3cm) beyond the flower edge.
Once the webbing is bonded to the wrong side of the fabric, roughly cut out the flower leaving a ¼in (6mm) allowance around the flower shape.
From Fabric 3 cut 7 flowers.
From Fabric 4 cut 9 flowers.
Note: Ample fabric has been listed to provide more flower motifs than required from each fabric but they may not be identical to those in the quilt. It will depend on how the individual yardage has been cut.

Border

From Fabric 5 cut 6 strips 4½in (11.4cm) wide.

Backing

From Fabric 6 cut 2 pieces 40in x 61in (101.6cm x 155cm).

Binding

From Fabric 7 cut 7 strips 2½in (6.4cm) wide. Remove selvedges and sew strips end to end with 45-degree seams (see page 141).

MAKING THE QUILT

Using a design wall will help to place pieces in the required layout.
Use ¼in (6mm) seams throughout.

Centre Background

Join the strips of each fabric end to end to make a long strip in each fabric, pressing seams open. Cut as follows:
From the long strip in Fabric 1 cut 5 lengths 59½in (151.1cm) long.
From the long strip in Fabric 2 cut 6 lengths 59½in (151.1cm) long.
Referring to the Quilt Assembly Diagram (overleaf) and quilt photograph, sew Fabric 1 and Fabric 2 background strips together, starting and ending with Fabric 2, to make a centre panel 59½in x 44½in (151.1cm x 113cm). Sew the strips from

FABRIC SWATCH DIAGRAM

Patchwork Fabrics

Fabric 1
SPOT
Duck Egg
GP70DE

Fabric 2
ABORIGINAL DOT
Orchid
GP71OD

Fabric 3
JAPANESE CHRYSANTHEMUM
Autumn
PJ41AU

Fabric 4
JAPANESE CHRYSANTHEMUM
Scarlet
PJ41SC

Fabric 5
SHOT COTTON
Paprika
SC101PP

Backing and Binding Fabrics

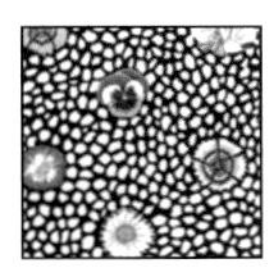

Fabric 6
GUINEA FLOWER
White
GP59WH

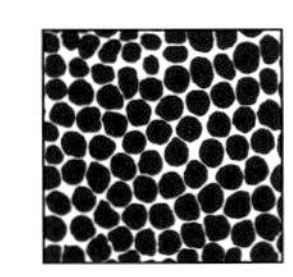

Fabric 7
JUMBLE
Black
BM53BK

alternate ends to prevent bowing and press all seam allowances towards the darker strips.

Appliqué Flowers

Once you have decided on the layout of the flowers, carefully trim the seam allowance back to the edge of the flower, using small, sharp embroidery scissors to cut as accurately as possible.

Once trimmed, pin the flowers in position. Fuse the flowers into position, referring to the fusible web manufacturer's instructions.

Appliqué the raw edges of the flowers with a free-motion machine straight stitch, or a stitch of your choice.

Note: Flowers in this quilt were appliquéd using a free-motion machine embroidery foot.

Borders

Press the quilt centre before adding the borders.

Join the strips end to end to make one long strip. Press the connecting seams open. From this long strip cut 2 pieces 59½in (151.1cm) long for the quilt sides and then cut 2 pieces 52½in (133.4cm) for the quilt top and bottom.

Pin (to prevent stretching) and sew the longer borders to the quilt sides, then press seams towards the quilt centre. Pin in place and sew the shorter borders to the top and bottom of the quilt. Press the seams towards the quilt centre.

FINISHING THE QUILT

Remove selvedges and sew the Fabric 6 backing fabric pieces together. Trim to form a piece 76in x 61in (193cm x 155cm).

Press the quilt top. Layer the quilt top, batting and backing, and baste together (see page 140).

Quilt as desired. (The original was machine quilted using an embroidery foot and with the feeder teeth dropped for free-motion quilting – refer to quilting detail photograph).

Trim the quilt edges and attach the binding (see page 141).

QUILT ASSEMBLY DIAGRAM

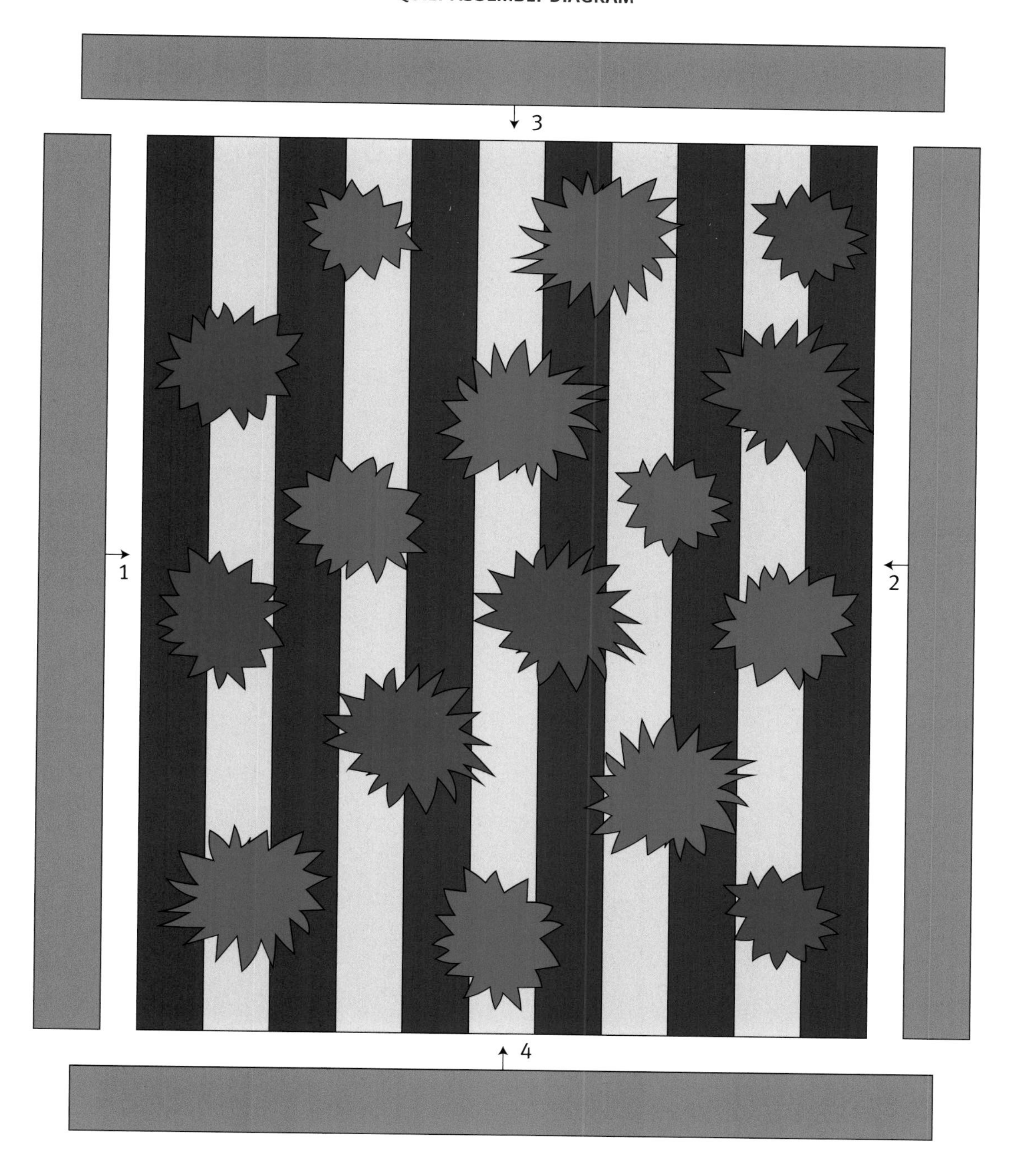

peach sunset *

Kaffe Fassett

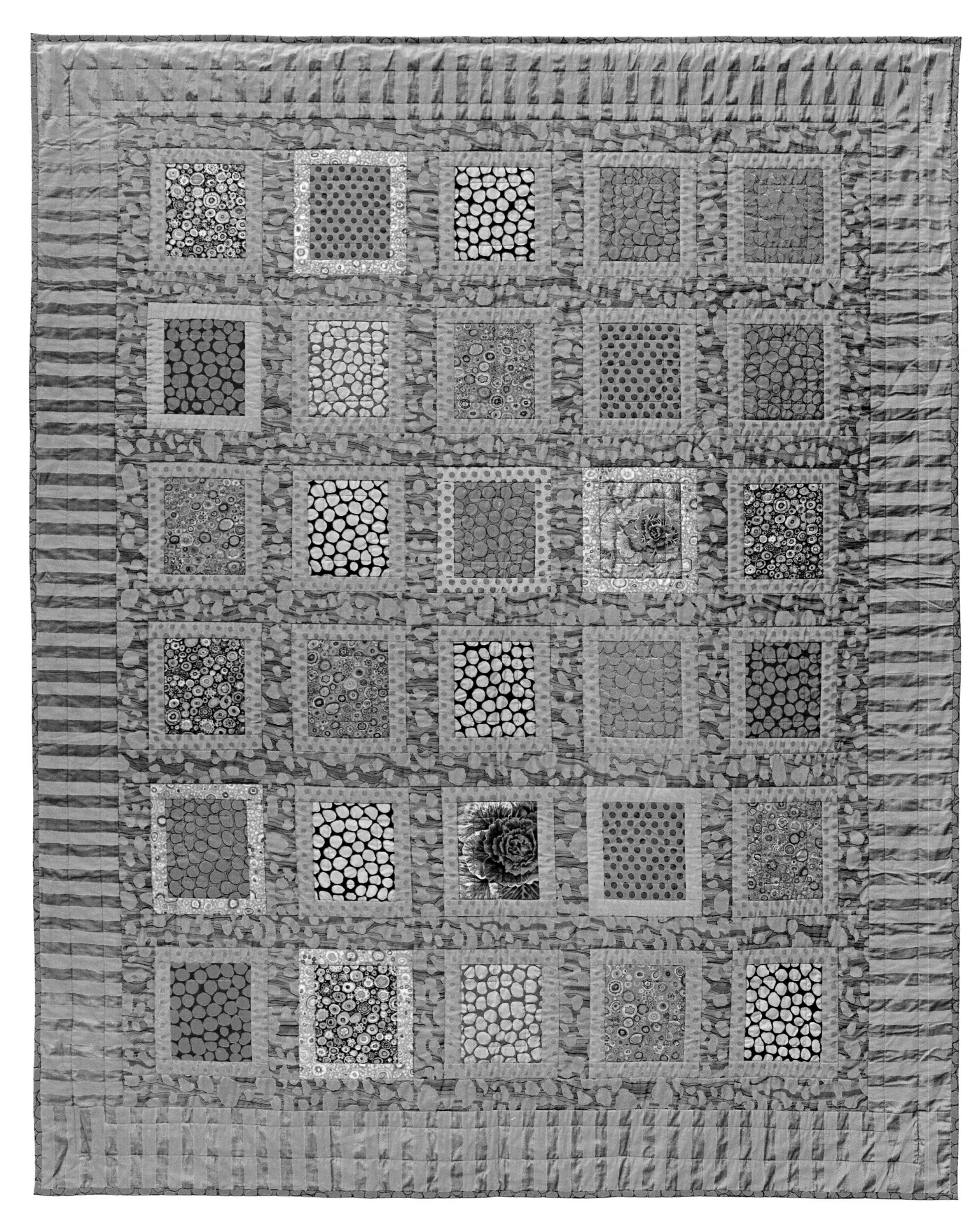

Framed rectangular blocks in shades of peach and orange are separated by sashing and completed with a wide border of directional stripes. Using warm colours only creates a quilt that positively glows.

FABRIC SWATCH DIAGRAM

Patchwork Fabrics

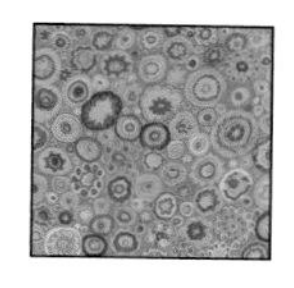

Fabric 1
PAPERWEIGHT
Pink
GP20PK

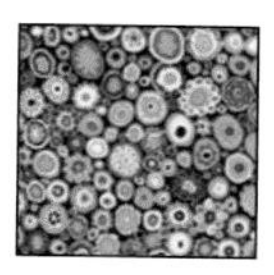

Fabric 2
PAPERWEIGHT
Pumpkin
GP20PN

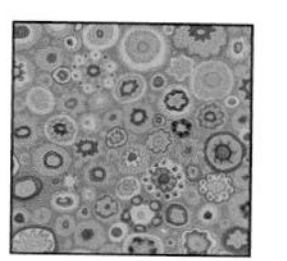

Fabric 3
PAPERWEIGHT
Red
GP20RD

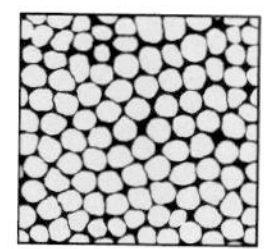

Fabric 4
JUMBLE
Rose
BM53RO

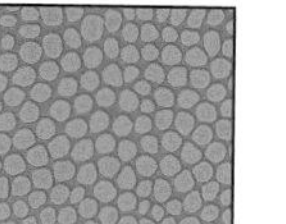

Fabric 5
JUMBLE
Tangerine
BM53TN

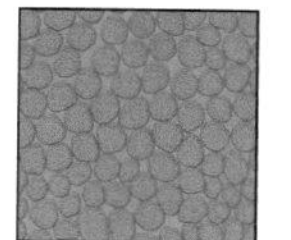

Fabric 6
JUMBLE
Pink
BM53PK

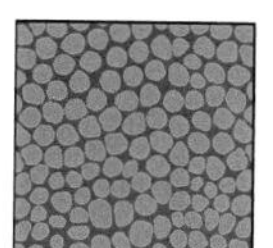

Fabric 7
JUMBLE
Orange
BM53OR

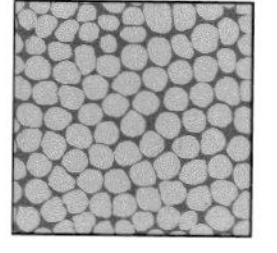

Fabric 8
JUMBLE
Saffron
BM53SX

Fabric 9
SPOT
Orange
GP70OR

Fabric 10
SPOT
Peach
GP70PH

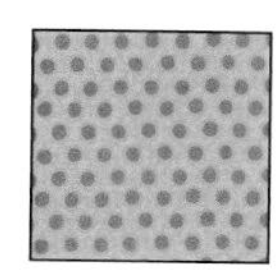

Fabric 11
SPOT
Gold
GP70GD

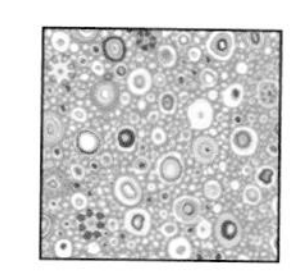

Fabric 12
ROMAN GLASS
Pink
GP01PK

Fabric 13
SHOT COTTON
Sunflower
SC112SF

Fabric 14
BRASSICA
Brown
PJ51BR

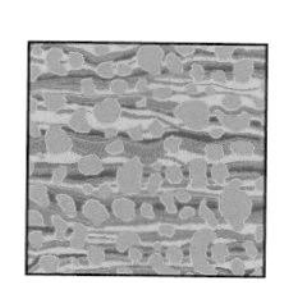

Fabric 15
STREAM
Orange
BM75OR

Fabric 16
WIDE STRIPE
Cantaloupe
SS01CA

Backing and Binding Fabrics

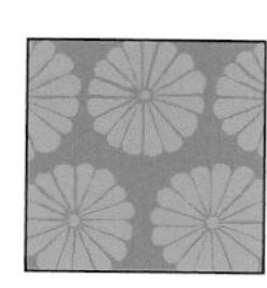

Fabric 17
DAMASK FLOWER
Orange
GP183OR

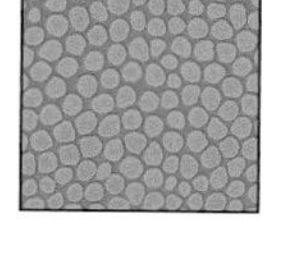

Fabric 5
JUMBLE
Tangerine
BM53TN

SIZE OF FINISHED QUILT
57½in x 72½in (146cm x 185cm)

FABRICS
Fabrics have been calculated at a maximum width of 40in (102cm). They have been given a number – see Fabric Swatch Diagram for details.

Patchwork Fabrics

PAPERWEIGHT		
Fabric 1	Pink	¼yd (25cm)
PAPERWEIGHT		
Fabric 2	Pumpkin	¼yd (25cm)
PAPERWEIGHT		
Fabric 3	Red	¼yd (25cm)
JUMBLE		
Fabric 4	Rose	¼yd (25cm)
JUMBLE		
Fabric 5	Tangerine	¼yd (25cm)
* see also Binding Fabric		
JUMBLE		
Fabric 6	Pink	¼yd (25cm)
JUMBLE		
Fabric 7	Orange	¼yd (25cm)
JUMBLE		
Fabric 8	Saffron	¼yd (25cm)
SPOT		
Fabric 9	Orange	¼yd (25cm)
SPOT		
Fabric 10	Peach	⅞yd (85cm)
SPOT		
Fabric11	Gold	⅛yd (15cm)
ROMAN GLASS		
Fabric 12	Pink	¼yd (25cm)
SHOT COTTON		
Fabric 13	Sunflower	⅛yd (15cm)
BRASSICA		
Fabric 14	Brown	¼yd (25cm)
STREAM		
Fabric 15	Orange	1½yd (1.4m)
WIDE STRIPE		
Fabric 16	Cantaloupe	1yd (95cm)

Backing and Binding Fabrics

DAMASK FLOWER		
Fabric 17	Orange	4½yd (4.2m)
JUMBLE		
Fabric 5	Tangerine	⅝yd (60cm)
* see also Patchwork Fabric		

Batting
66in x 81in (168cm x 206cm)

PATCHES

Framed blocks are made of 1 rectangle patch 5in x 6in (12.7cm x 15.2cm) finished, framed by a 1in (2.5cm) finished border. Each framed block measures 7in x 8in (17.8cm x 20.3cm) finished.
The 30 framed blocks are set in 6 rows of 5 blocks with directional sashing 2in (5.1cm) wide finished and a 5in (12.7cm) wide border completing the quilt.

CUTTING OUT

Fabrics are cut across the width, unless otherwise stated. When required strips are longer than 40in (102cm) – the width of the fabric – join strips end to end to obtain the required length. Use ¼in (6mm) seam allowance and press seams open.

Blocks

Cut a strip 5½in (14cm) wide across the width of each of Fabrics 1–9 and cross cut 30 rectangles 5½in x 6½in (14cm x 16.5cm) from strips as follows:
Fabric 1 2 rectangles;
Fabric 2 4 rectangles;
Fabric 3 3 rectangles;
Fabric 4 5 rectangles;
Fabric 5 4 rectangles;
Fabric 6 2 rectangles;
Fabric 7 3 rectangles;
Fabric 8 2 rectangles;
Fabric 9 3 rectangles.
From Fabric 14 fussy cut 2 rectangles 5½in x 6½in (14cm x 16.5cm) that each show a large part of a Brassica head, referring to the quilt photograph for guidance.

Block Frames

Each block frame requires:
2 pieces cut 1½in x 6½in (3.8cm x 16.5cm) for the sides, and 2 pieces cut 1½in x 7½in (3.8cm x 19.1cm) for the top and bottom.
Cut strips 1½in (3.8cm) wide. Each strip will give you either 6 side pieces or 5 top or bottom pieces. Cut a total of 120 pieces (30 sets of sides, tops and bottoms) from fabrics as follows:
Fabric 10 (17 strips) 46 side pieces, 46 top and bottom pieces;
Fabric 11 (1 strip) 2 side pieces, 2 top and bottom pieces;
Fabric 12 (3 strips) 8 side pieces, 8 top and bottom pieces;
Fabric 13 (2 strips) 4 side pieces, 4 top and bottom pieces.

Sashing

Sashing is cut directionally so that the horizontal lines of the fabric run across the quilt on all pieces.
From Fabric 15 cut as follows:
For vertical sashing: Cut 3 strips 8½in (21.6cm) wide and cross cut 2½in (6.4cm) pieces. Each strip will yield 16 pieces. Cut a total of 36 pieces 8½in x 2½in (21.6cm x 6.4cm).
For horizontal sashing: Cut 9 strips 2½in (6.4cm) wide, remove selvedges and sew them end to end. Cross cut 7 horizontal sashing strips, each measuring 2½in x 47½in (6.4cm x 120.7cm).

Border

From Fabric 16 cut 6 strips 5½in (14cm) wide across the width of the fabric, remove selvedges and join them end to end. From the length cut:
2 pieces 5½in x 62½in (14cm x 158.8cm) for the side borders.
2 pieces 5½in x 57½in (14cm x 146.1cm) for the top and bottom borders.

Backing

From Fabric 17 cut 1 piece 40in x 81in (101.6cm x 206cm) and 1 piece 26½in x 81in (67.3cm x 206cm).

Binding

From Fabric 7 cut 7 strips 2½in (6.4cm) wide. Remove selvedges and sew end to end with 45-degree seams (see page 141).

BLOCK ASSEMBLY DIAGRAM

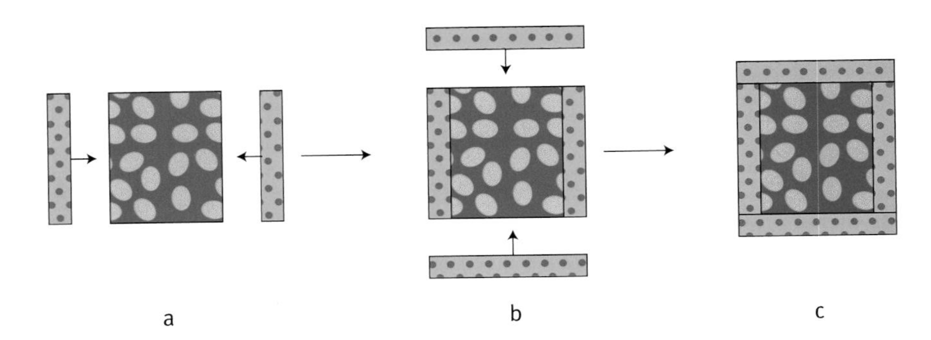

MAKING THE QUILT

Using a design wall will help to place patches in the required layout.
Use ¼in (6mm) seams throughout.

Making the Blocks

To make the framed blocks, refer to the Block Assembly Diagram. Take 1 rectangle piece and attach side strips (a). Press and attach top and bottom strips (b) to complete the block (c).
Make 30 blocks in total.

Centre

Referring to the Quilt Assembly Diagram and quilt photograph for block placement, lay out the blocks. Each row has 5 framed blocks, each of which is connected with vertical sashing strips. Sew the blocks and sashing strips together into rows, starting and ending each row with a sashing strip. Press seams towards the sashing.
Add the long horizontal sashing strips to the rows of blocks. To avoid stretching the long pieces, pin and then sew them to each row of blocks and to the top and bottom of the quilt centre. Press seams towards the sashing.

Border

Referring to the Quilt Assembly Diagram, pin each side border, 5½in x 62½in (14cm x 158.8cm), to the quilt centre and sew, pressing seams towards the sashing. Then pin and sew the top and bottom borders, 5½in x 57½in (14cm x 146.1cm), to the quilt, again pressing seams towards the sashing.

QUILT ASSEMBLY DIAGRAM

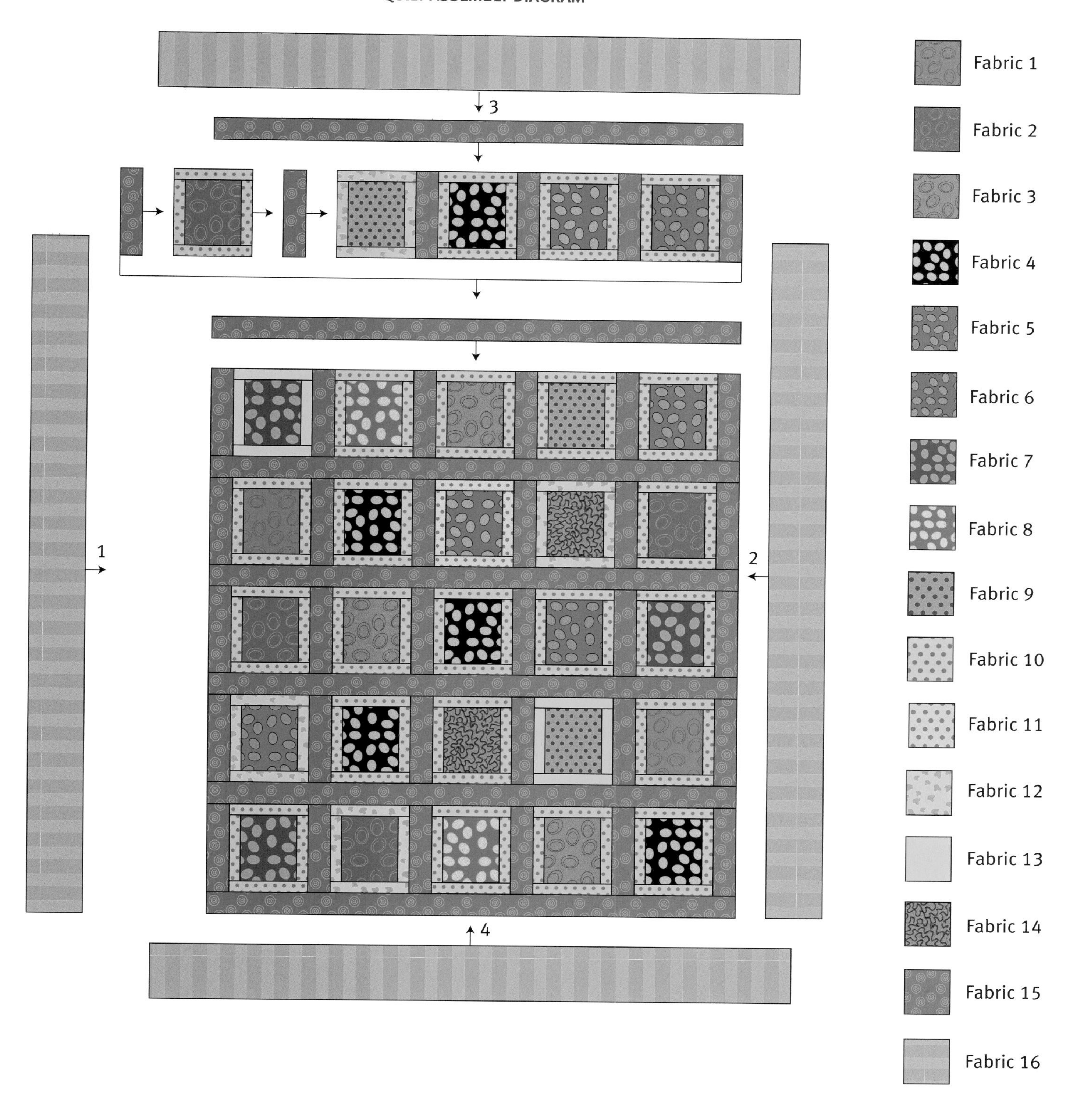

FINISHING THE QUILT

Sew the two Fabric 17 backing pieces together and trim to form a piece 66in x 81in (168cm x 206cm).

Press the quilt top. Layer the quilt top, batting and backing, and baste together (see page 140).

Quilt as desired.

Trim the quilt edges and attach the binding (see page 141).

dark watermelons *

Kaffe Fassett

Deep blues, purples and reds, with an occasional flash of green, echo the shades in the Watermelons Earth fabric central panel and the Wisteria Black borders. The result is a strong statement quilt in an eye-catching yet very easy design.

FINISHED SIZE
70in x 76in (178cm x 194cm)

FABRICS
Fabrics have been calculated at a maximum width of 40in (102cm). They have been given a number – see Fabric Swatch Diagram for details.

Patchwork Fabrics

WATERMELONS		
Fabric 1	Earth	¾yd (70cm)
Fabric 2	Blue	¼yd (25cm)
Fabric 3	Red	¼yd (25cm)
ANIMAL		
Fabric 4	Pink	¼yd (25cm)
Fabric 5	Green	¼yd (25cm)
Fabric 6	Sage	¼yd (25cm)
Fabric 7	Purple	¼yd (25cm)
Fabric 8	Orange	¼yd (25cm)
MILLEFIORE		
Fabric 9	Dusty	¼yd (25cm)
STREAM		
Fabric 10	Magenta	¼yd (25cm)
OCTOPUS		
Fabric 11	Red	¼yd (25cm)
LOTUS LEAF		
Fabric 12	Vintage	¼yd (25cm)
AGATE		
Fabric 13	Red	¼yd (25cm)
Fabric 14	Ochre	¼yd (25cm)
DANCING DAHLIAS		
Fabric 15	Dark	¼yd (25cm)
Fabric 16	Blue	¼yd (25cm)
BEARDED IRIS		
Fabric 17	Dark	¼yd (25cm)
WISTERIA		
Fabric 18	Teal	¼yd (25cm)
Fabric 19	Black	2yd (1.9m)

Backing and Binding

ORANGES		
Fabric 20	Purple	4¾yd (4.4m)
SPOT		
Fabric 21	Burgundy	⅝yd (60cm)

Batting
79in x 85in (200cm x 216cm)

FABRIC SWATCH DIAGRAM

Patchwork Fabrics

Fabric 1
WATERMELONS
Earth
PJ103ER

Fabric 2
WATERMELONS
Blue
PJ103BL

Fabric 3
WATERMELONS
Red
PJ103RD

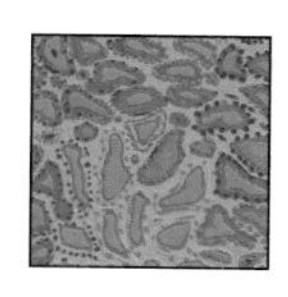

Fabric 4
ANIMAL
Pink
BM076PK

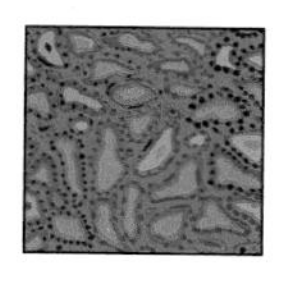

Fabric 5
ANIMAL
Green
BM076GN

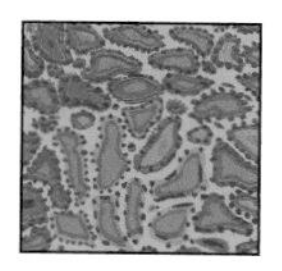

Fabric 6
ANIMAL
Sage
BM076SJ

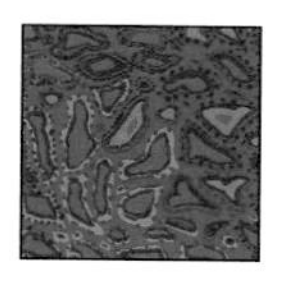

Fabric 7
ANIMAL
Purple
BM076PU

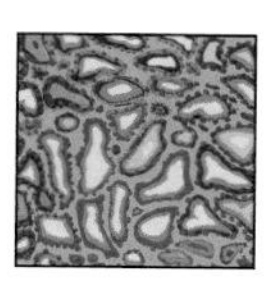

Fabric 8
ANIMAL
Orange
BM076OR

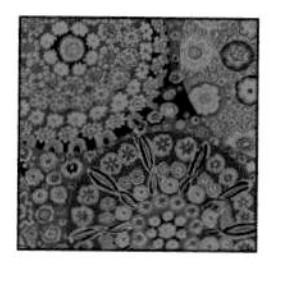

Fabric 9
MILLEFIORE
Dusty
GP092DY

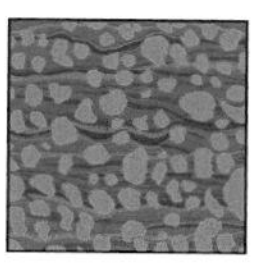

Fabric 10
STREAM
Magenta
BM075MG

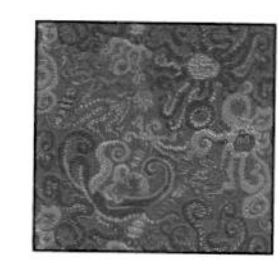

Fabric 11
OCTOPUS
Red
BM074RD

Fabric 12
LOTUS LEAF
Vintage
GP029VN

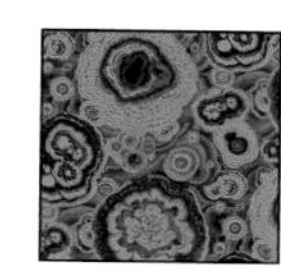

Fabric 13
AGATE
Red
PJ106RD

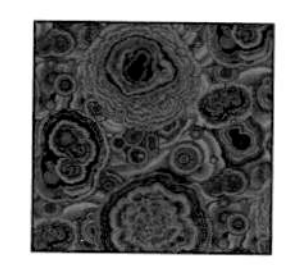

Fabric 14
AGATE
Ochre
PJ106OC

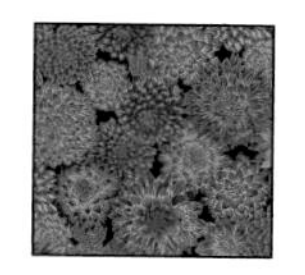

Fabric 15
DANCING DAHLIAS
Dark
PJ101DK

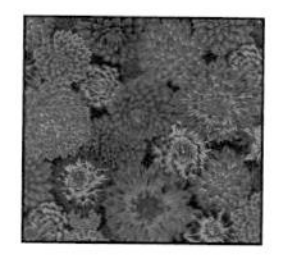

Fabric 16
DANCING DAHLIAS
Blue
PJ101BL

Fabric 17
BEARDED IRIS
Dark
PJ105DK

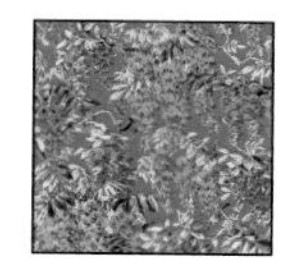

Fabric 18
WISTERIA
Teal
PJ102TE

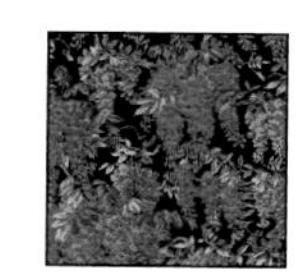

Fabric 19
WISTERIA
Black
PJ102BK

Backing and Binding Fabrics

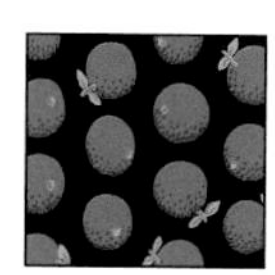

Fabric 20
ORANGES
Purple
PG177PU

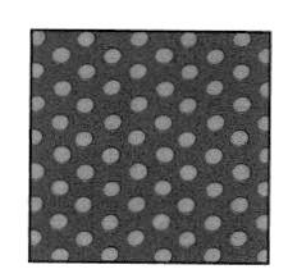

Fabric 21
SPOT
Burgundy
GP70BG

PATCHES

A large rectangle forms the centre of this quilt, surrounded by square patches cut 6½in (16.5cm) square, sewn in rows.

CUTTING OUT

Fabric is cut across the width unless otherwise stated.
When required strips are longer than 40in (102 cm) – the width of the fabric – remove selvedges and join strips end to end to obtain the required length. Use a ¼in (6mm) seam allowance and press seams open.

Centre Panel

From Fabric 1 cut the centre panel 18½in (47cm) wide x 24½in (62.2cm) long, making sure the melons fill the panel in a pleasing way.

Squares

From the remaining Fabric 1 cut 2 strips 6½in (16.5cm) wide and cross cut 6 squares at 6½in (16.5cm).
Cut 1 strip 6½in (16.5cm) wide and cross cut squares 6½in (16.5cm) from each fabric as follows:

Fabric 2 6 squares;
Fabric 3 5 squares;
Fabric 4 3 squares;
Fabric 5 3 squares;
Fabric 6 3 squares;
Fabric 7 4 squares;
Fabric 8 4 squares;
Fabric 9 3 squares;
Fabric 10 4 squares;
Fabric 11 5 squares;
Fabric 12 5 squares;
Fabric 13 2 squares;
Fabric 14 6 squares;
Fabric 15 6 squares;
Fabric 16 5 squares;
Fabric 17 5 squares;
Fabric 18 3 squares.
Total of 78 squares.

Border

The border is cut directionally – horizontal strips for the top and bottom, vertical strips for the sides – to showcase the wisteria flowers.
Side Borders: From Fabric 19 cut 1 strip 30½in (77.5cm) across the width of the fabric. Cross cut 4 pieces 8½in (21.6cm) wide down the length of the piece.
Top and Bottom Borders: From the remaining Fabric 19 cut 4 strips 8½in (21.6cm) wide across the width of the fabric.

Backing

From Fabric 20 cut 2 pieces 40in x 85in (102cm x 216cm).

Binding

From Fabric 21 cut 8 strips 2½in (6.4cm) wide. Remove selvedges and sew strips end to end with 45-degree seams (see page 141).

MAKING THE QUILT

Using a design wall will help to place patches in the required layout.
Use ¼in (6mm) seams throughout.
Lay out the centre panel and patches referring to the Quilt Assembly Diagram and quilt photograph.
Note: Press the seams in each row in the same direction on alternate rows – odd rows to the left, even rows to the right – to allow finished seams to lie flat.
Referring to the Quilt Assembly Diagram, sew the 4 rows of 3 patches each into two blocks for the sides of the centre panel, before sewing the two blocks to each side of the centre panel.
Sew the 9 patches together for the top 3 rows, press as described in the Note above, then sew the 3 rows together.
Repeat for the 3 rows of patches at the bottom of the quilt.
To complete the quilt centre, sew the top and bottom rows of patches to the centre section of the quilt.

Border

Sew 2 side border pieces of Fabric 19 together to create each side border measuring 8½in x 60½in (21.6cm x 153.7cm). Press seams open. Pin to each side of the quilt centre, sew and press seams towards the borders.
Sew 2 top and bottom border pieces of Fabric 19 together to create each top and bottom border measuring 8½in x 70½in (21.6cm x 179.1cm). Press seams open. Pin to the top and bottom of the quilt centre, sew and press seams towards the borders.

FINISHING THE QUILT

Remove selvedges, sew the backing pieces together and trim to form a piece 79in x 85in (200cm x 216cm).
Press the quilt top. Layer the quilt top, batting and backing, and baste together (see page 140).
Quilt as desired.
Trim the quilt edges and attach the binding (see page 141).

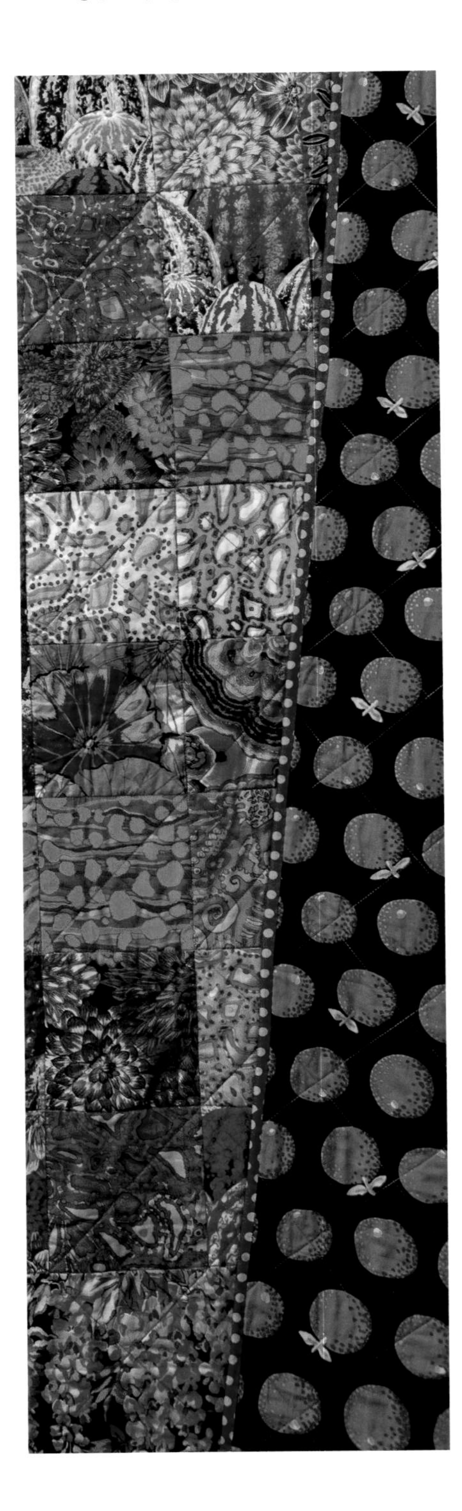

QUILT ASSEMBLY DIAGRAM

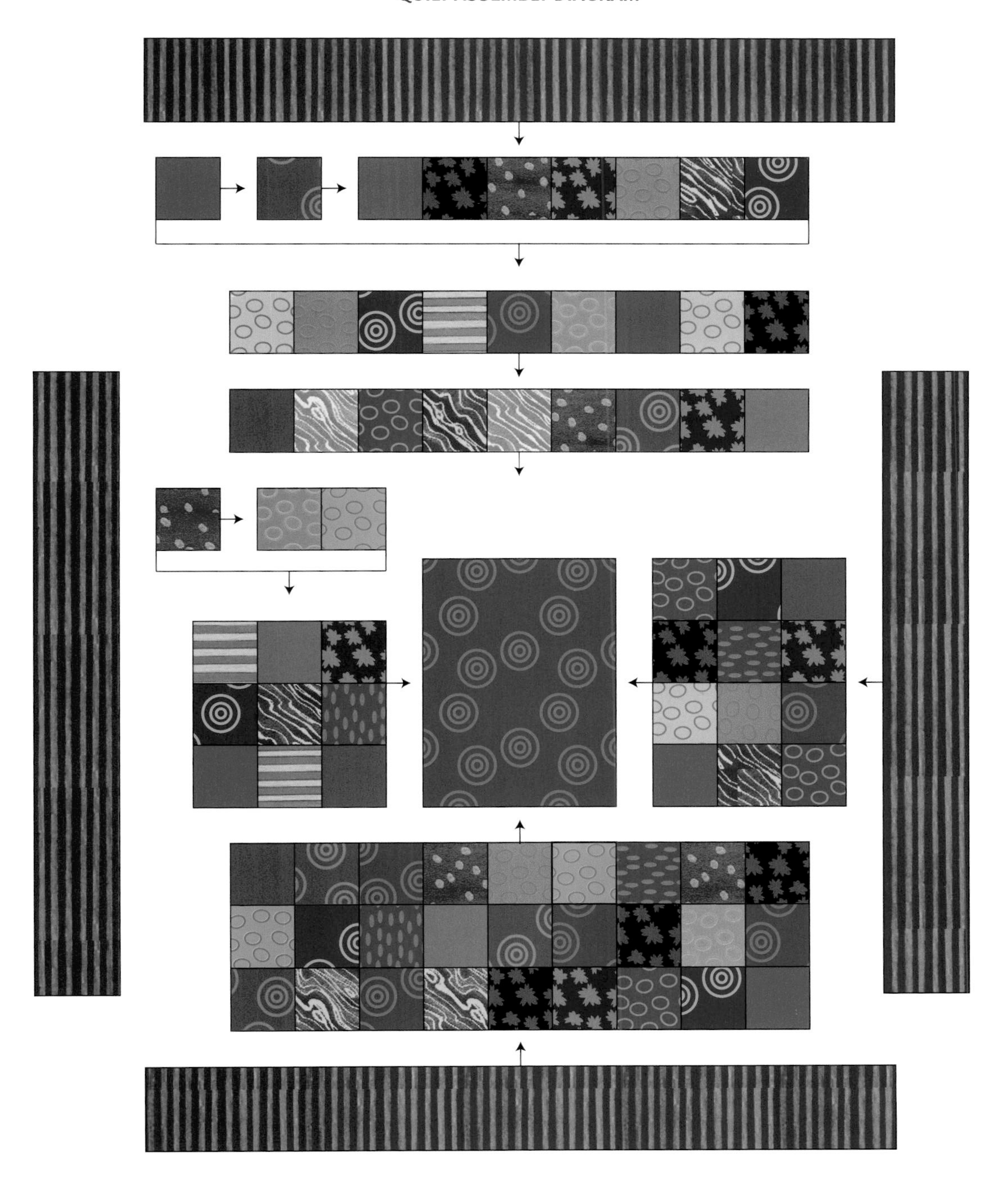

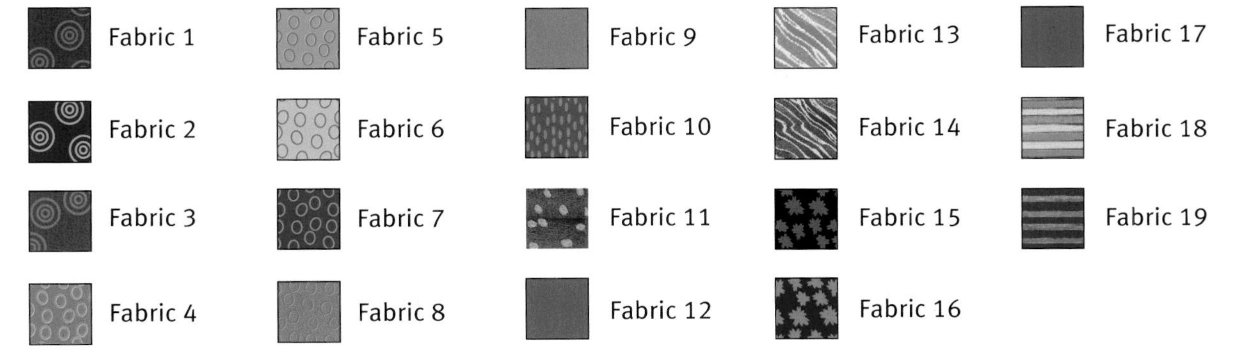

mirror columns *

Kaffe Fassett

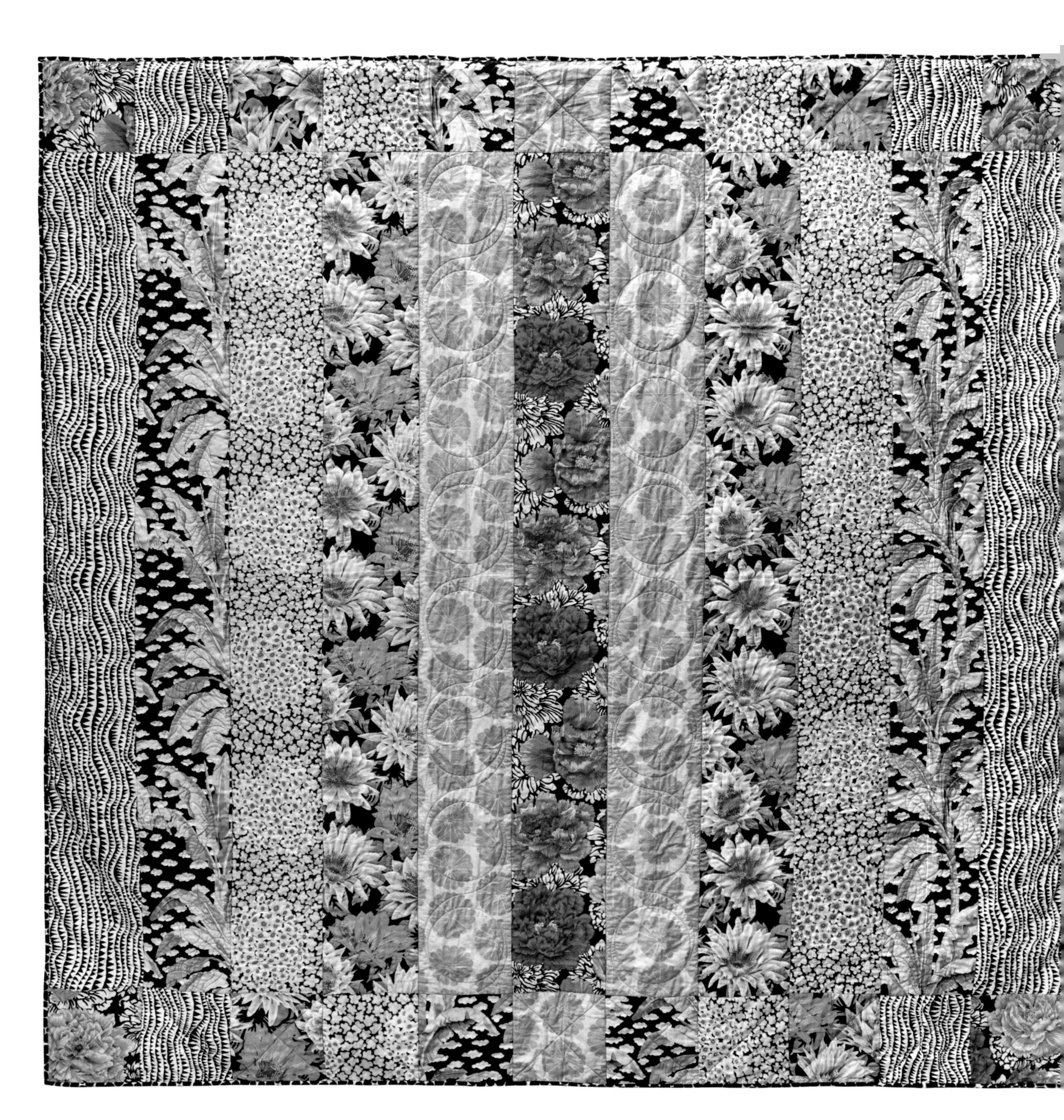

The long strips in this quilt create vertical bands that are repeated on each side of the central Brocade Peony column as though mirrored. The borders are the same width as the columns. The Shark's Teeth fabric side borders, unlike the central columns, are cut across the width of the fabric and invisibly joined to give the appearance of 11 columns in total.

SIZE OF FINISHED QUILT

88in x 88in (224cm x 224cm)

FABRICS

Fabrics have been calculated at a maximum width of 40in (102cm) and cut across the width. They have been given a number – see Fabric Swatch Diagram for details.

Patchwork Fabrics

SHARK'S TEETH
Fabric 1 Black 1⅜yd (1.3m)
BANANA TREE
Fabric 2 Grey 2⅛yd (2m)
HYDRANGEA
Fabric 3 Grey 2⅛yd (2m)
CACTUS FLOWER
Fabric 4 Contrast 2⅛yd (2m)
DAMASK FLOWER
Fabric 5 Lilac 2⅛yd (2m)
BROCADE PEONY
Fabric 6 Crimson 2⅛yd (2m)

Backing and Binding Fabrics

MILLEFIORE (wide)
Fabric 7 Pastel 2¾yd (2.6m)
JUMBLE
Fabric 8 Black ¾yd (70cm)

Batting

97in x 97in (246cm x 246cm)

PATCHES

Long strips are set into 9 columns and completed with a wide border and 4 corner squares. Strips for the side borders look as though they are cut from one piece but are pieced and invisibly joined, while top and bottom borders are each pieced from 9 squares and completed with corner squares.

CUTTING OUT

All columns are cut from strips cut down the length of the fabric. The side borders are cut from strips cut across the width of the fabric, which are then joined invisibly to form a similar length column to the other 9. Use ¼in (6mm) seams throughout.

Centre Columns

Cut the following fabrics down the length of the fabric to form columns 8½in x 72½in (21.6cm x 184.2cm):
Fabric 2 2 columns
Fabric 3 2 columns
Fabric 4 2 columns
Fabric 5 2 columns
Fabric 6 1 column

Side Borders

Fabric 1 is cut across the **width** of the fabric to get the best effect of the pattern. Enough fabric has been allowed to enable you to cut strips at the same point in the fabric pattern so that, when 2 pieces are sewn together, the joined piece looks continuous.
From Fabric 1 cut 4 matchings strips 8½in (21.6cm) wide to form 2 side borders. Sew 2 strips end to end to obtain the required length for each border. Use a ¼in (6mm) seam and press seams open, then trim to 8½in x 72½in (21.6cm x 184.2cm).

Top and Bottom Borders

From the remaining fabrics, cut strips 8½in (21.6cm) wide and cross cut squares 8½in x 8½in (21.6cm x 21.6cm) from fabrics as follows:
Fabric 1 4 squares;
Fabric 2 4 squares;
Fabric 3 4 squares;
Fabric 4 4 squares;
Fabric 5 2 squares.

Corner Squares

From the remaining Fabric 6 fussy cut 4 different flower motifs into squares 8½in x 8½in (21.6cm x 21.6cm).

Backing

From Fabric 7 extra-wide backing fabric cut a piece 97in x 97in (246cm x 246cm).

Binding

From Fabric 8 cut 10 strips 2½in (6.4cm) wide. Remove selvedges and sew strips end to end with 45-degree seams (see page 141).

FABRIC SWATCH DIAGRAM

Patchwork Fabrics

Fabric 1
SHARK'S TEETH
Black
BM060BK

Fabric 2
BANANA TREE
Grey
GP179GY

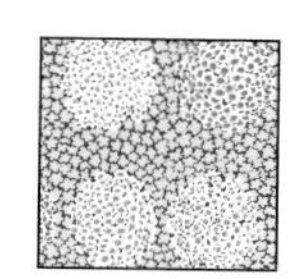
Fabric 3
HYDRANGEA
Grey
GP180GY

Fabric 4
CACTUS FLOWER
Contrast
PJ096CN

Fabric 5
DAMASK FLOWER
Lilac
GP183LI

Fabric 6
BROCADE PEONY
Crimson
PJ062CJ

Backing and Binding Fabrics

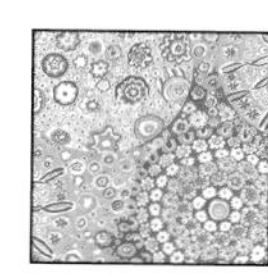
Fabric 7
MILLEFIORE (wide)
Pastel
QB006PT

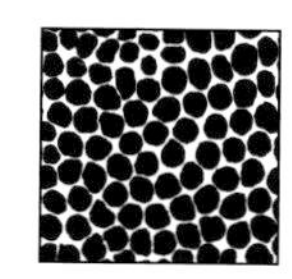
Fabric 8
JUMBLE
Black
BM053BK

MAKING THE QUILT

Using a design wall helps to place patches in the required layout.
Use $1/4$in (6mm) seams throughout.

Side Borders

Sew matching pairs of Fabric 1 together end to end so the pattern remains unbroken. Press seams open. Trim each joined piece to $8\frac{1}{2}$in x $72\frac{1}{2}$in (21.6cm x 184.2cm).

Centre

Lay out the columns on a design wall, including the side border columns, referring to the Quilt Assembly Diagram and quilt photograph. Sew the columns together, pinning each strip before sewing to avoid stretching the long pieces.

Top and Bottom Borders

Add the top and bottom Fabric 16 border squares to the layout as shown in the Quilt Assembly Diagram, positioning them at each end of each border. Sew each row of 11 squares together to form the borders. Press seams, pin and then sew the borders to the quilt, taking care to match the crossing seams.

FINISHING THE QUILT

Cut the Fabric 7 extra-wide backing piece to 97in x 97in (246cm x 246cm). Press the quilt top. Layer the quilt top, batting and backing, and baste together (see page 140).
Quilt as desired.
Trim the quilt edges and attach the binding (see page 141).

QUILT ASSEMBLY DIAGRAM

Fabric 1

Fabric 2

Fabric 3

Fabric 4

Fabric 5

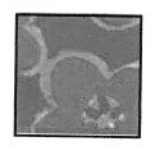
Fabric 6

leafy diamonds **

Kaffe Fassett

A new variation of the 60 degree diamond quilt, with large floral prints used in the vertical rows and the smaller, more graphic prints in the horizontal rows.

FABRIC SWATCH DIAGRAM

Patchwork Fabrics

Fabric 1
CACTUS FLOWER
Contrast
PJ096CN

Fabric 2
CACTUS FLOWER
Brown
PJ96BR

Fabric 3
CACTUS FLOWER
Emerald
PJ96EM

Fabric 4
BROCADE PEONY
Cool
PJ062CL

Fabric 5
BROCADE PEONY
Moss
PJ62MS

Fabric 6
FEATHERS
Lime
PJ55LM

Fabric 7
BANANA TREE
Purple
GP179PU

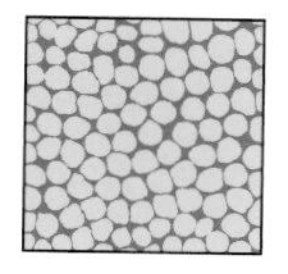

Fabric 8
JUMBLE
Lime
BM53LM

Fabric 9
BUTTON MOSAIC
Green
GP182GN

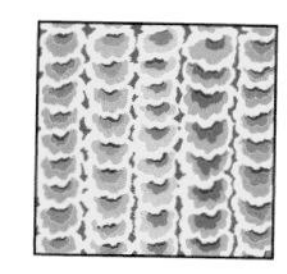

Fabric 10
GARLANDS
Green
GP181GN

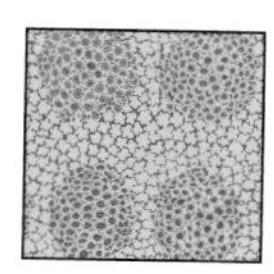

Fabric 11
HYDRANGEA
Green
GP180GN

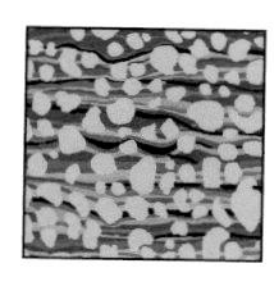

Fabric 12
STREAM
Green
BM075GN

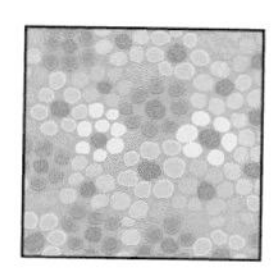

Fabric 13
FLOWER DOT
Aqua
BM077AQ

Backing and Binding Fabrics

Fabric 14
LOTUS LEAF
Jade
QB007JA

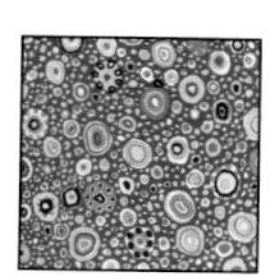

Fabric 15
ROMAN GLASS
Leafy
GP01LF

SIZE OF FINISHED QUILT

$54\frac{1}{2}$in x $84\frac{1}{2}$in (138cm x 215cm)

FABRICS

Fabrics have been calculated at a maximum width of 40in (102cm). They have been given a number – see Fabric Swatch Diagram for details.

Patchwork Fabrics

CACTUS FLOWER		
Fabric 1	Contrast	$\frac{5}{8}$yd (60cm)
Fabric 2	Brown	$\frac{1}{2}$yd (50cm)
Fabric 3	Emerald	$\frac{5}{8}$yd (60cm)
BROCADE PEONY		
Fabric 4	Cool	$\frac{1}{2}$yd (50cm)
Fabric 5	Moss	$\frac{1}{2}$yd (50cm)
FEATHERS		
Fabric 6	Lime	$\frac{1}{2}$yd (50cm)
Fabric 7	Purple	$\frac{1}{2}$yd (50cm)
JUMBLE		
Fabric 8	Lime	$\frac{1}{4}$yd (25cm)
BUTTON MOSAIC		
Fabric 9	Green	$\frac{1}{2}$yd (50cm)
GARLANDS		
Fabric 10	Green	$\frac{7}{8}$yd (85cm)
HYDRANGEA		
Fabric 11	Green	$\frac{7}{8}$yd (85cm)
STREAM		
Fabric 12	Green	$\frac{3}{4}$yd (70cm)
FLOWER DOT		
Fabric 13	Aqua	$\frac{1}{4}$yd (25cm)

Backing and Binding Fabrics

LOTUS LEAF		
Fabric 14	Jade	$1\frac{3}{4}$yd (1.7m)
ROMAN GLASS		
Fabric 15	Leafy	$\frac{5}{8}$yd (60cm)

Batting

63in x 93in (160cm x 236cm)

TEMPLATES

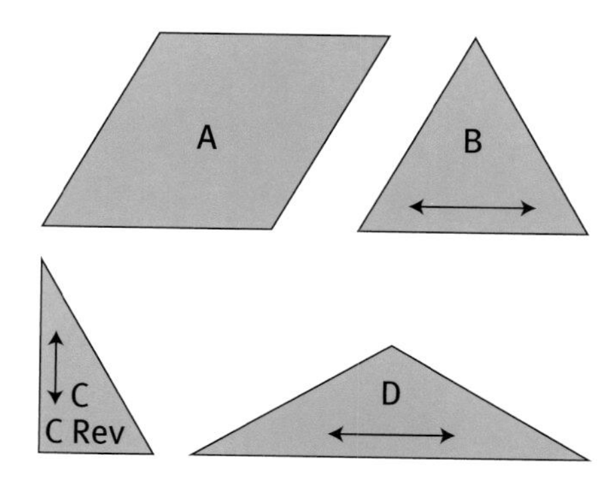

PATCHES

The quilt is made up of 60 degree diamond and triangle patches that can be cut from strips using a 60 degree ruler or by using Templates A, B, C/C Reverse and D (see pages 131–133).

CUTTING OUT

Fabric is cut across the width unless otherwise stated.
Use ¼in (6mm) seams throughout.

Diamonds

Referring to the Cutting Diagram, cut 6½in (16.5cm) strips across the width of the fabric. Each strip will yield 5 Template A diamonds using either Cutting Diagram Method 1 or Method 2. Using the different cutting methods means each bias-cut edge is sewn to a grain line edge, thereby strengthening the quilt and preventing it from stretching.
Note: If using a 60 degree ruler, use the manufacturer's instructions for cutting diamonds.

Vertical Floral Diamonds

Using Cutting Diagram Method 1, cut strips and patches as follows:
Fabric 1 (3 strips) 14 diamonds;
Fabric 2 (2 strips) 7 diamonds;
Fabric 3 (3 strips) 14 diamonds;
Fabric 4 (2 strips) 7 diamonds;
Fabric 5 (2 strips) 7 diamonds;
Fabric 6 (2 strips) 7 diamonds;
Fabric 7 (2 strips) 7 diamonds.

Horizontal Graphic Diamonds

Using Cutting Diagram Method 2, cut strips and patches as follows:
Fabric 8 (1 strip) 4 diamonds;
Fabric 9 (2 strips) 8 diamonds;
Fabric 10 (4 strips) 16 diamonds;
Fabric 11 (4 strips) 16 diamonds;
Fabric 13 (1 strip) 4 diamonds.

Top and Bottom Triangles

From Fabric 12 cut 2 strips 6¾in (17.1cm) wide and cross cut 16 triangles using Template B, placing it on the grain line and rotating the ruler/template 180 degrees after each cut. From the remaining pieces cut 2 Template C and 2 Template C Reverse by turning the template to reverse side, for the 4 corners of the quilt.

CUTTING DIAGRAM

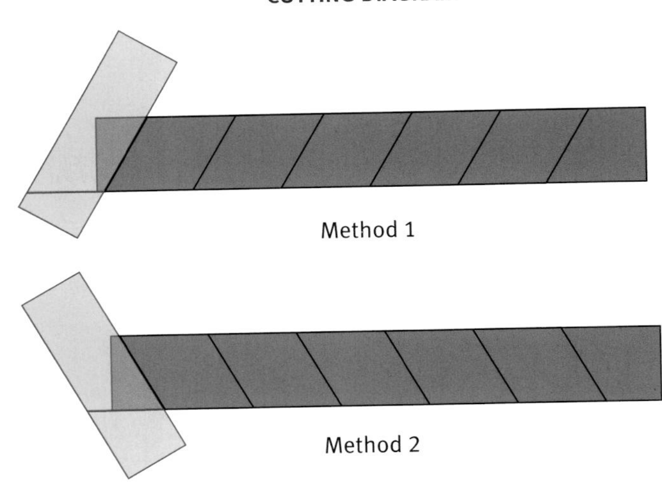

Template D Side Triangles

From the remaining Fabric 12 cut 3 strips 4in (10.2cm) wide. Using Template D, cut 12 side triangles, rotating the template 180 degrees after each triangle (5 triangles can be cut from each strip).

Backing

From Fabric 14 extra-wide backing cut a piece 63in x 93in (160cm x 236cm).

Binding

From Fabric 15 cut 8 strips 2½in (6.4cm) wide. Remove selvedges and sew strips end to end with 45-degree seams (see page 141).

MAKING THE QUILT

Using a design wall will help to place patches in the required layout. Use ¼in (6mm) seams throughout.
Arrange the diamond patches following the Quilt Assembly Diagram and quilt photograph, making sure the vertical and horizontal fabrics are placed correctly.
Try to vary the direction of the pattern by rotating some patches 180 degrees, to create a sense of movement.
Add the side, top and bottom triangles and position the corner triangles.
Take care when handling the patches as they have some bias edges. A spritz of spray starch helps stabilize the raw edges.
Referring to the Quilt Assembly Diagram, sew the patches into diagonal rows, pressing the seams in the same direction on alternate rows – odd rows to the left, even rows to the right – to allow the finished seams to lie flat.
Sew the diagonal rows together and press seams to complete the quilt top.

FINISHING THE QUILT

Press the quilt top and backing. Layer the quilt top, batting and backing, and baste together (see page 140).
Quilt as desired.
Trim the quilt edges and attach the binding (see page 141).

QUILT ASSEMBLY DIAGRAM

 Fabric 1

 Fabric 2

 Fabric 3

 Fabric 4

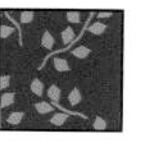 Fabric 5

 Fabric 6

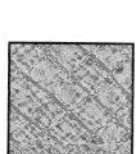 Fabric 7

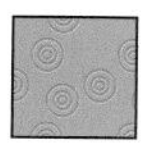 Fabric 8

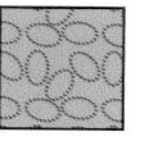 Fabric 9

 Fabric 10

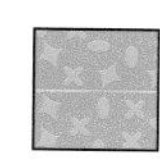 Fabric 11

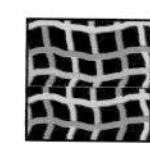 Fabric 12

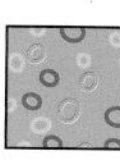 Fabric 13

dark boxes *

Kaffe Fassett

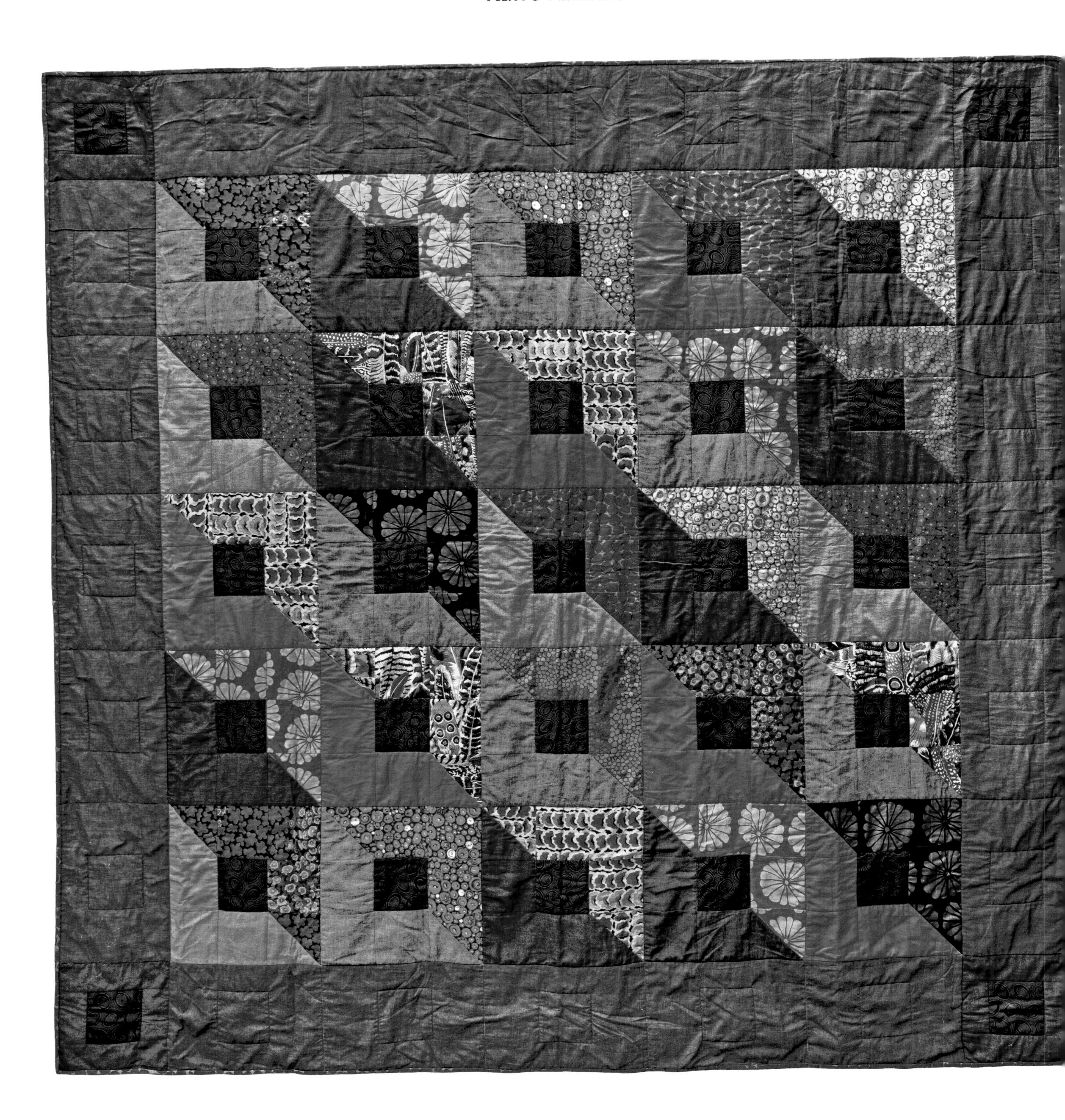

A simple layout that punches above its weight, thanks to the eye-catching use of deep, rich colours.

SIZE OF FINISHED QUILT

76½in x 76½in (194cm x 194cm)

FABRICS

Fabrics have been calculated at a maximum width of 40in (102cm). They have been given a number – see Fabric Swatch Diagram for details.

Patchwork Fabrics

FEATHERS

Fabric 1	Autumn	½yd (50cm)

BUTTON MOSAIC

Fabric 2	Red	⅜yd (40cm)
Fabric 3	Blue	⅜yd (40cm)
Fabric 4	Purple	⅜yd (40cm)

DAMASK FLOWER

Fabric 5	Blue	⅜yd (40cm)
Fabric 6	Purple	⅜yd (40cm)
Fabric 7	Brown	⅜yd (40cm)

GARLANDS

Fabric 8	Dark	½yd (50cm)

PEBBLE MOSAIC

Fabric 9	Prune	⅜yd (40cm)

HYDRANGEA

Fabric 10	Purple	½yd (50cm)

JUMBLE

Fabric 11	Prune	⅜yd (40cm)

* see also Binding Fabric

SHOT COTTON

Fabric 12	Pimento	¾yd (70cm)
Fabric 13	Pine	⅝yd (60cm)
Fabric 14	Plum	½yd (50cm)
Fabric 15	Heliotrope	⅝yd (60cm)
Fabric 16	Teal	½yd (50cm)
Fabric 17	Aubergine	2yd (1.9m)

ABORIGINAL DOT

Fabric 18	Orchid	⅝yd (60cm)

Backing and Binding Fabrics

MILLEFIORE (wide)

Fabric 19	Blue	2⅜yd (2.3m)

extra wide backing fabric.

JUMBLE

Fabric 11	Prune	⅝yd (60cm)

* see also PatchworkFabric

Batting

85in x 85in (216cm x 216cm)

FABRIC SWATCH DIAGRAM

Patchwork Fabrics

Fabric 1
FEATHERS
Autumn
PJ55AU

Fabric 2
BUTTON MOSAIC
Red
GP182RD

Fabric 3
BUTTON MOSAIC
Blue
GP182BL

Fabric 4
BUTTON MOSAIC
Purple
GP182PU

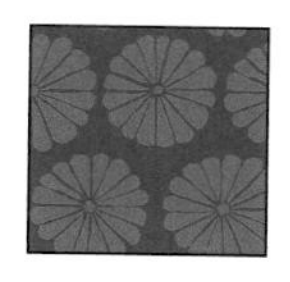

Fabric 5
DAMASK FLOWER
Blue
GP183BL

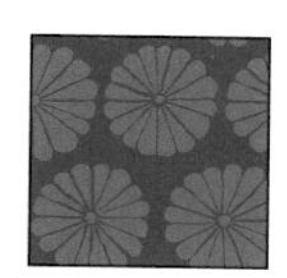

Fabric 6
DAMASK FLOWER
Purple
GP183PU

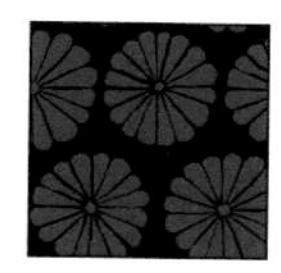

Fabric 7
DAMASK FLOWER
Brown
GP183BR

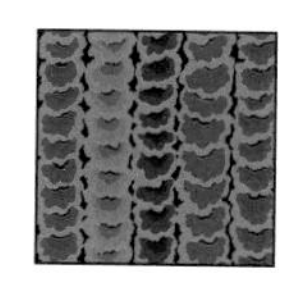

Fabric 8
GARLANDS
Dark
GP181DK

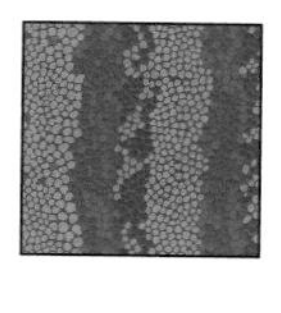

Fabric 9
PEBBLE MOSAIC
Prune
BM42PV

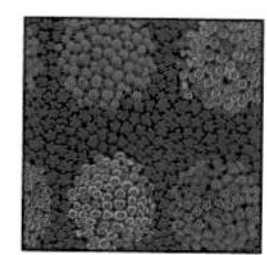

Fabric 10
HYDRANGEA
Purple
GP180PU

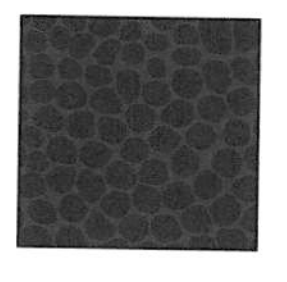

Fabric 11
JUMBLE
Prune
BM53PV

Fabric 12
SHOT COTTON
Pimento
SC116PI

Fabric 13
SHOT COTTON
Pine
SC120PY

Fabric 14
SHOT COTTON
Plum
SC119PL

Fabric 15
SHOT COTTON
Heliotrope
SC106HL

Fabric 16
SHOT COTTON
Teal
SC105TE

Fabric 17
SHOT COTTON
Aubergine
SC117AB

Fabric 18
ABORIGINAL DOT
Orchid
GP71OD

Backing and Binding Fabrics

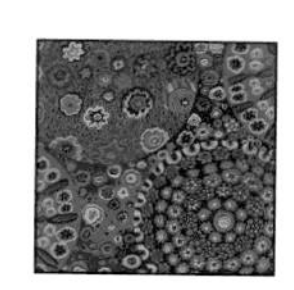

Fabric 19
MILLEFIORE (wide)
Blue
QB006BL

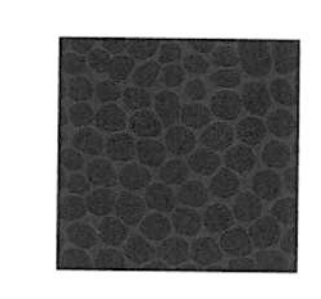

Fabric 11
JUMBLE
Prune
BM53PV

PATCHES

All patches are cross cut from strips cut across the width of the fabric.

The split 9-patch block is 12in (30.5cm) square finished and is made using square and half-square triangle (HST) patches, both forming squares 4in x 4in (10.2cm x 10.2cm) finished. The blocks are straight set into 5 rows of 5.

CUTTING OUT

Cut strips across the width of the fabric then cross cut as instructed.

Use ¼in (6mm) seams throughout.

Triangle Patches

Cut a strip 4⅞in (12.3cm) wide from each of the following fabrics and cross cut 4⅞in (12.3cm) squares. Cut each square diagonally once to form two HSTs.

Cut a total of 100 HSTs from fabrics as follows:

Fabric 1 3 squares, 6 triangles;
Fabric 2 2 squares, 4 triangles;
Fabric 3 2 squares, 4 triangles;
Fabric 4 2 squares, 4 triangles;
Fabric 5 2 squares, 4 triangles;
Fabric 6 2 squares, 4 triangles;
Fabric 7 2 squares, 4 triangles;
Fabric 8 3 squares, 6 triangles;
Fabric 9 2 squares, 4 triangles;
Fabric 10 3 squares, 6 triangles;
Fabric 11 2 squares, 4 triangles;
Fabric 12 5 squares, 10 triangles;
Fabric 13 7 squares, 14 triangles;
Fabric 14 3 squares, 6 triangles;
Fabric 15 6 squares, 12 triangles;
Fabric 16 4 squares, 8 triangles.

Square Patches

Cut strips 4½in (11.4cm) wide and cross cut 4½in (11.4cm) squares. Each strip will yield 8 squares. Cut a total of 179 squares from fabrics as follows:

Fabric 1 (2 strips) 9 squares;
Fabric 2 (1 strip) 6 squares;
Fabric 3 (1 strip) 6 squares;
Fabric 4 (1 strip) 6 squares;
Fabric 5 (1 strip) 6 squares;
Fabric 6 (1 strip) 6 squares;
Fabric 7 (1 strip) 6 squares;
Fabric 8 (2 strips) 9 squares;
Fabric 9 (1 strip) 6 squares;
Fabric 10 (2 strips) 9 squares;
Fabric 11 (1 strip) 6 squares;
Fabric 12 (2 strips) 15 squares;
Fabric 13 (3 strips) 21 squares;

BLOCK ASSEMBLY DIAGRAM

a

b

c

Fabric 14 (2 strips) 9 squares;
Fabric 15 (3 strips) 18 squares;
Fabric 16 (2 strips) 12 squares;
Fabric 18 (4 strips) 29 squares (including 4 for the corner blocks).

Borders

From Fabric 17, cutting **down the length** of the fabric, cut 4 strips 8½in (21.6cm) wide. Trim each border piece to 60½in (153.7cm) long.

Corner Blocks

From the remaining Fabric 12 cut 3 strips 2½in (6.4cm) wide and cross cut 8 pieces 2½in x 8½in (6.4cm x 21.6cm) and 8 pieces 2½in x 4½in (6.4cm x 11.4cm).

Backing

From Fabric 19 extra wide backing fabric, cut a piece 85in x 85in (216cm x 216cm).

Binding

From Fabric 11 cut 8 strips 2½in (6.4cm) wide. Remove selvedges and sew end to end with 45-degree seams (see page 141).

MAKING THE QUILT

Using a design wall will help to place the patches in the required layout.
Use ¼in (6mm) seams throughout.

Making the Centre Blocks

Using the Block Assembly Diagram as a guide, for each block select 3 matching plain square patches, 3 matching patterned square patches and 1 centre square patch in Fabric 18. Also select 2 matching plain and 2 matching patterned triangle patches.

Referring to the Block Diagram, sew the plain and patterned triangles together along their long edge to make 2 HST squares (a). Arrange the pieced squares with the other patches as shown in (b) and sew together, matching seam joins, to create the finished block (c).
Make 25 blocks.
Using the Quilt Assembly Diagram and quilt photograph for fabric placement, sew the blocks into rows, pressing seams in the same direction on alternate rows – odd rows to the left, even rows to the right – to allow the finished seams to lie flat. Sew the 5 rows together taking care to match crossing seams.

Corner Blocks

Referring to the Corner Block Assembly Diagram, make 4 corner blocks. First sew a 4½in (11.4cm) piece in Fabric 12 to each side of a Fabric 18 centre square, then sew an 8½in (21.6cm) piece in Fabric 12 to the top and bottom. Press seams away from the centre square.

Borders

Pin and then sew border pieces to both sides of the quilt centre. Sew a corner square block to either end of the remaining 2 border sections. Pin and then sew these to the top and bottom of the quilt top to complete the quilt top.

FINISHING THE QUILT

Press the quilt top and backing piece.
Layer the quilt top, batting and backing, and baste together (see page 140).
Quilt as desired.
Trim the quilt edges and attach the binding (see page 141).

CORNER BLOCK ASSEMBLY DIAGRAM

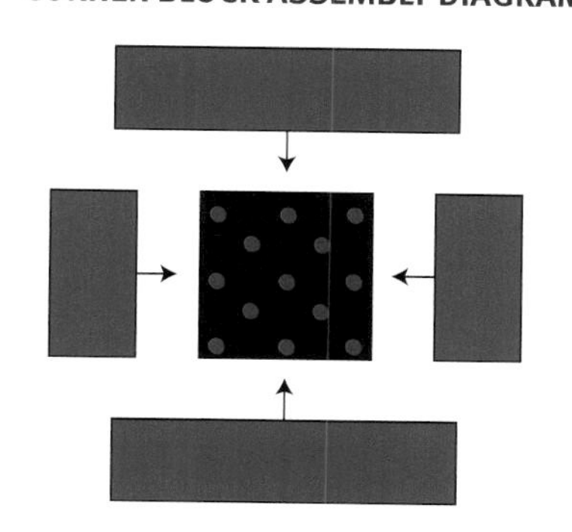

QUILT ASSEMBLY DIAGRAM

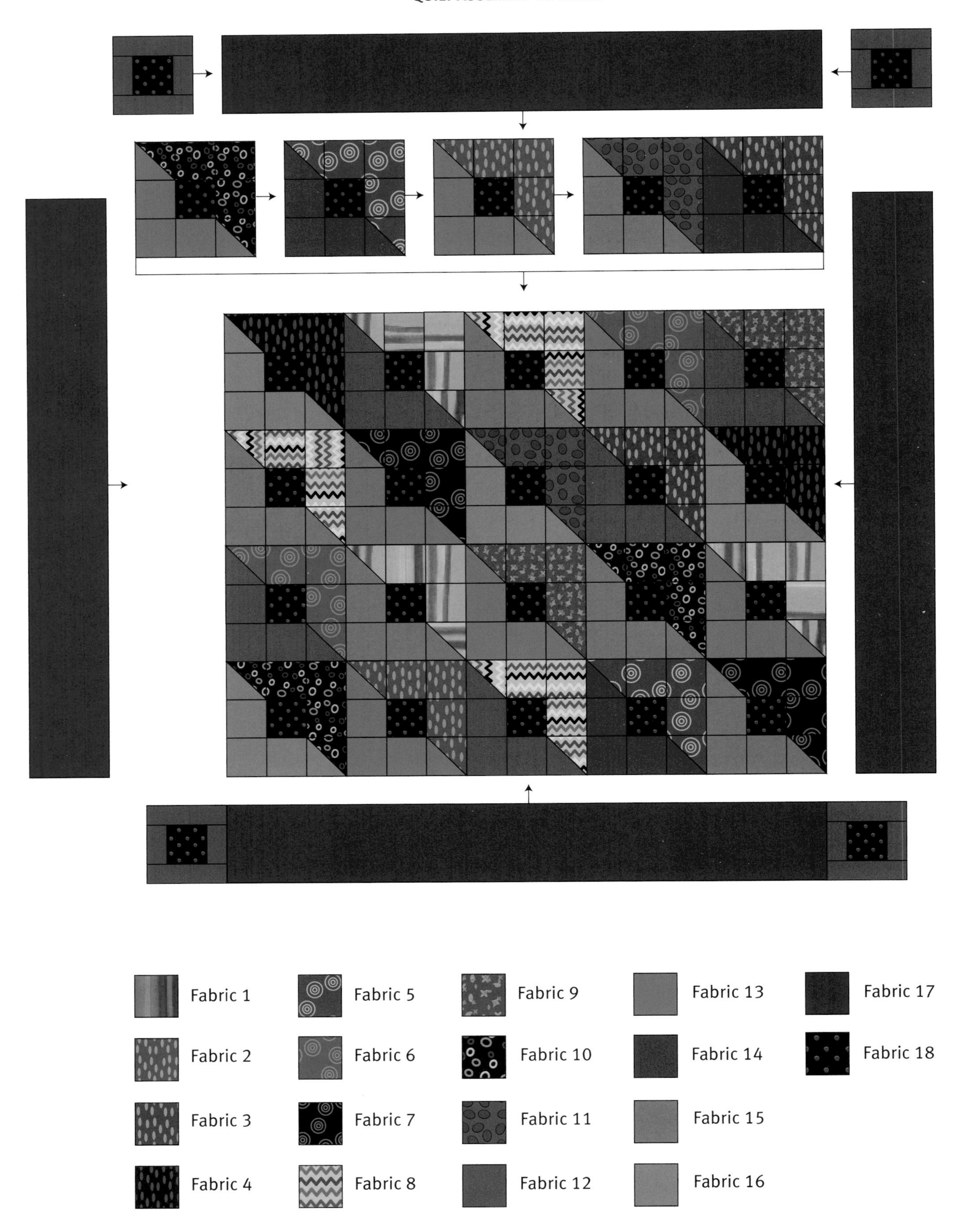

shaded squares *

Kaffe Fassett

This strikingly graphic yet simple quilt is created from a glowing mixture of my Shot Cottons and Woven Stripe fabrics.

SIZE OF FINISHED QUILT

46in x 59in (117cm x 150cm)

FABRICS

Fabrics have been calculated at a maximum width of 40in (102cm). They have been given a number – see Fabric Swatch Diagram for details.

Patchwork Fabrics

SHOT COTTON
Fabric 1 Paprika ¼yd (25cm)
SHOT COTTON
Fabric 2 Nutmeg ¼yd (25cm)
SHOT COTTON
Fabric 3 Wine ¼yd (25cm)
SHOT COTTON
Fabric 4 Teal ¼yd (25cm)
SHOT COTTON
Fabric 5 Heliotrope ¼yd (25cm)
SHOT COTTON
Fabric 6 Khaki ¼yd (25cm)
SHOT COTTON
Fabric 7 Camellia ¼yd (25cm)
SHOT COTTON
Fabric 8 Blood Orange ¼yd (25cm)
SHOT COTTON
Fabric 9 Pistachio ¼yd (25cm)
SHOT COTTON
Fabric 10 Lupin ¼yd (25cm)
SHOT COTTON
Fabric 11 Opal ¼yd (25cm)
SHOT COTTON
Fabric 12 Harissa ¼yd (25cm)
SHOT COTTON
Fabric 13 Pimento ¼yd (25cm)
WIDE STRIPE
Fabric 14 Aloe ¼yd (25cm)
WIDE STRIPE
Fabric 15 Cantaloupe ⅜yd (40cm)
WIDE STRIPE
Fabric 16 Chestnut ⅜yd (40cm)
WIDE STRIPE
Fabric 17 Embers ¼yd (25cm)
WIDE STRIPE
Fabric 18 Fjord ¼yd(25cm)
WIDE STRIPE
Fabric 19 Peat ¼yd (25cm)
NARROW STRIPE
Fabric 20 Cocoa ¼yd (25cm)
NARROW STRIPE
Fabric 21 Gooseberry ⅜yd (40cm)
NARROW STRIPE
Fabric 22 Mallard ¼yd (25cm)
NARROW STRIPE
Fabric 23 Plaster ⅜yd (40cm)
NARROW STRIPE
Fabric 24 Seaweed ¼yd (25cm)

Backing and Binding Fabrics

FLOWER DOT
Fabric 25 Warm 3⅛yd (2.9m)
MAD PLAID
Fabric 26 Maroon ½yd (50cm)

Batting

54in x 67in (137cm x 170cm)

PATCHES

The quilt is pieced using half-square triangle patches to make square blocks. Plain Shot Cotton triangles are cut from squares that are cut from strips cut across the width of the fabric.
Striped triangles are cut with the long edge placed parallel with the stripes of the fabric. Strips are cut across the width of the fabric then cross cut at 45 degrees. The combination of bias edges sewn to grain edges stabilizes each seam and prevents stretching.
Square blocks are set in 9 rows of 7 blocks.

FABRIC SWATCH DIAGRAM

Patchwork Fabrics

Fabric 1
SHOT COTTON
Paprika
SC101PP

Fabric 2
SHOT COTTON
Nutmeg
SC102NM

Fabric 3
SHOT COTTON
Wine
SC103WN

Fabric 4
SHOT COTTON
Teal
SC105TE

Fabric 5
SHOT COTTON
Heliotrope
SC106HL

Fabric 6
SHOT COTTON
Khaki
SC107KH

Fabric 7
SHOT COTTON
Camellia
SC109CX

Fabric 8
SHOT COTTON
Blood Orange
SC110BO

Fabric 9
SHOT COTTON
Pistachio
SC111PX

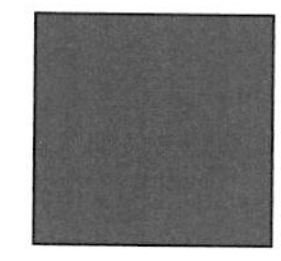

Fabric 10
SHOT COTTON
Lupin
SC113LU

Fabric 11
SHOT COTTON
Opal
SC114OP

Fabric 12
SHOT COTTON
Harissa
SC115HA

Fabric 13
SHOT COTTON
Pimento
SC116PI

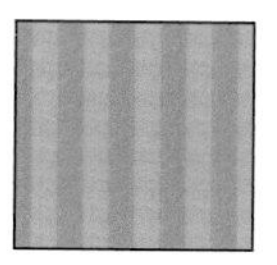

Fabric 14
WIDE STRIPE
Aloe
SS01AO

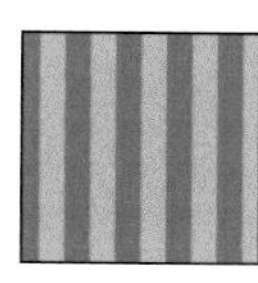

Fabric 15
WIDE STRIPE
Cantaloupe
SS01CA

Fabric 16
WIDE STRIPE
Chestnut
SS01CX

Fabric 17
WIDE STRIPE
Embers
SS01EB

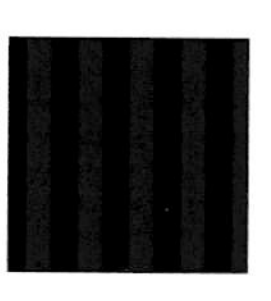

Fabric 18
WIDE STRIPE
Fjord
SS01FJ

Fabric 19
WIDE STRIPE
Peat
SS01PZ

Fabric 20
NARROW STRIPE
Cocoa
SS02CO

Fabric 21
NARROW STRIPE
Gooseberry
SS02GY

Fabric 22
NARROW STRIPE
Mallard
SS02ML

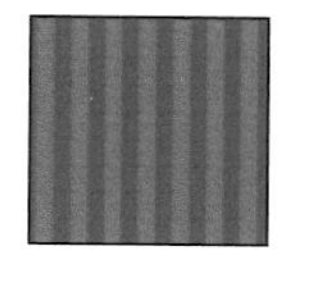

Fabric 23
NARROW STRIPE
Plaster
SS02PJ

Fabric 24
NARROW STRIPE
Seaweed
SS02SW

Backing and Binding Fabrics

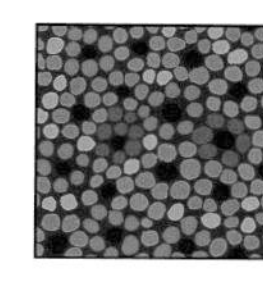

Fabric 25
FLOWER DOT
Warm
BM77WM

Fabric 26
MAD PLAID
Maroon
BM37MM

CUTTING OUT

Fabric is cut across the width unless otherwise stated. If you spray the fabrics with starch before cutting them, it will help to prevent the bias edges from stretching when sewn.

Plain Triangles

Cut strips 7⅜in (18.7cm) wide and cross cut squares at 7⅜in (18.7cm). Each strip will give you 5 squares. Cross cut squares once diagonally to yield 2 triangles from each square. Cut a total of 63 triangles from fabrics as follows:

Fabric 1 (1 strip) 4 squares, 7 triangles;
Fabric 2 (1 strip) 2 squares, 3 triangles;
Fabric 3 (1 strip) 2 squares, 3 triangles;
Fabric 4 (1 strip) 2 squares, 3 triangles;
Fabric 5 (1 strip) 1 square, 2 triangles;
Fabric 6 (1 strip) 3 squares, 6 triangles;
Fabric 7 (1 strip) 4 squares, 8 triangles;
Fabric 8 (1 strip) 2 squares, 5 triangles;
Fabric 9 (1 strip) 3 squares, 6 triangles;
Fabric 10 (1 strip) 4 squares, 7 triangles;
Fabric 11 (1 strip) 3 squares, 6 triangles;
Fabric 12 (1 strip) 3 squares, 5 triangles;
Fabric 13 (1 strip) 2 squares, 2 triangles.

Striped Triangles

Cut strips 5¼in (13.3cm) wide. Using the 45-degree marking on your ruler to align with the edge, cut a line at 45 degrees across the strip as shown in Striped Triangle Cutting Diagram (a), then cut triangles along the strip as shown in (b) and (c), pivoting the ruler and lining up the 45-degree marking along the edge of the strip for each cut. Each strip yields 6 triangles.
Cut strips and a total of 63 triangles from fabrics as follows:

Fabric 14 (1 strip) 6 triangles;
Fabric 15 (2 strips) 7 triangles;
Fabric 16 (2 strips) 8 triangles;
Fabric 17 (1 strip) 6 triangles;
Fabric 18 (1 strip) 4 triangles;
Fabric 19 (1 strip) 2 triangles;
Fabric 20 (1 strip) 4 triangles;
Fabric 21 (2 strips) 8 triangles;
Fabric 22 (1 strip) 4 triangles;
Fabric 23 (2 strips) 8 triangles;
Fabric 24 (1 strip) 6 triangles.

Backing

From Fabric 25 backing fabric cut 2 pieces 40in x 54in (101.6cm x 137cm).

STRIPED TRIANGLE CUTTING DIAGRAM

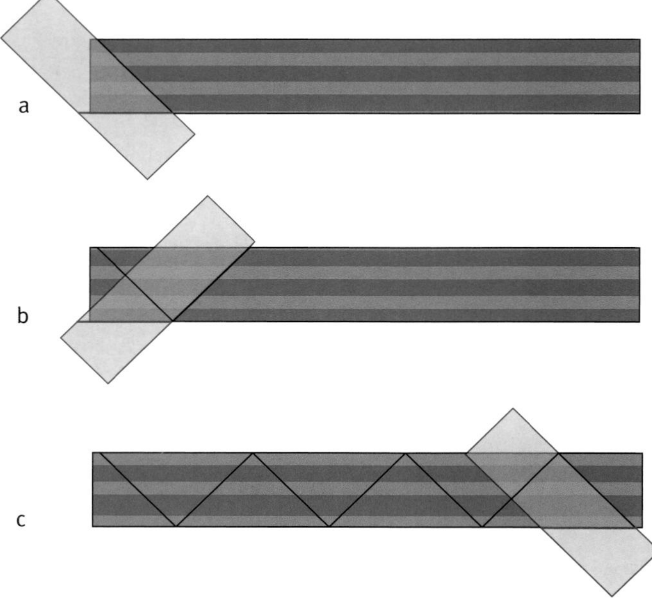

BLOCK ASSEMBLY DIAGRAM

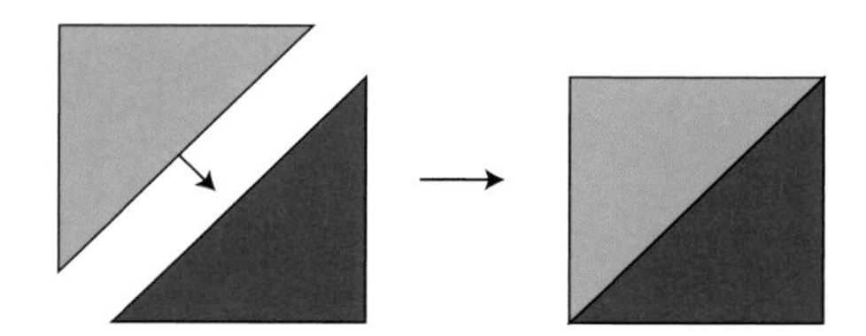

Binding

From Fabric 26 cut 6 strips 2½in (6.4cm) wide. Remove selvedges and sew strips end to end with 45-degree seams (see page 141).

MAKING THE QUILT

Using a design wall will help to place patches in the required layout.
Use ¼in (6mm) seams throughout.

Blocks

Each block is made from one Shot Cotton triangle and one Stripe Cotton triangle sewn together along the long diagonal edges to form a half-square triangle block as shown in the Block Assembly Diagram. Make a total of 63 half-square triangle blocks.

Centre

Sew the blocks into 9 rows of 7 squares referring to the Quilt Assembly Diagram and the quilt photograph.
Press seams in the same direction on alternate rows – odd rows to the left, even rows to the right – to allow the finished seams to lie flat. Sew the rows together to complete the quilt top.

FINISHING THE QUILT

Remove selvedges and sew the two Fabric 25 backing pieces together and trim to form a piece 54in x 67in (137cm x 170cm).
Press the quilt top. Layer the quilt top, batting and backing, and baste together (see page 140).
Quilt as desired.
Trim the quilt edges and attach the binding (see page 141).

QUILT ASSEMBLY DIAGRAM

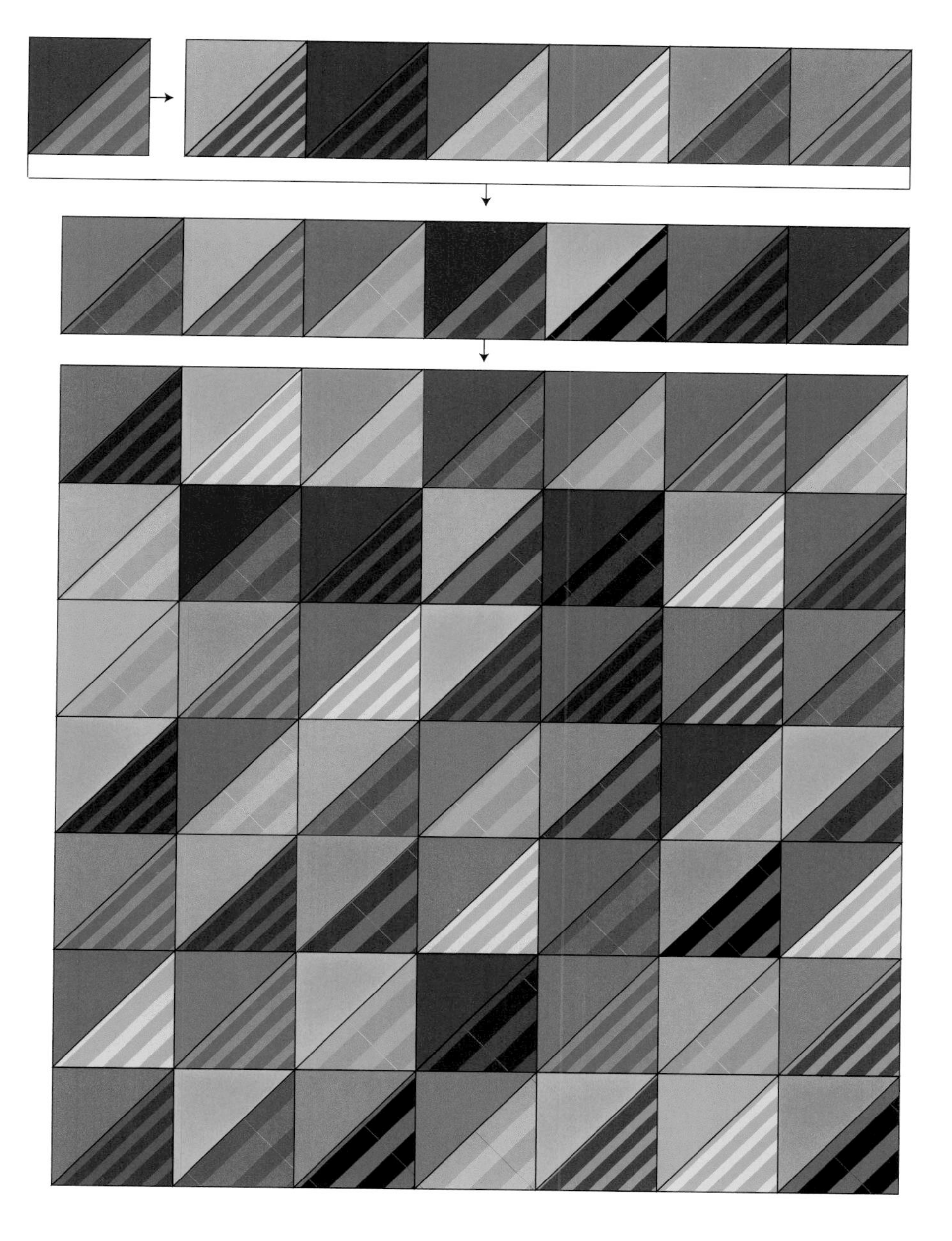

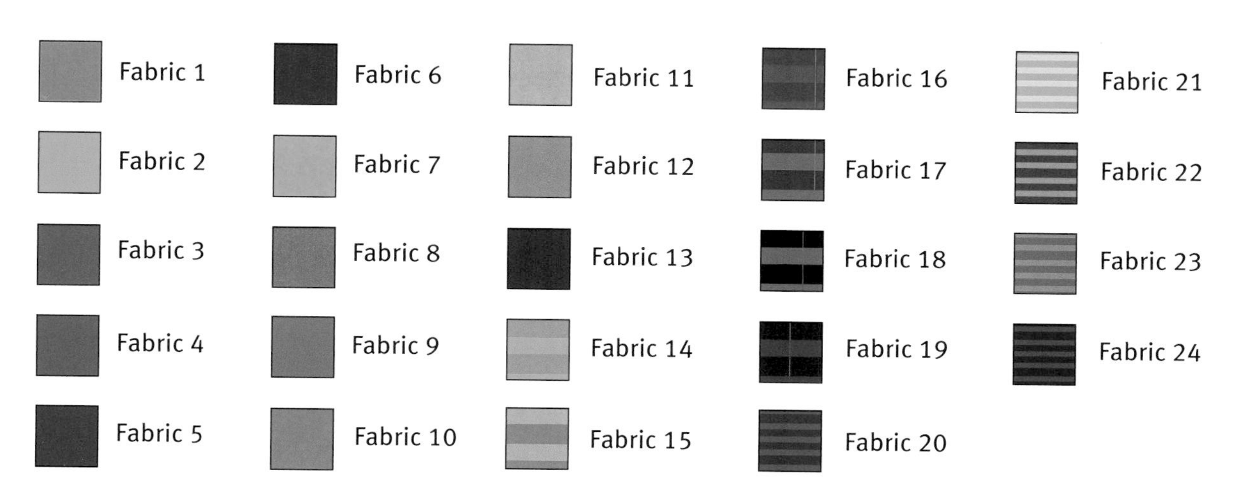

cotton candy pinwheels **

Kaffe Fassett

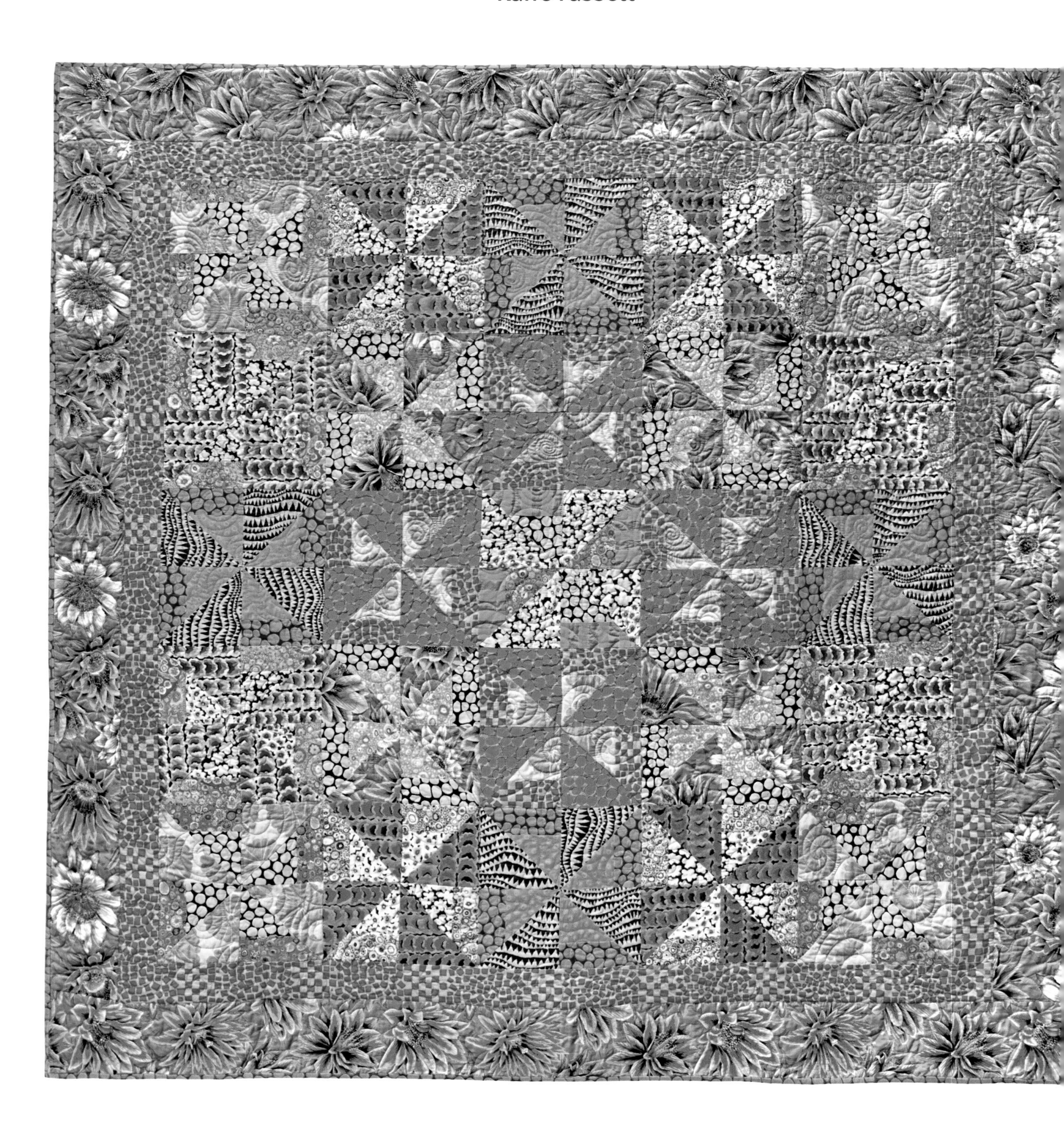

This version of pinwheels is one made from blocks that are a combination of an alternating simple pinwheel and an extended pinwheel. Some blocks have the extended pinwheel blades (formed from triangles) in the feature colour while others are in the paler background colour, which creates the effect of the pinwheels spinning in opposite directions.

SIZE OF FINISHED QUILT
79in x79in (201cm x 201cm)

FABRICS
Fabrics have been calculated at a maximum width of 40in (102cm). Fabrics have been given a number – see Fabric Swatch Diagram for details.

Patchwork Fabrics

GARLANDS		
Fabric 1	Blue	½yd (50cm)
Fabric 2	Red	½yd (50cm)
HYDRANGEA		
Fabric 3	Grey	⅝yd (60cm)
DAMASK FLOWER		
Fabric 4	Lilac	⅝yd (60cm)
SHARKS TEETH		
Fabric 5	Pine	½yd (50cm)
JUMBLE		
Fabric 6	Pink	½yd (50cm)
Fabric 7	Rose	⅝yd (60cm)
Fabric 8	Bubblegum	¼yd (25cm)
* see also Binding Fabric		
SPOT		
Fabric 9	Peach	¼yd (25cm)
ROMAN GLASS		
Fabric 10	Pink	¼yd (25cm)
PAPERWEIGHT		
Fabric 11	Pink	½yd (50cm)
Fabric 12	Sludge	¼yd (25cm)
MILLEFIORE		
Fabric 13	Mauve	¼yd (25cm)
WIDE STRIPE		
Fabric 14	Cantaloupe	⅛yd (15cm)
CHIPS		
Fabric 15	Fog	1yd (95cm)
CACTUS FLOWER		
Fabric 16	Tawny	2¼yd (2.1m)

Backing and Binding Fabrics

ONION RINGS extra-wide		
Fabric 17	Pink	2½yd (2.3m)
JUMBLE		
Fabric 8	Bubblegum	¾yd (70cm)
* see also Patchwork Fabric		

Batting
88in x 88in (224cm x 224cm)

FABRIC SWATCH DIAGRAM

Patchwork Fabrics

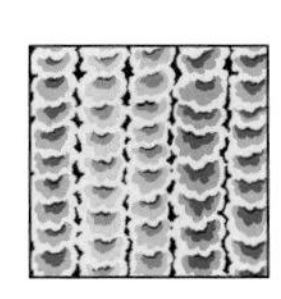

Fabric 1
GARLANDS
Blue
GP181BL

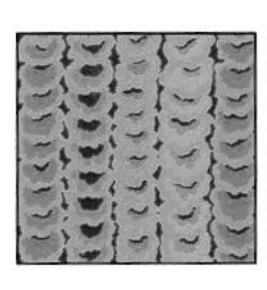

Fabric 2
GARLANDS
Red
GP181RD

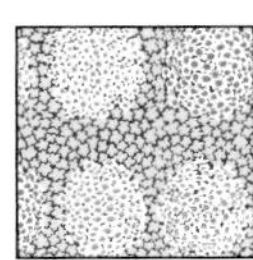

Fabric 3
HYDRANGEA
Grey
GP180GY

Fabric 4
DAMASK FLOWER
Lilac
GP183LI

Fabric 5
SHARK'S TEETH
Pine
BM60PY

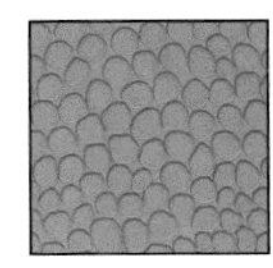

Fabric 6
JUMBLE
Pink
BM53PK

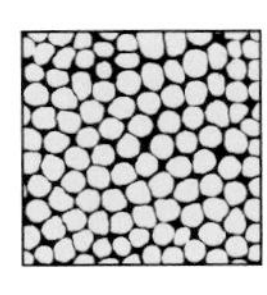

Fabric 7
JUMBLE
Rose
BM53RO

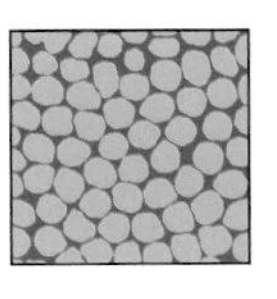

Fabric 8
JUMBLE
Bubblegum
BM53BB

Fabric 9
SPOT
Peach
GP70PH

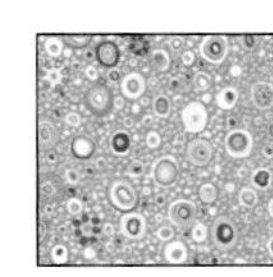

Fabric 10
ROMAN GLASS
Pink
GP01PK

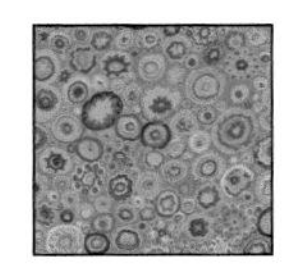

Fabric 11
PAPERWEIGHT
Pink
GP20PK

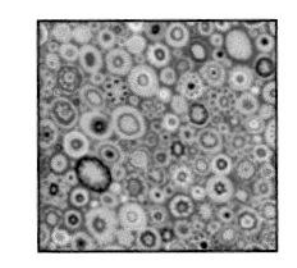

Fabric 12
PAPERWEIGHT
Sludge
GP20SL

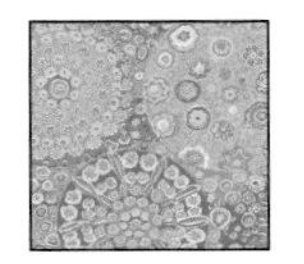

Fabric 13
MILLEFIORE
Mauve
GP92MV

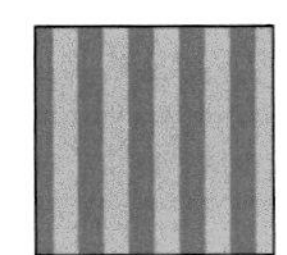

Fabric 14
WIDE STRIPE
Cantaloupe
SS001CA

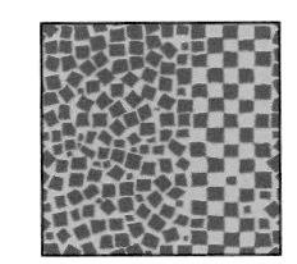

Fabric 15
CHIPS
Fog
BM73FG

Fabric 16
CACTUS FLOWER
Tawny
PJ96TY

Backing and Binding Fabrics

Fabric 17
ONION RINGS WIDE
Pink
QB001PK

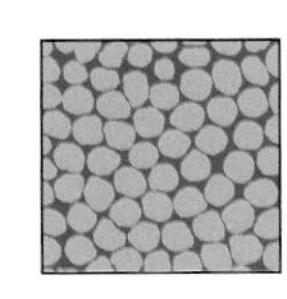

Fabric 8
JUMBLE
Bubblegum
BM53BB

TEMPLATES

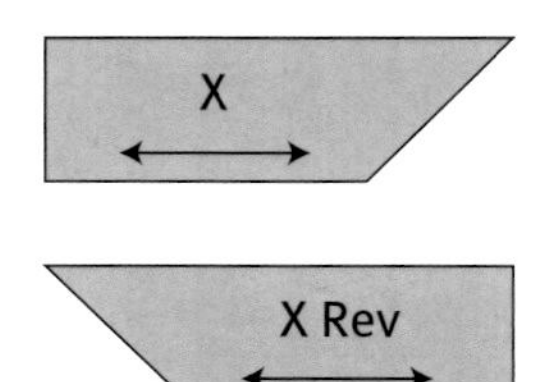

PATCHES

Blocks are made from 3 patches that are all cut from strips cut across the width of the fabric; large triangles and small triangles both cut from squares; and trapezoids cut using Templates X and X reverse (see page 137).

BLOCKS

There are 2 different blocks, Block A and Block B (see Making the Quilt), that are mirror images of each other. In Block A the points of the trapezoids point clockwise around the pinwheel. In Block B the points of the trapezoids point anti-clockwise around the pinwheel. Blocks are arranged in 5 rows of 5 blocks, alternating between block layouts A and B.

CUTTING OUT

Fabric is cut across the width unless otherwise stated.

Borders

Inner Border

From Fabric 15 cut 7 strips 3½in (8.9cm) wide. Remove selvedges and sew end to end, casually matching the pattern. Cut 2 lengths 66½in (167.6cm) for the top and bottom. Cut 2 lengths 60½in (153.7cm) for the sides. Retain the remaining fabric for the trapezoid patches.

Outer Border

From Fabric 16 remove selvedges and, cutting **down the length** of the fabric, cut 2 pieces 6½in x 78½in (16.5cm x 199.4cm) for the top and bottom borders. Also cutting **down the length,** cut 2 pieces 6½in x 66½in (16.5cm x 167.6cm) for the side borders. Retain the remaining fabric for the large triangles.

Large Triangles

Cut strips 6⅞in (17.5cm) wide and cross cut squares as required. Cut each square diagonally once from corner to corner to make 2 half-square triangles from each square. Each strip will yield 5 squares (10 triangles). Cut strips and squares from fabrics as follows:
Fabric 1 (2 strips) 8 squares – 16 triangles;
Fabric 2 (2 strips) 8 squares – 16 triangles;
Fabric 3 (1 strip) 2 squares – 4 triangles;
Fabric 4 (2 strips) 8 squares – 16 triangles;
Fabric 5 (2 strips) 8 squares – 16 triangles;
Fabric 6 (2 strips) 8 squares – 16 triangles;
From the remaining Fabric 16 (1 strip, cut down the length) 8 squares – 16 triangles.
Total: 100 triangles.

Small Triangles

Cut strips 4⅞in (12.4cm) wide and cross cut squares as required. Cut each square diagonally once from corner to corner to make 2 half-square triangles from each square. Each strip will yield 8 squares (16 triangles). Cut strips and squares from fabrics as follows:
From the remaining Fabric 3 (2 strips) 16 squares – 32 triangles;
From the remaining Fabric 4 (1 strip) 8 squares – 16 triangles;
Fabric 7 (2 strips) 9 squares – 18 triangles;
Fabric 9 (1 strip) 8 squares – 16 triangles;
Fabric 10 (1 strip) 8 squares – 16 triangles;
Fabric 11 (1 strip) 1 square – 2 triangles.
Total: 100 triangles.

Trapezoids

Note: When using Templates X and X reverse, cut through a single layer of fabric only.
Cut strips 2½in (6.4cm) wide. Each strip will yield 6 trapezoids if the template is rotated 180 degrees after each cut.

Block A: Cut strips and trapezoids using Template X from fabrics as follows:
Fabric 12 (3 strips) 16 trapezoids;
Fabric 13 (3 strips) 16 trapezoids;
From the remaining Fabric 15 (3 strips) 16 trapezoids.
Total: 48 trapezoids.

Block B: Cut strips and trapezoids using Template X Reverse from fabrics as follows:
From the remaining Fabric 7 (3 strips) 16 trapezoids;
Fabric 8 (3 strips) 16 trapezoids;
From the remaining Fabric 11 (3 strips) 16 trapezoids;
Fabric 14 (1 strip) 4 trapezoids.
Total: 52 trapezoids.

Backing

Trim Fabric 17 backing fabric to 88in x 881in (224cm x 224cm).

Binding

From Fabric 8 cut 9 strips 2½in (6.4cm) wide. Remove selvedges and sew strips end to end with 45-degree seams (see page 141).

BLOCK LAYOUT DIAGRAM

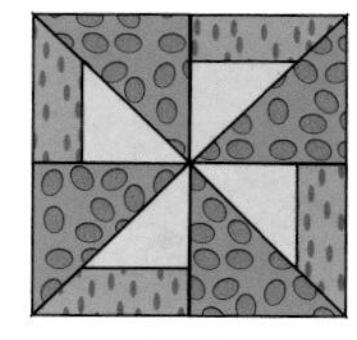

Block A

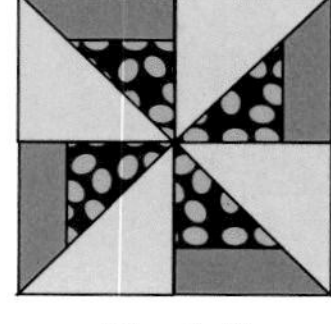

Block B

BLOCK ASSEMBLY DIAGRAM

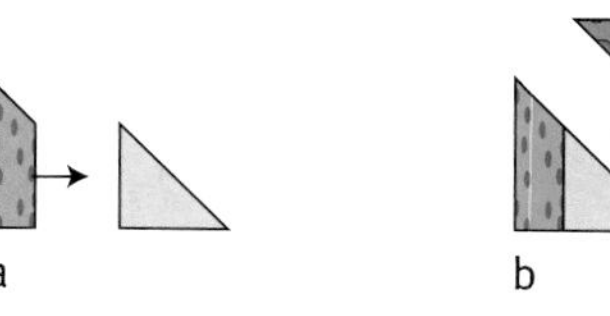

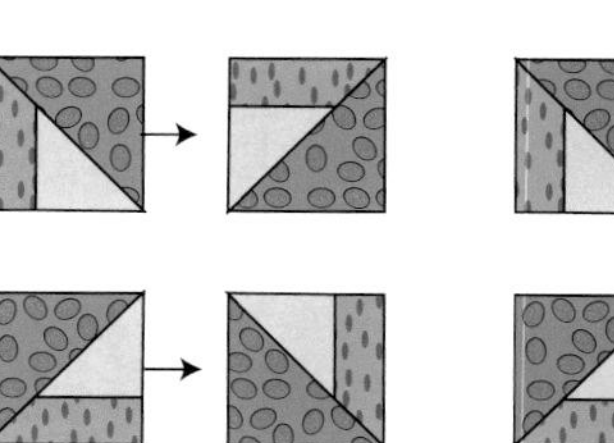

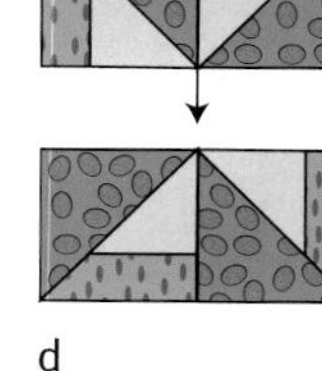

MAKING THE QUILT
Using a design wall will help to place patches in the required layout.
Use ¼in (6mm) seams throughout.

Blocks
Referring to the Block Layout Diagram and Block Assembly Diagram, use 4 large triangles, 4 small triangles and 4 trapezoids to create each block.
Sew the 4 small triangles to the trapezoids and press seams towards the trapezoids (a). Sew each small triangle/ trapezoid unit to a large triangle to create squares (b). Sew the squares together in pairs, checking the position of the centre points (c). Sew the 2 halves of the block together to complete the block (d).
Make 12 Block A and 13 Block B as follows:

Block A
Make the following numbers of blocks:
Using Fabric 1 large triangles, Fabric 3 small triangles and Fabric 13 trapezoids (4 blocks)
Using Fabric 2 large triangles, Fabric 3 small triangles and Fabric 12 trapezoids (4 blocks);
Using Fabric 6 large triangles, Fabric 4 small triangles and Fabric 15 trapezoids (4 blocks).

Block B
Using Fabric 3 large triangles, Fabric 7 and Fabric 11 small triangles and Fabric 14 trapezoids (1 block);
Using Fabric 4 large triangles, Fabric 7 small triangles and Fabric 11 trapezoids (4 blocks);
Using Fabric 5 large triangles, Fabric 9 small triangles and Fabric 8 trapezoids (4 blocks);
Using Fabric 16 large triangles, Fabric 10 small triangles and Fabric 7 trapezoids (4 blocks).

ASSEMBLING THE BLOCKS
Arrange the blocks on a design wall in 5 rows of 5 blocks, paying attention to the precise placement of each pinwheel and referring to the Quilt Assembly Diagram overleaf and quilt photograph for placement. Except for the centre block, all the others are repeated 4 times around the quilt. Sew each row of 5 blocks together, pressing seams in the same direction alternate rows – odd rows to the left, even rows to the right – to allow the finished seams to lie flat. Sew the 5 rows together.

Borders
Pin each border in place before sewing to prevent stretching. Sew the shorter Fabric 15 inner borders to each side, then sew the longer inner borders to the top and bottom.
Sew the shorter Fabric 16 outer borders to each side, then sew the longer outer borders to the top and bottom to complete the quilt top.

FINISHING THE QUILT
Press the quilt top. Layer the quilt top, batting and backing, and baste together (see page 140).
Quilt as desired.
Trim the quilt edges and attach the binding (see page 141).

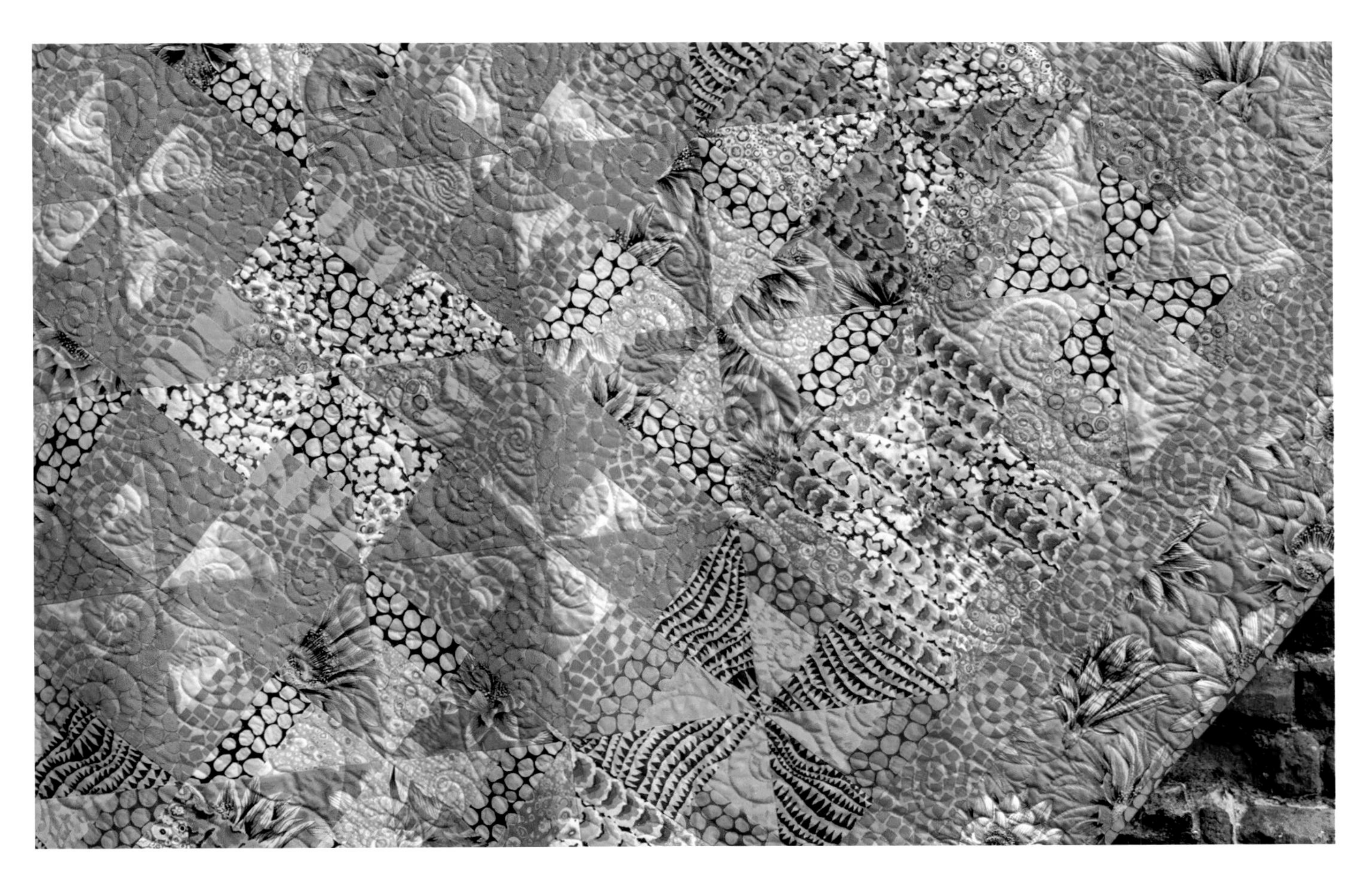

QUILT ASSEMBLY DIAGRAM

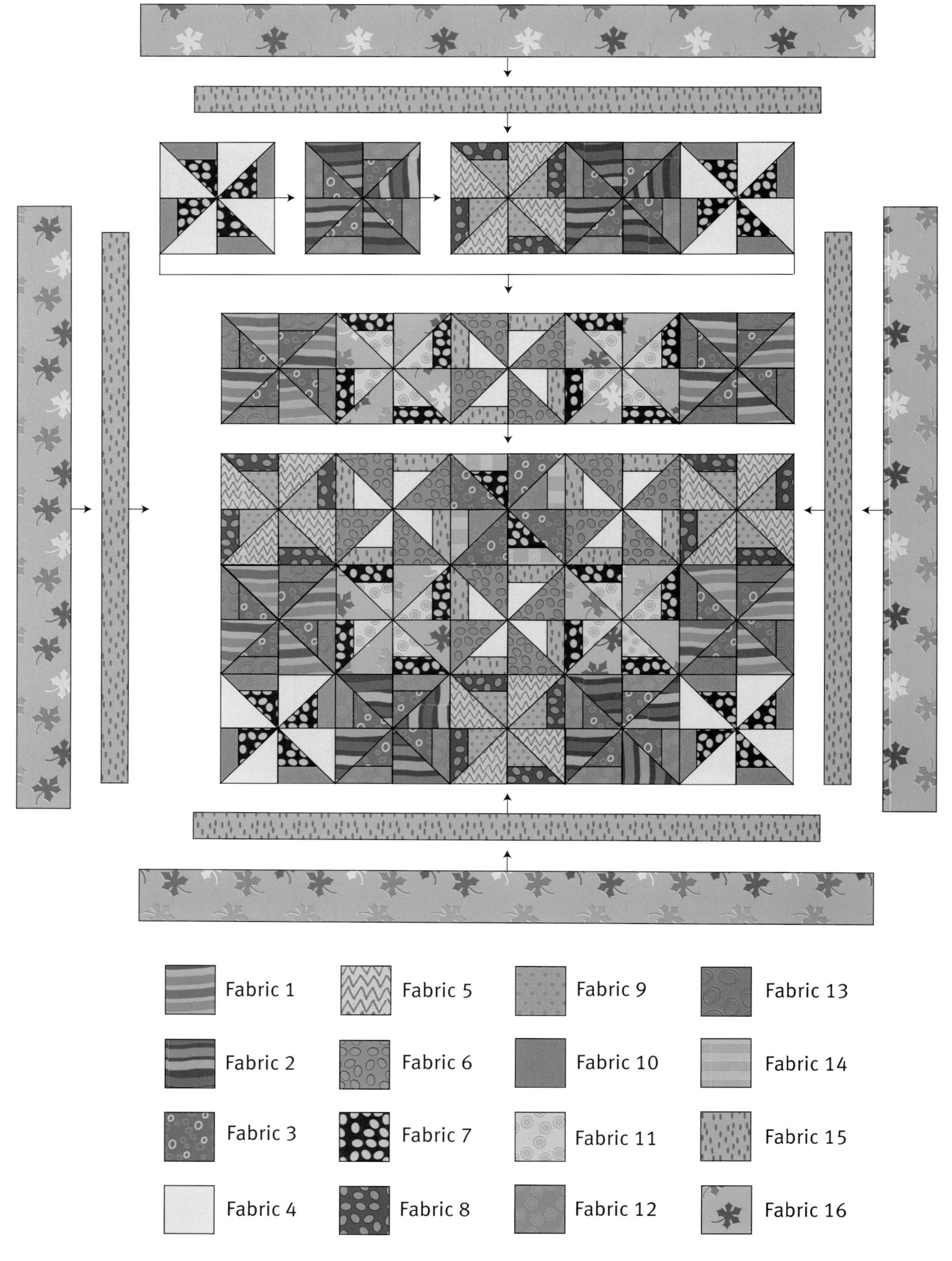

templates

Refer to the individual quilt instructions for the templates needed. Look for the quilt name on the templates to make sure you are using the correct shapes for the project. Arrows on templates should be lined up with the straight grain of the fabric, which runs either along the selvedge or at 90 degrees to the selvedge. Following marked grain lines is important to avoid bias edges, which can cause distortion.

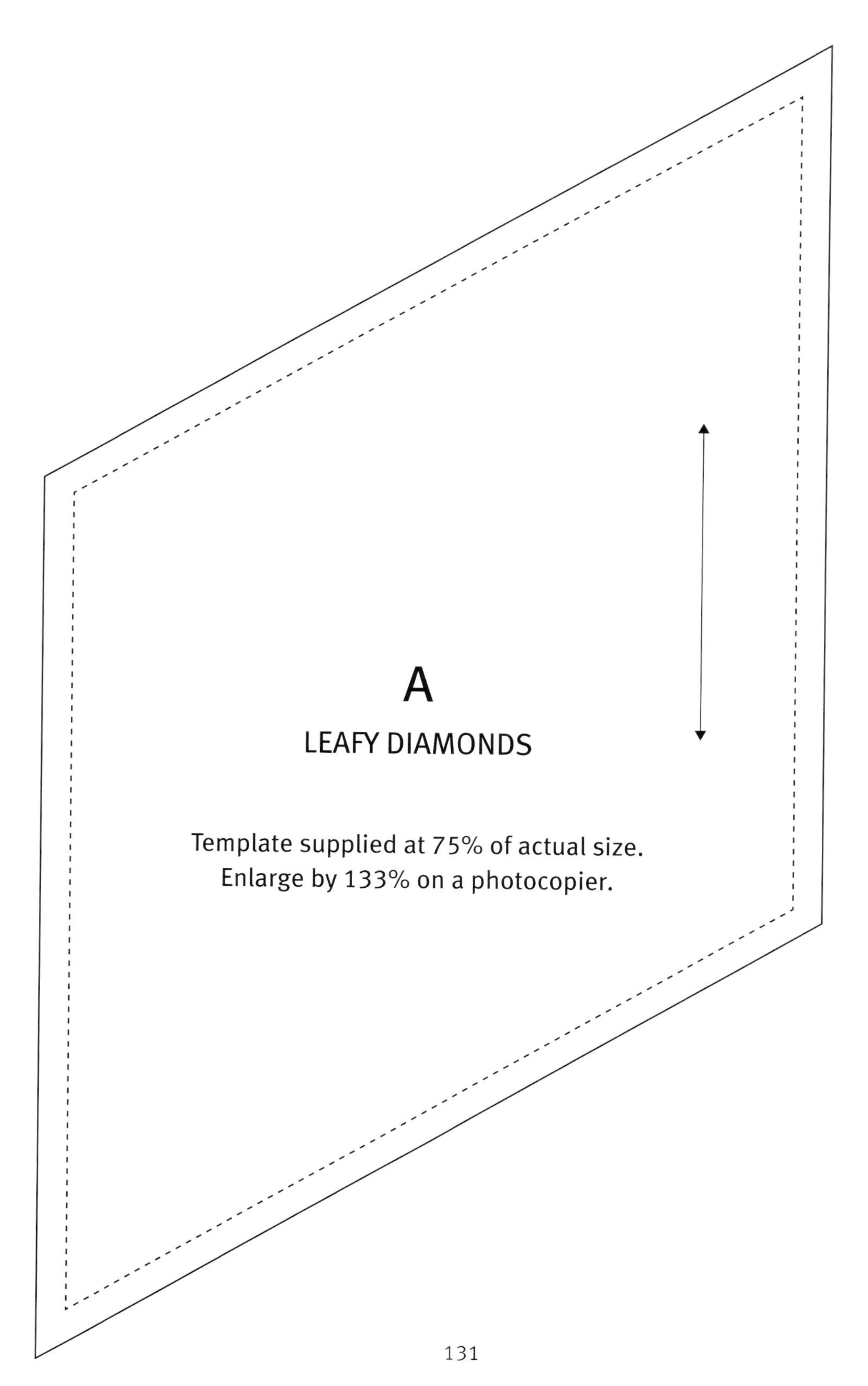

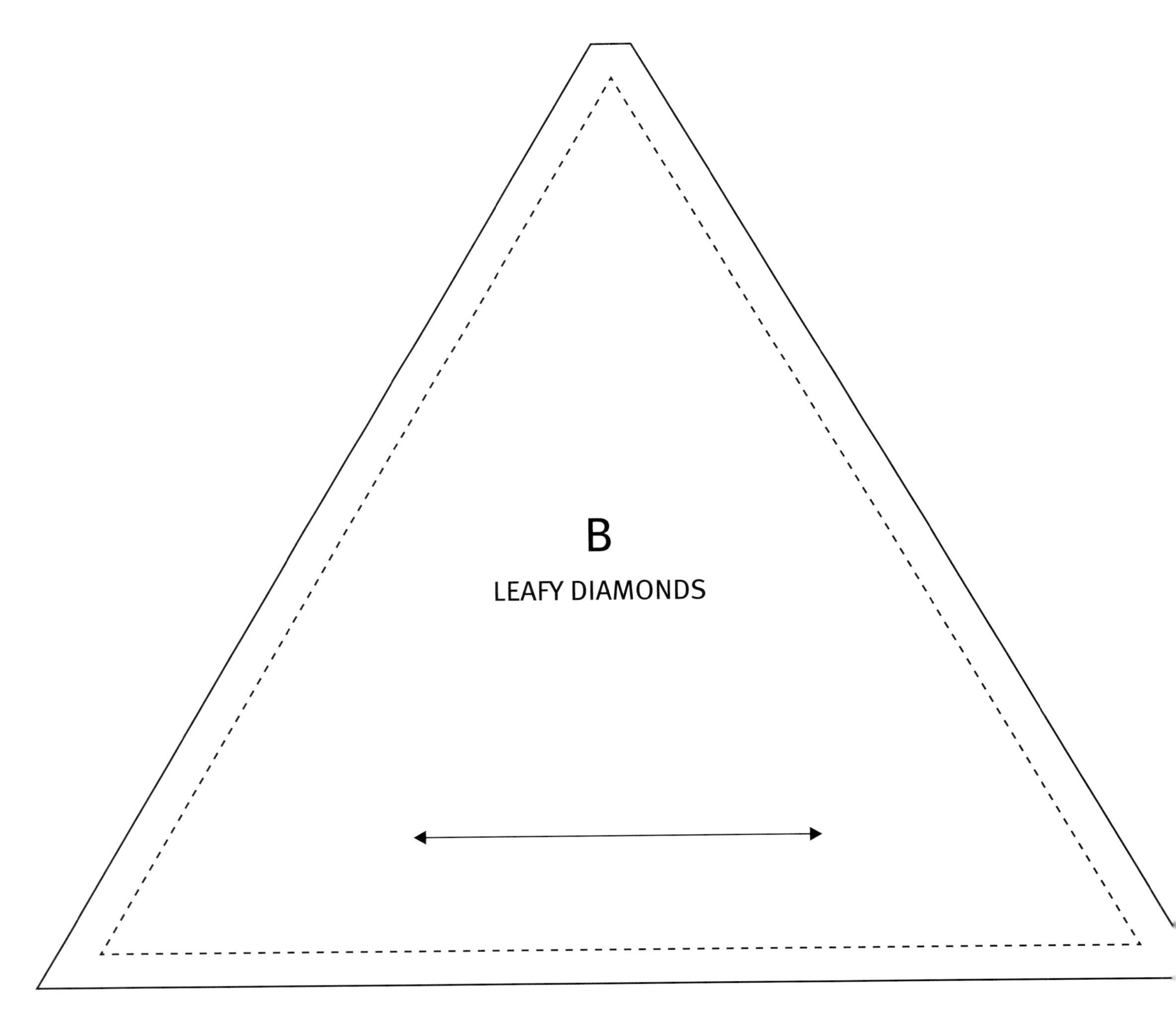
B
LEAFY DIAMONDS

C

LEAFY DIAMONDS

C REVERSE

LEAFY DIAMONDS

D

LEAFY DIAMONDS

Place on fold of paper to complete the template

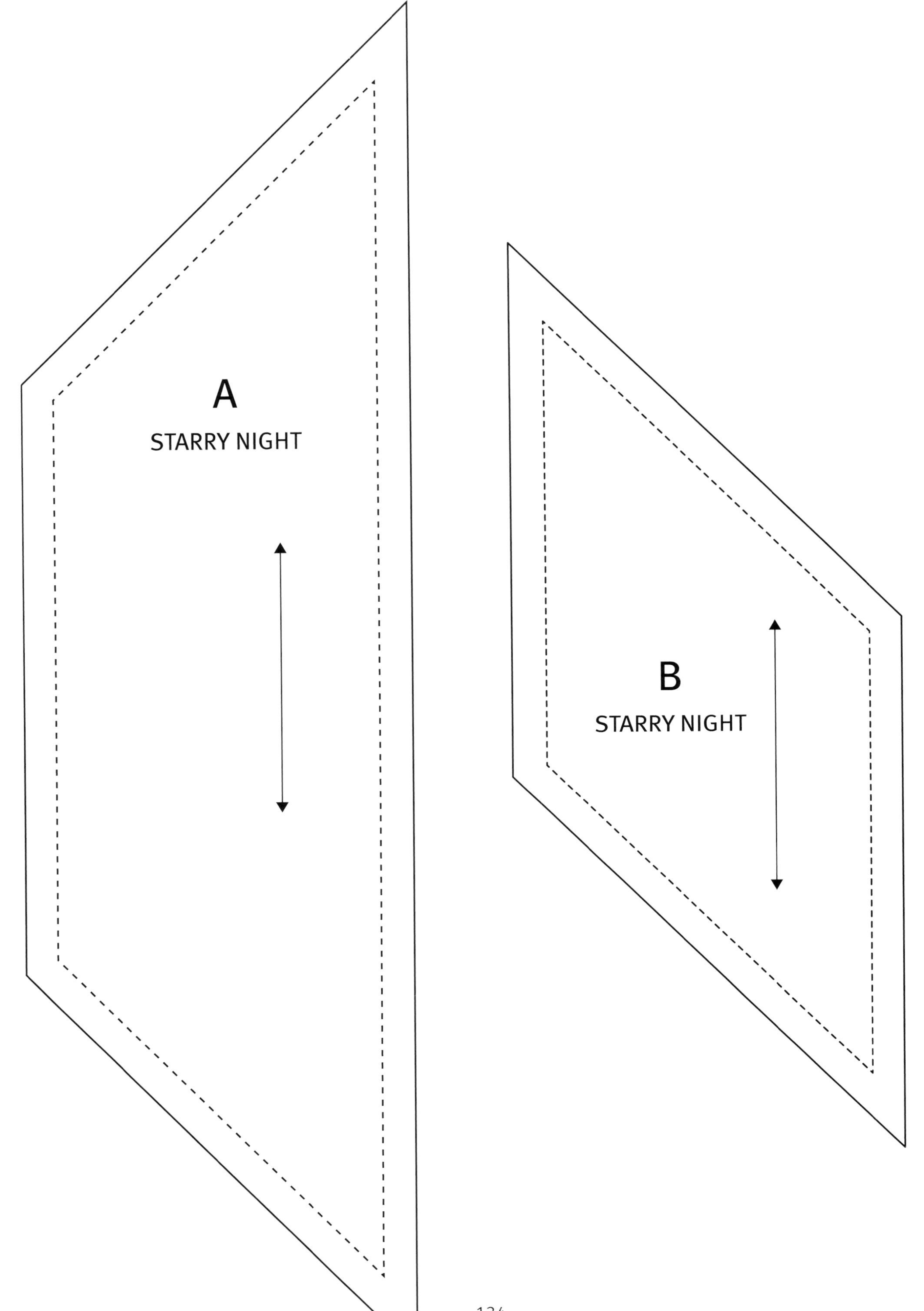
A
STARRY NIGHT
B
STARRY NIGHT

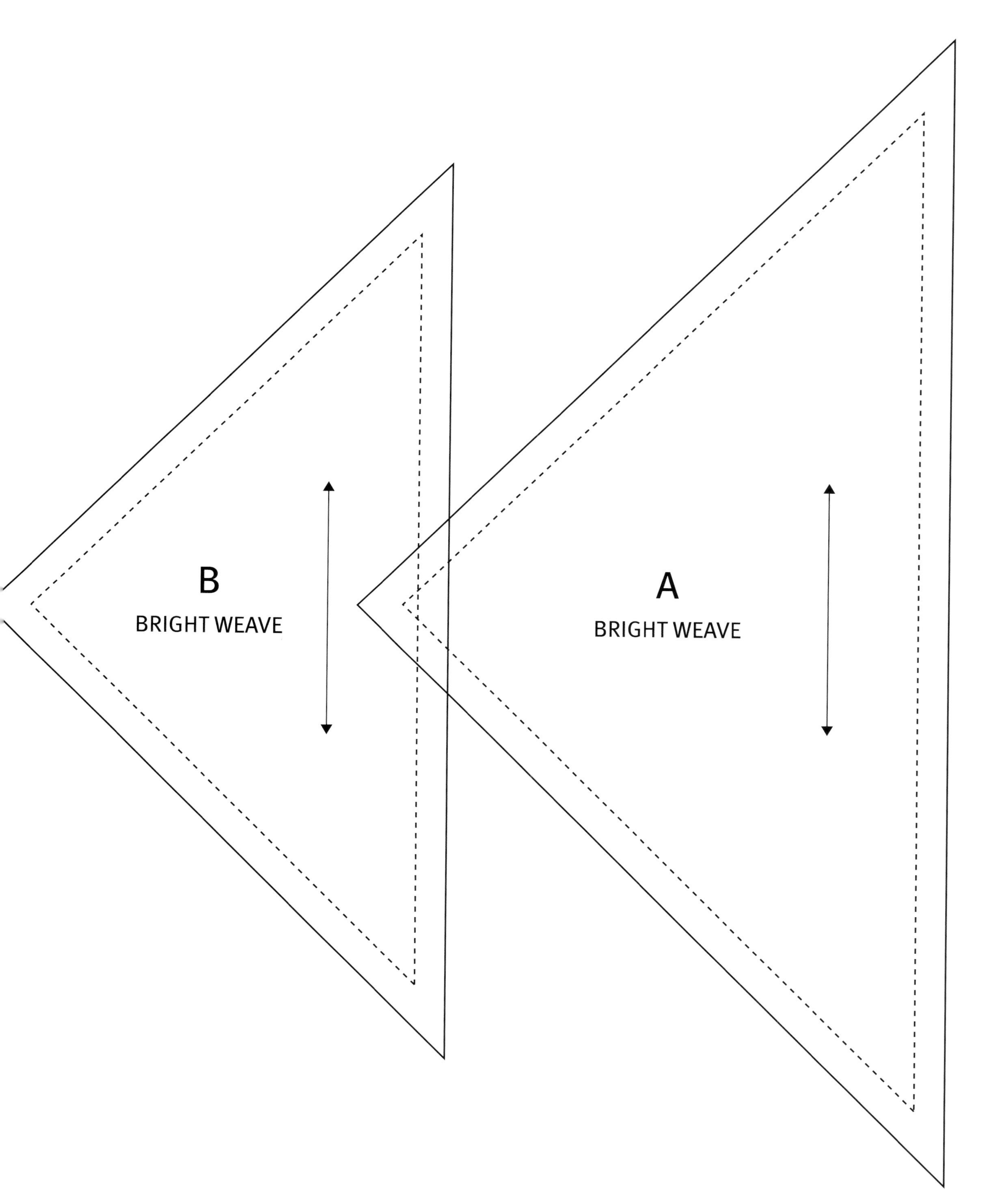
B
BRIGHT WEAVE
A
BRIGHT WEAVE

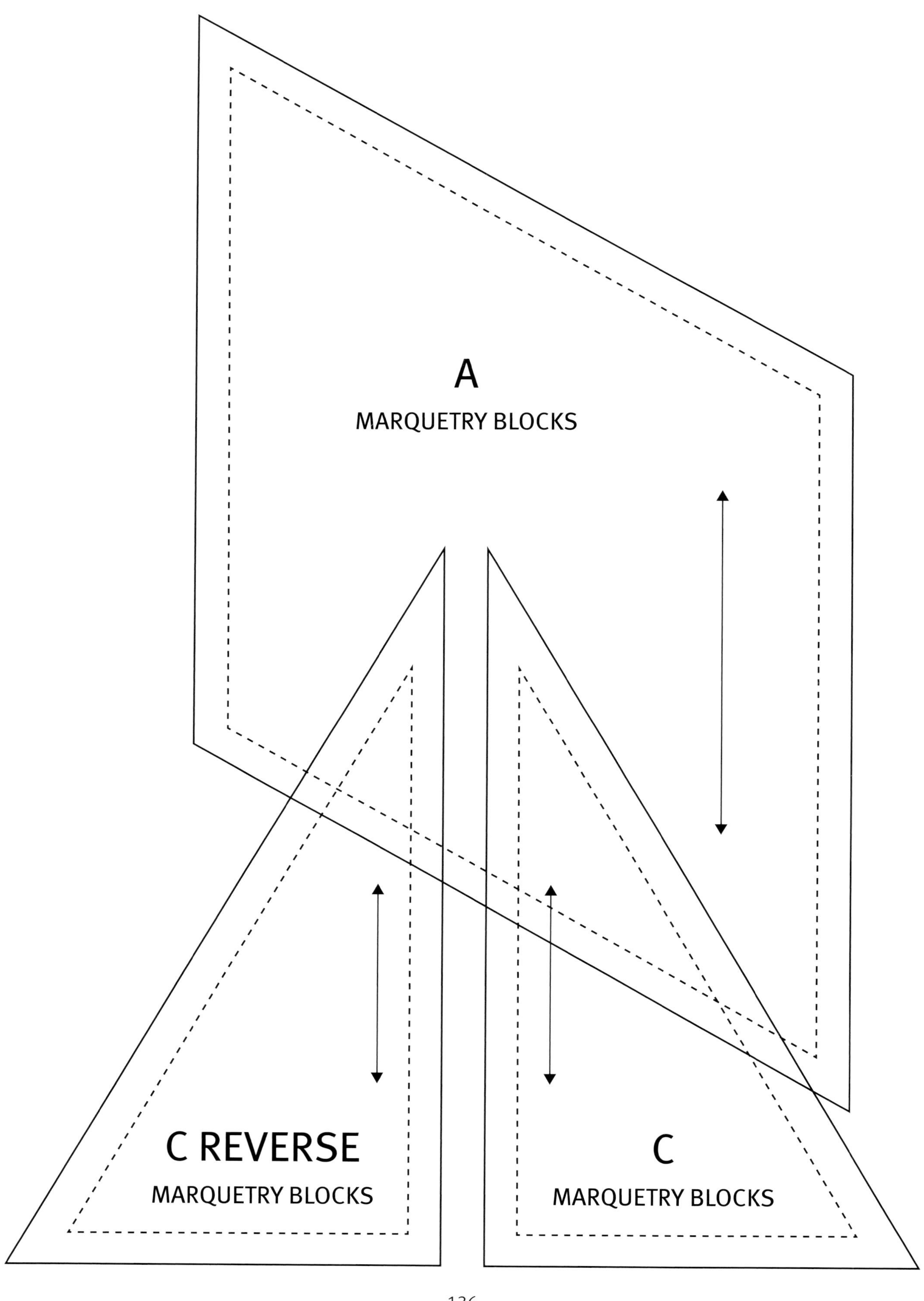
A
MARQUETRY BLOCKS
C REVERSE
MARQUETRY BLOCKS
C
MARQUETRY BLOCKS

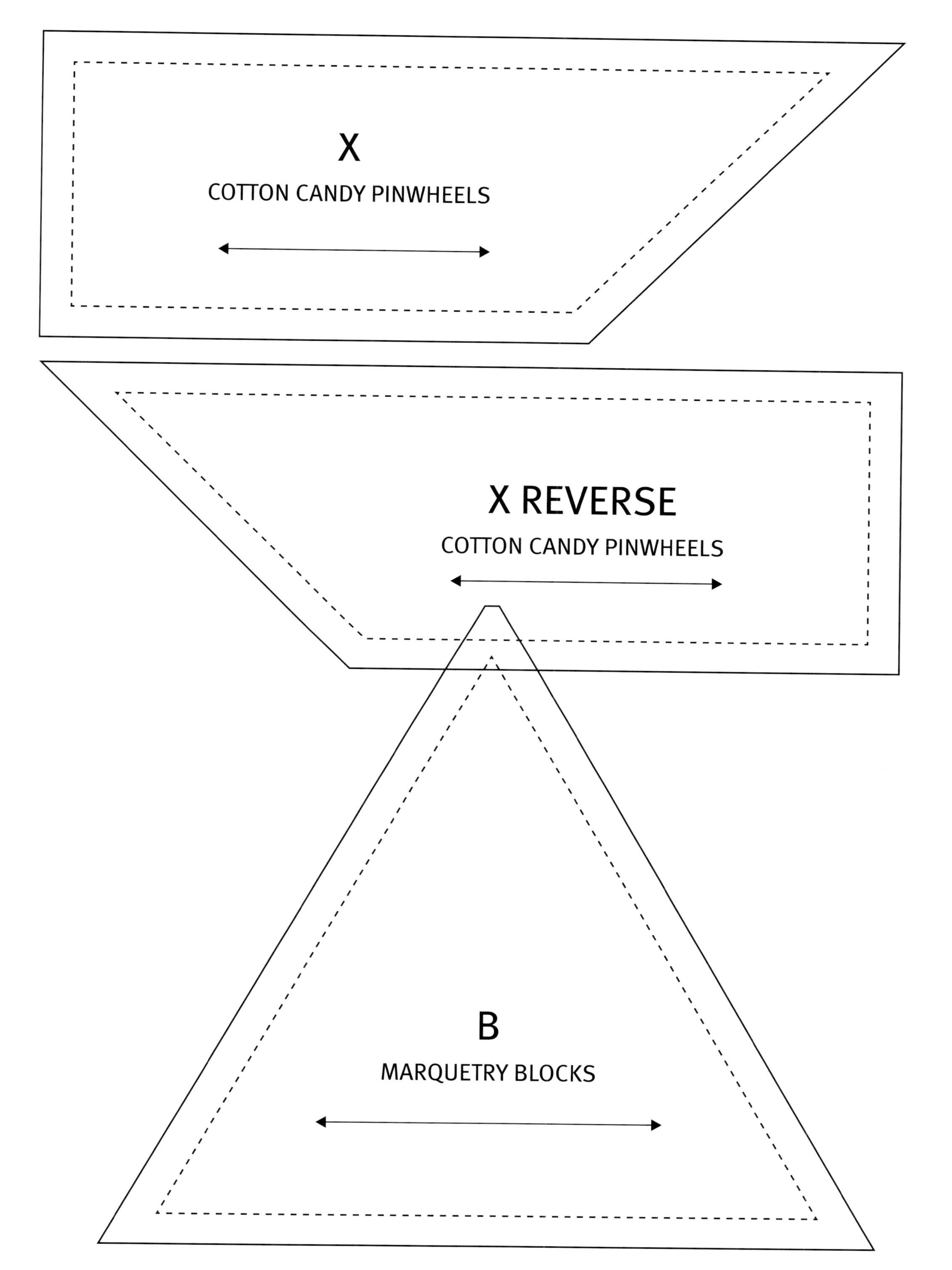
X
COTTON CANDY PINWHEELS
X REVERSE
COTTON CANDY PINWHEELS
B
MARQUETRY BLOCKS

patchwork and quilting know-how

These instructions are intended for the novice quilt maker, providing the basic information needed to make the projects in this book, along with some useful tips.

EXPERIENCE RATINGS
* Easy, straightforward, suitable for a beginner.
** Suitable for the average patchworker and quilter.
*** For the more experienced patchworker and quilter.

ABOUT THE FABRICS
The fabrics used for the quilts in this book are mainly from Kaffe Fassett Collective:
GP is the code for Kaffe Fassett's designs,
PJ for Philip Jacobs' and **BM** for Brandon Mably's.
The other fabrics used are Shot Cottons and Stripes with SC or SS prefixes as well as wide backing fabrics with QB prefixes.

PREPARING THE FABRIC
Prewash all new fabrics before you begin, to ensure that there will be no uneven shrinkage and no bleeding of colours when the finished quilt is laundered. Press the fabric whilst it is still damp to return crispness to it. All fabric requirements in this book are calculated on a 40in (102cm) usable fabric width, to allow for shrinkage and selvedge removal.

MAKING TEMPLATES
Transparent template plastic is the best material to use: it is durable and allows you to see the fabric and select certain motifs. You can also use tracing paper and thin stiff cardboard.

Templates for machine piecing
1 Trace off the actual-sized template provided either directly on to template plastic, or on to tracing paper and then on to thin cardboard. Use a ruler to help you trace off the straight cutting line, dotted seam line and grain lines.

Sometimes templates are too large to print complete. Transfer the template on to the fold of a large sheet of paper, cut out and open out for the full template. Some templates are printed at a reduced size and need to be scaled up on a photocopier.
2 Cut out the traced off template using a craft knife, a ruler and a self-healing cutting mat.
3 Punch holes in the corners of the template, at each point on the seam line, using a hole punch.

Templates for hand piecing
• Make a template as for machine piecing, but do not trace off the cutting line. Use the dotted seam line as the outer edge of the template.

• This template allows you to draw the seam lines directly on to the fabric. The seam allowances can then be cut by eye around the patch.

CUTTING THE FABRIC
On the individual instructions for each project, you will find a summary of all the patch shapes used.

Always mark and cut out any border and binding strips first, followed by the largest patch shapes and finally the smallest ones, to make the most efficient use of your fabric. The border and binding strips are best cut using a rotary cutter.

Rotary cutting
Rotary cut strips are usually cut across the fabric from selvedge to selvedge, but some projects may vary, so please read through all the instructions before you start cutting the fabrics.

1 Before beginning to cut, press out any folds or creases in the fabric. If you are cutting a large piece of fabric, you will need to fold it several times to fit the cutting mat. When there is only a single fold, place the fold facing you. If the fabric is too wide to be folded only once, fold it concertina-style until it fits your mat. A small rotary cutter with a sharp blade will cut up to six layers of fabric; a large cutter up to eight layers.

2 To ensure that your cut strips are straight and even, the folds must be placed exactly parallel to the straight edges of the fabric and along a line on the cutting mat.

3 Place a rotary ruler over the raw edge of the fabric, overlapping it about ½in (1.25cm). Make sure that the ruler is at right angles to both the straight edges and the fold to ensure that you cut along the straight grain. Press down on the ruler and wheel the cutter away from you along the edge of the ruler.

4 Open out the fabric to check the edge. Don't worry if it's not perfectly straight – a little wiggle will not show when the quilt is stitched together. Re-fold the fabric, then place the ruler over the trimmed edge, aligning the edge with the markings on the ruler that match the correct strip width. Cut strip along the edge of the ruler.

USING TEMPLATES
The most efficient way to cut out templates is by first rotary cutting a strip of fabric to the width stated for your template, and then marking off your templates along the strip, edge to edge at the required angle. This method leaves hardly any waste and gives a random effect to your patches.

A less efficient method is to fussy cut them, where the templates are cut individually by placing them on particular motifs or stripes, to create special effects. Although this method is more wasteful, it yields very interesting results.

1 Place the template face down, on the wrong side of the fabric, with the grain-line arrow following the straight grain of the fabric, if indicated. Be careful though – check with your individual instructions, as some instructions may ask you to cut patches on varying grains.

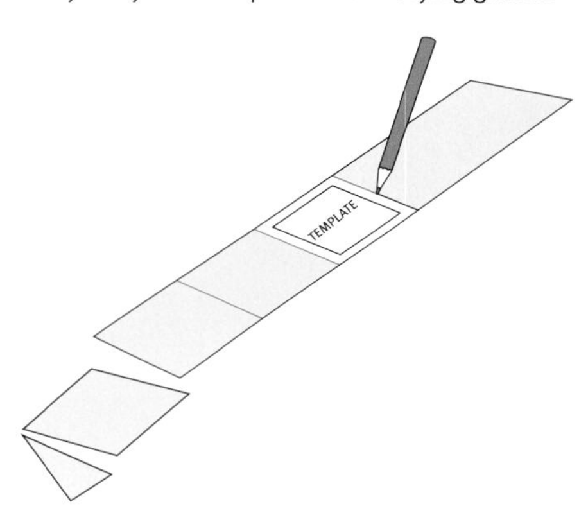

2 Hold the template firmly in place and draw around it with a sharp pencil or crayon, marking in the corner dots or seam lines. To save fabric, position patches close together or even touching. Don't worry if outlines positioned on the straight grain when drawn on striped fabrics do not always match the stripes when cut – this will add a degree of visual excitement to the patchwork!

3 Once you've drawn all the pieces needed, you are ready to cut the fabric, with either a rotary cutter and ruler or a pair of sharp sewing scissors.

BASIC HAND AND MACHINE PIECING
Patches can be stitched together by hand or machine. Machine stitching is quicker, but hand assembly allows you to carry your patches around with you and work on them in every spare moment. The choice is yours. For techniques that are new to you, practise on scrap pieces of fabric until you feel confident.

Hand piecing

1 Pin two patches with right sides together, so that the marked seam lines are facing outwards.

2 Using a single strand of strong thread, secure the corner of a seam line with a couple of back stitches.

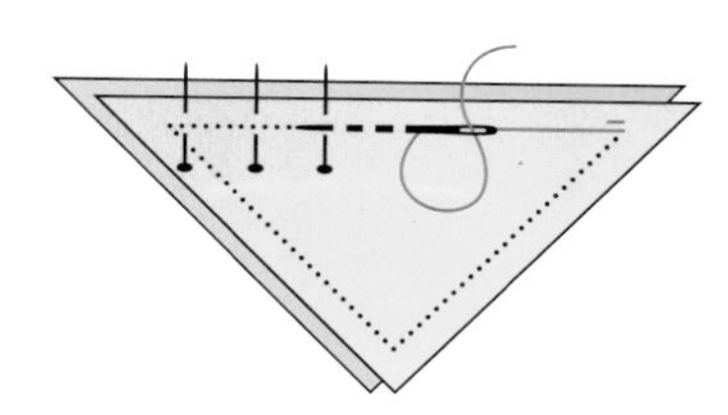

3 Sew running stitches along the marked line, working 8–10 stitches per inch (2.5cm) and ending at the opposite seam line corner with a few back stitches. When hand piecing never stitch over the seam allowances.

4 Press the seams to one side, as shown in machine piecing (Step 2).

Machine piecing

Follow the quilt instructions for the order in which to piece the individual patchwork blocks and then assemble the blocks together in rows.

1 Seam lines are not marked on the fabric for simple shapes, so stitch ¼in (6mm) seams using the machine needle plate, a ¼in (6mm) wide machine foot, or tape stuck to the machine as a guide. Pin two patches with right sides together, matching edges.

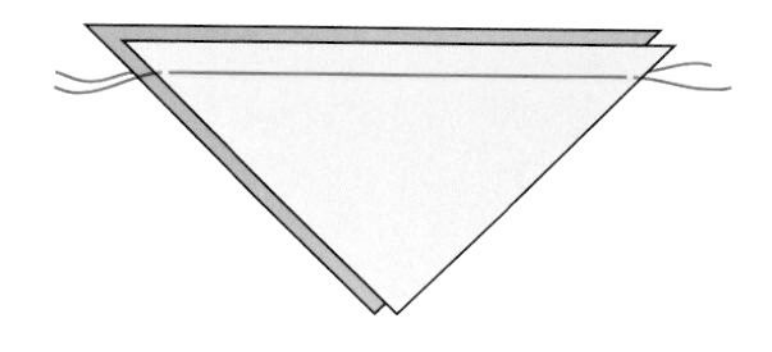

For some shapes, particularly diamonds, you need to match the sewing lines, not the fabric edges. Place 2 diamonds right sides together but offset so that the sewing lines intersect at the correct position. Use pins to secure for sewing.

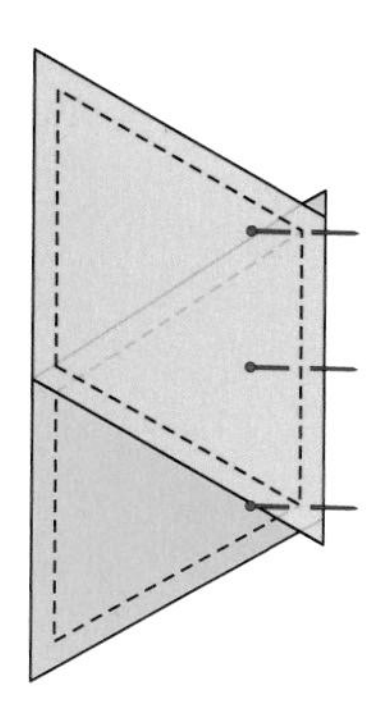

Set your machine at 10–12 stitches per inch (2.5cm) and stitch seams from edge to edge, removing pins as you feed the fabric through the machine.

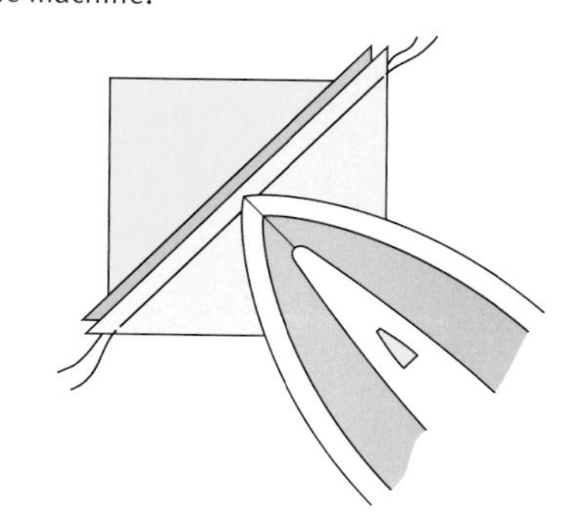

2 Press the seams of each patchwork block to one side before attempting to join it to another block. When joining diamond shaped blocks you will need to offset the blocks in the same way as diamond shaped patches, matching the sewing lines, not the fabric edges.

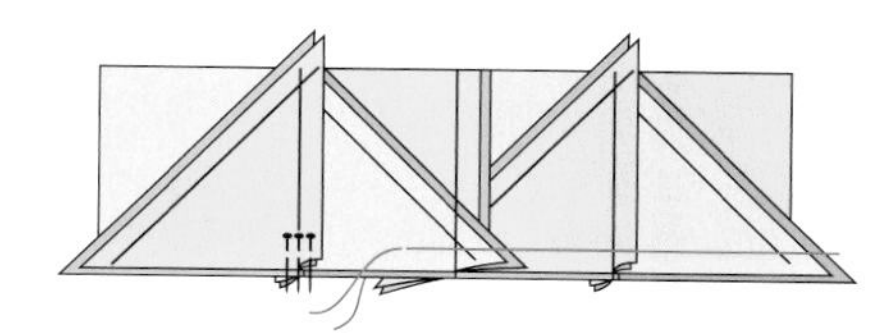

3 When joining rows of blocks, make sure that adjacent seam allowances are pressed in opposite directions to reduce bulk and make matching easier. Pin pieces together directly through the stitch line and to the right and left of the seam. Remove pins as you sew. Continue pressing seams to one side as you work.

Inset (Y) seams

When 3 or more patches have seams that come together without making a rectangle (i.e. in a Y-shape), an inset seam is needed. As shown in the diagram, with RS together, first sew the A–B seam. Then, starting from an inner point to an outer point, sew the A–C seam, and finally the A–D seam. Make sure you start and finish each ¼in (6mm) seam exactly at the beginning and end (as marked by dots on the diagram) and do not stitch into the seam allowance.

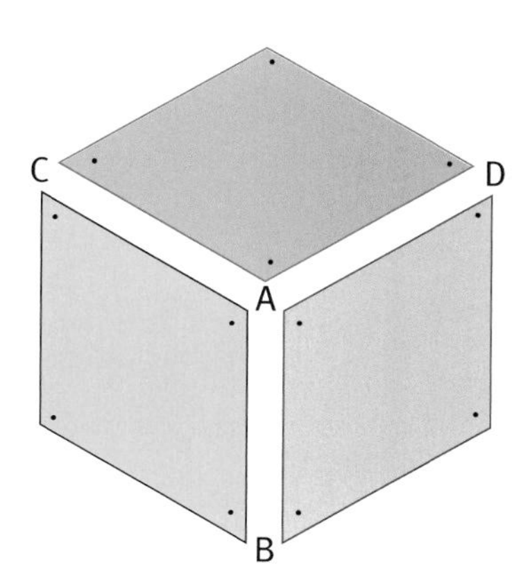

MACHINE APPLIQUÉ WITH ADHESIVE WEB

To make appliqué very easy you can use adhesive web (which comes attached to a paper backing sheet) to bond the motifs to the background fabric. There are two types of web available: the first keeps the pieces in place while they are stitched, the second permanently attaches the pieces so that no sewing is required. Follow steps 1 and 2 for the non-sew type and steps 1–3 for the type that requires sewing.

1 Trace the reversed appliqué design onto the paper side of the adhesive web, leaving a ¼in (6mm) gap between all the shapes. Roughly cut out the motifs ⅛in (3mm) outside your drawn line.

2 Bond the motifs to the reverse of your chosen fabrics. Cut out on the drawn line with very sharp scissors. Remove the backing paper by scoring the centre of the motif carefully with a scissor point and peeling the paper away from the centre out (to prevent damage to the edges). Place the motifs onto the background, noting any which may be layered. Cover with a clean cloth and bond with a hot iron (check instructions for temperature setting as adhesive web can vary depending on the manufacturer).

3 Using a contrasting or toning coloured thread in your machine, work small close zig zag stitches (or a blanket stitch if your machine has one) around the edge of the motifs; the majority of the stitching should sit on the appliqué shape. When stitching up to points, stop with the machine needle in the down position, lift the foot of your machine, pivot the work, lower the foot and continue to stitch. Make sure all the raw edges are stitched.

HAND APPLIQUÉ

Good preparation is essential for speedy and accurate hand appliqué. The finger-pressing method is suitable for needle-turning application, used for simple shapes like leaves and flowers. Using a card template is the best method for bold simple motifs such as circles.

Finger–pressing method

1 To make your template, transfer the appliqué design using carbon paper on to stiff card, and cut out the template. Trace around the outline of your appliquéd shape on to the right side of your fabric using a well sharpened pencil. Cut out shapes, adding by eye a ¼in (6mm) seam allowance all around.

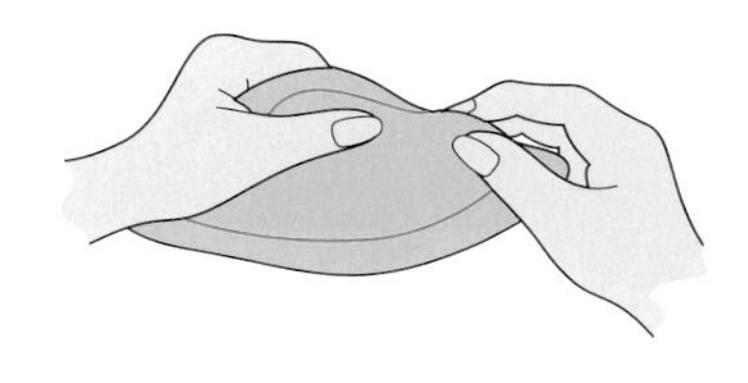

2 Hold the shape right side up and fold under the seam, turning along your drawn line, pinch to form a crease. Dampening the fabric makes this very easy. When using shapes with points such as leaves, turn in the seam allowance at the point first, as shown in the diagram. Then continue all round the shape. If your shapes have sharp curves, you can snip the seam allowance to ease the curve. Take care not to stretch the appliqué shapes as you work.

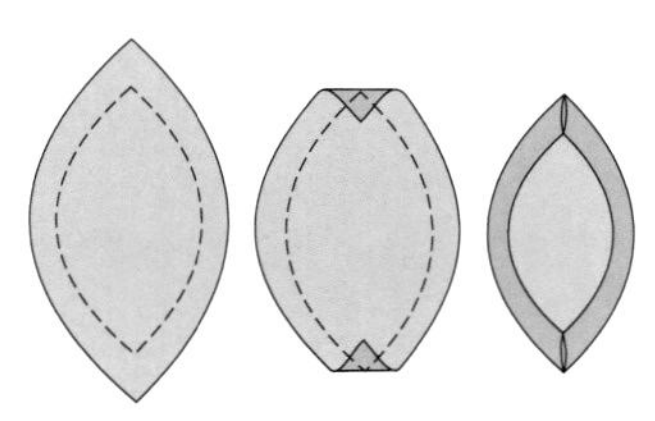

Straight stems

Place fabric face down and simply press over the ¼in (6mm) seam allowance along each edge. You don't need to finish the ends of stems that are layered under other appliqué shapes. Where the end of the stem is visible, simply tuck under the end and finish neatly.

Needle-turning application

Take the appliqué shape and pin in position. Stroke the seam allowance under with the tip of the needle as far as the creased pencil line, and hold securely in place with your thumb. Using a matching thread, bring the needle up from the back of the block into the edge of the shape and proceed to blind-hem in place. (This stitch allows the motifs to appear to be held on invisibly.) To do this, bring the thread out from below through the folded edge of the motif, never on the top. The stitches must be small, even and close together to prevent the seam allowance from unfolding and from frayed edges appearing. Try to avoid pulling the stitches too tight, as this will cause the motifs to pucker up. Work around the whole shape, stroking under each small section before sewing.

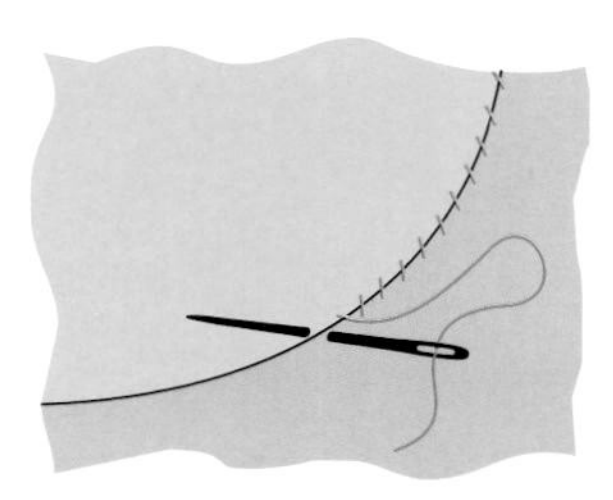

QUILTING

When you have finished piecing your patchwork and added any borders, press it carefully. It is now ready for quilting.

Marking quilting designs and motifs

Many tools are available for marking quilting patterns, check the manufacturer's instructions for use and test on scraps of fabric from your project. Use an acrylic ruler for marking straight lines.

Stencils

Some designs require stencils; these can be made at home, by transferring the designs on to template plastic, or stiff cardboard. The design is then cut away in the form of long dashes, to act as guides for both internal and external lines. These stencils are a quick method for producing an identical set of repeated designs.

BACKING FABRIC

The quilts in this book use two different widths of backing fabric – the standard width of 44in (112cm) and a wider one of 108in (274cm). If you can't find (or don't want to use) the wider fabric then select a standard-width fabric instead and adjust the amount accordingly. For most of the quilts in the book, using a standard-width fabric will probably mean joins in the fabric. The material list for each quilt assumes that an extra 4in of backing fabric is needed all round (8in in total) when making up the quilt sandwich, to allow for long-arm quilting if needed. We have assumed a usable width of 40in (102cm), to allow for selvedge removal and possible shrinkage after washing.

Preparing the backing and batting

- Remove the selvedges and piece together the backing fabric to form a backing at least 4in (10cm) larger all around than the patchwork top.

- Choose a fairly thin batting, preferably pure cotton, to give your quilt a flat appearance. If your batting has been rolled up, unroll it and let it rest before cutting it to the same size as the backing.

- For a large quilt it may be necessary to join two pieces of batting to fit. Lay the pieces of batting on a flat surface so that they overlap by around 8in (20cm). Cut a curved line through both layers.

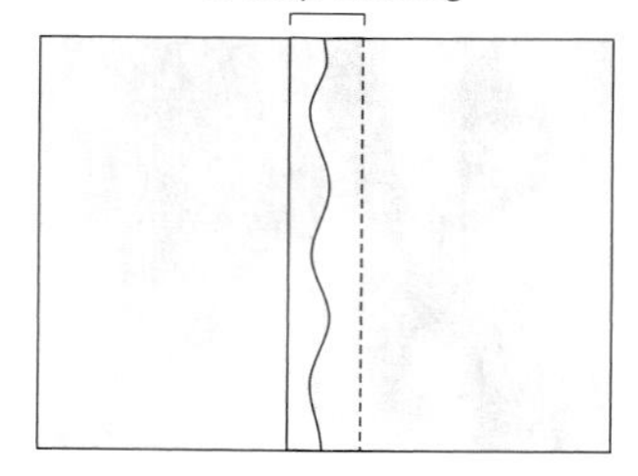

- Carefully peel away the two narrow pieces and discard. Butt the curved cut edges back together. Stitch the two pieces together using a large herringbone stitch.

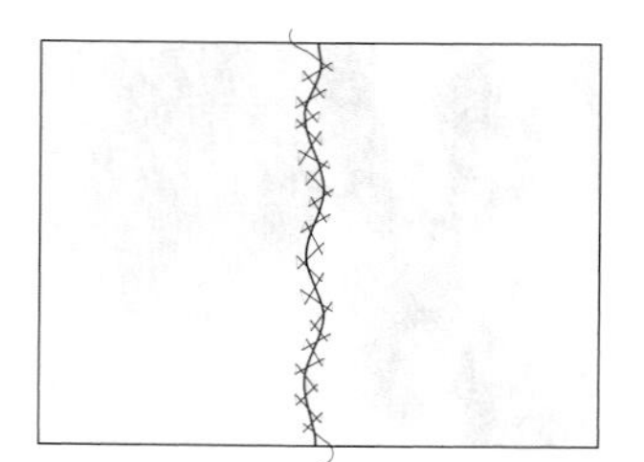

BASTING THE LAYERS TOGETHER

1 On the floor or on a large work surface, lay out the backing with wrong side uppermost. Use weights along the edges to keep it taut.

2 Lay the batting on the backing and smooth it out gently. Next lay the patchwork top, right side up, on top of the batting and smooth gently until there are no wrinkles. Pin at the corners and at the midpoints of each side, close to the edges.

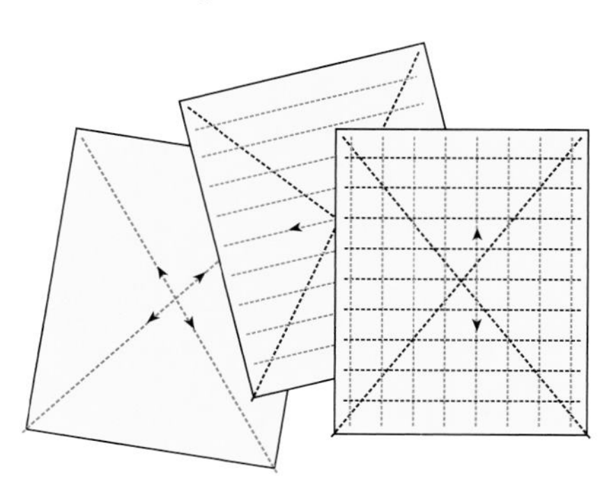

3 Beginning at the centre, baste diagonal lines outwards to the corners, making your stitches about 3in (7.5cm) long. Then, again starting at the centre, baste horizontal and vertical lines out to the edges. Continue basting until you have basted a grid of lines about 4in (10cm) apart over the entire quilt.

4 For speed, when machine quilting, some quilters prefer to baste their quilt sandwich layers together using rust-proof safety pins, spaced at 4in (10cm) intervals over the entire quilt.

HAND QUILTING

This is best done with the quilt mounted on a quilting frame or hoop, but as long as you have basted the quilt well, a frame is not essential. With the quilt top facing upwards, begin at the centre of the quilt and make even running stitches following the design. It is more important to make even stitches on both sides of the quilt than to make small ones. Start and finish your stitching with back stitches and bury the ends of your threads in the batting.

TIED QUILTING

If you prefer you could use tied quilting rather than machine quilting. For tied quilting, use a strong thread that will withstand being pulled through the quilt layers and tied in a knot. You can tie with the knot on the front of the quilt or the back, as preferred. Leaving tufts of thread gives an attractive, rustic look.

Thread a needle with a suitable thread, using the number of strands noted in the project. Put the needle and thread through from the front of the work, leaving a long tail. Go through to the back of the quilt, make a small stitch and then come back through to the front. Tie the threads together using a reef knot and trim the thread ends to the desired length. For extra security, you could tie a double knot or add a spot of fabric glue on the knot.

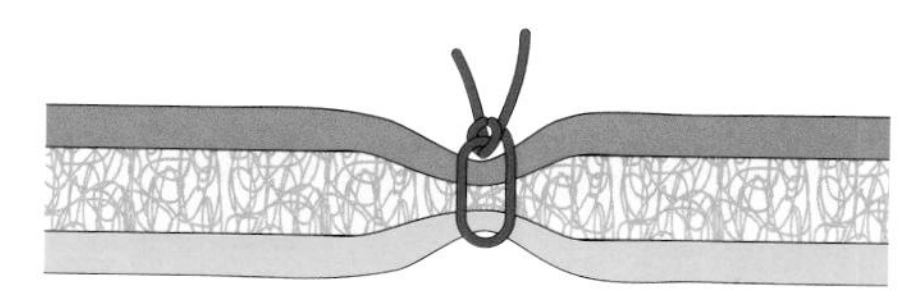

MACHINE QUILTING

- For a flat looking quilt, always use a walking foot on your machine for stitching straight lines, and a darning foot for free-motion quilting.

- It is best to start your quilting at the centre of the quilt and work out towards the borders, doing the straight quilting lines first (stitch-in-the-ditch) followed by the free-motion quilting.

- When free-motion quilting, stitch in a loose meandering style as shown in the diagrams. Do not stitch too closely as this will make the quilt feel stiff when finished. If you wish you can include floral themes or follow shapes on the printed fabrics for added interest.

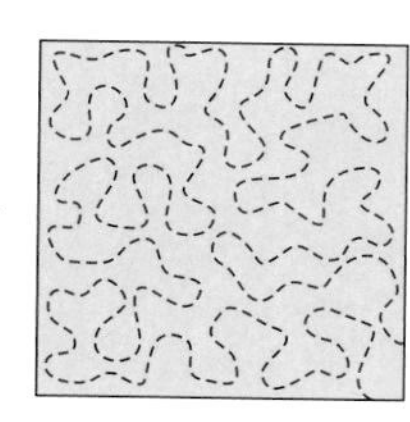

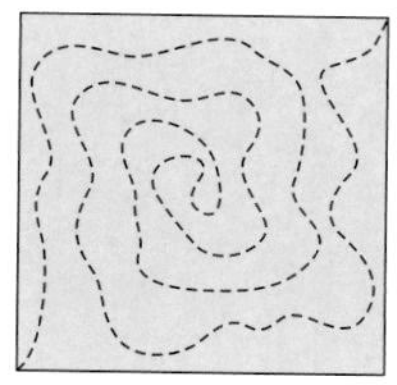

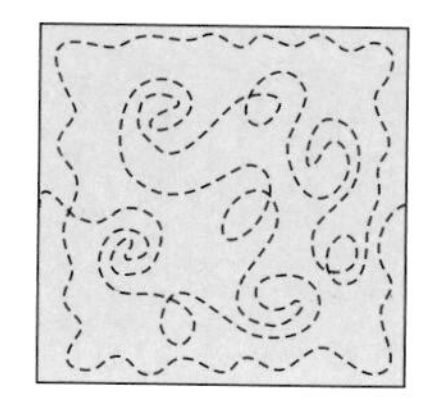

- Make it easier for yourself by handling the quilt properly. Roll up the excess quilt neatly to fit under your sewing machine arm, and use a table or chair to help support the weight of the quilt that hangs down the other side.

FINISHING

Preparing to bind the edges

Once you have quilted or tied your quilt sandwich together, remove all the basting stitches. Then, baste around the outer edge of the quilt ¼in (6mm) from the edge of the top patchwork layer. Trim the back and batting to the edge of the patchwork and straighten the edge of the patchwork if necessary.

Binding and 45-degree seams

1 Cut bias or straight grain strips the width required for your binding, making sure the grain-line is running the correct way on your straight grain strips. Cut enough strips until you have the required length to go around the edge of your quilt.

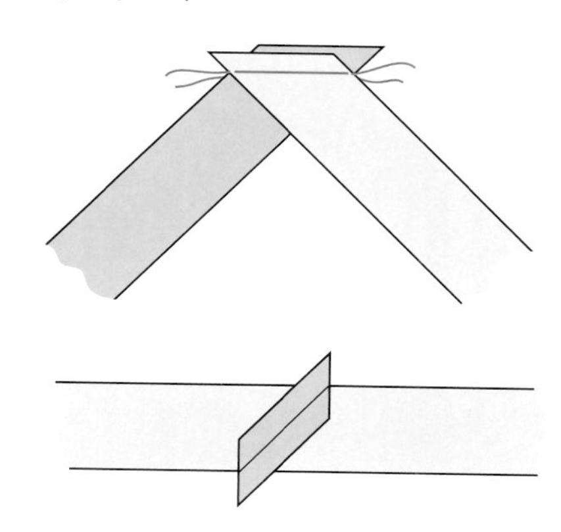

2 To join strips together, the two ends that are to be joined must be cut at a 45-degree angle, as above. Stitch right sides together, trim turnings and press seam open.

Binding the edges

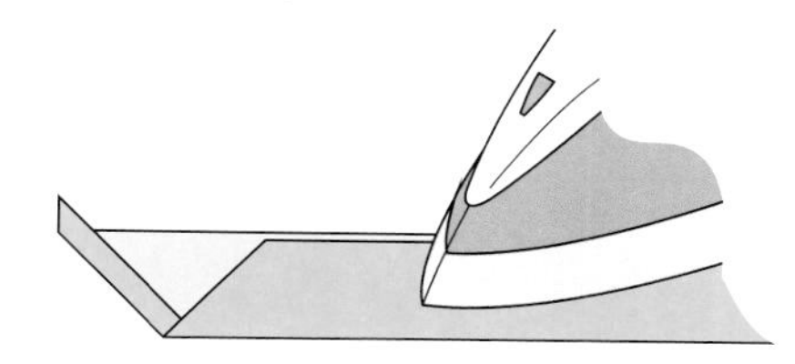

1 Cut the starting end of binding strip at a 45-degree angle, fold a ¼in (6mm) turning to wrong side along cut edge and press in place. With wrong sides together, fold strip in half lengthways, keeping raw edges level, and press.

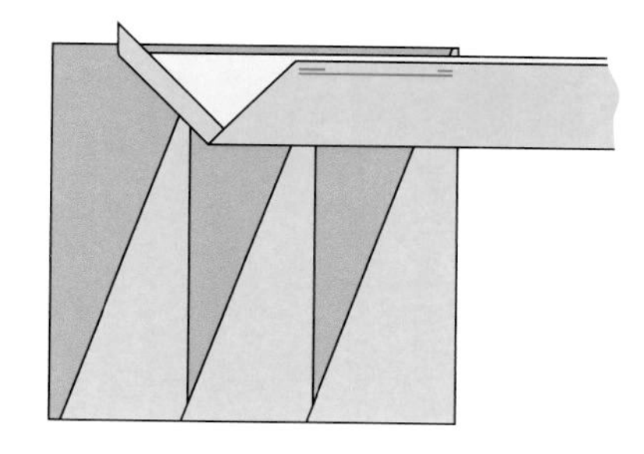

2 Starting at the centre of one of the long edges, place the doubled binding on to the right side of the quilt keeping raw edges level. Stitch the binding in place. starting ¼in (6mm) in from the diagonal folded edge. Reverse stitch to secure, and work ¼in (6mm) in from edge of the quilt towards first corner of quilt. Stop ¼in (6mm) in from corner and work a few reverse stitches.

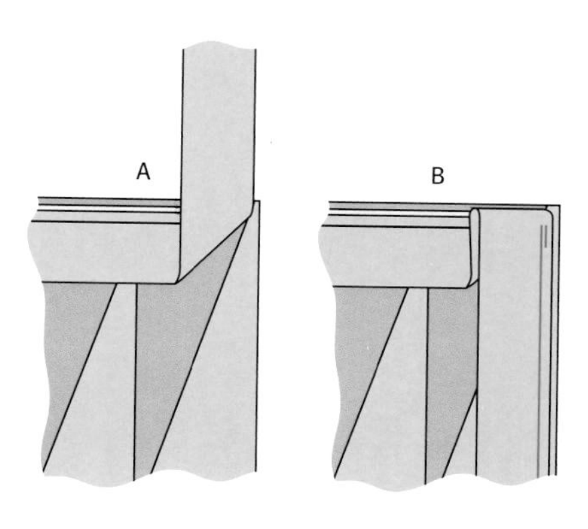

3 Fold the loose end of the binding up, making a 45-degree angle (see A). Keeping the diagonal fold in place, fold the binding back down, aligning the raw edges with the next side of the quilt. Starting at the point where the last stitch ended, stitch down the next side (see B).

4 Continue to stitch the binding in place around all the quilt edges in this way, tucking the finishing end of the binding inside the diagonal starting section.

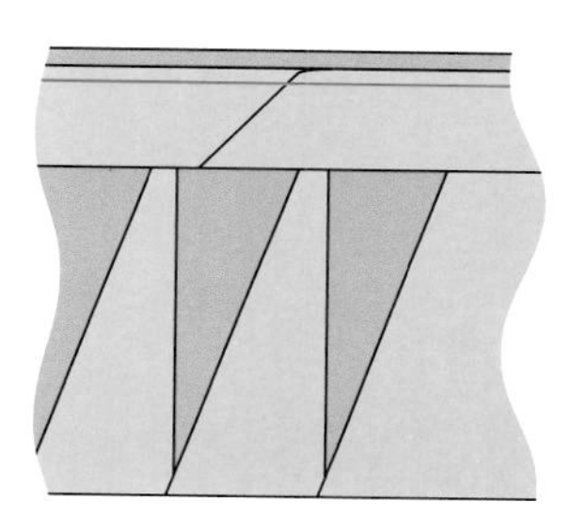

5 Turn the folded edge of the binding on to the back of the quilt. Hand stitch the folded edge in place just covering binding machine stitches, and folding a mitre at each corner.

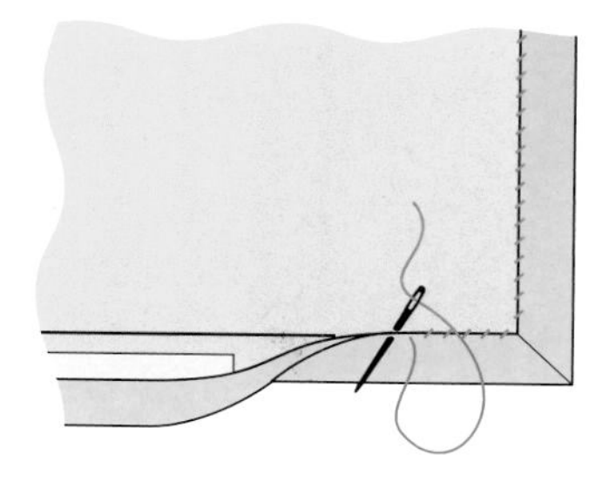

glossary of terms

Adhesive or fusible web This comes attached to a paper-backed sheet and is used to bond appliqué motifs to a background fabric. There are 2 types of web available, the first keeps the pieces in place whilst they are stitched, the second permanently attaches the pieces so that no sewing is required.

Appliqué The technique of stitching fabric shapes on to a background to create a design. It can be applied either by hand or machine with a decorative embroidery stitch, such as buttonhole, or satin stitch.

Backing The bottom layer of a quilt sandwich. It is made of fabric pieced to the size of the quilt top with the addition of about 4in (10cm) all around to allow for quilting take-up.

Basting or tacking This is a means of holding two fabric layers or the layers of a quilt sandwich together temporarily with large hand stitches or pins.

Batting or wadding This is the middle layer, or padding in a quilt. It can be made of cotton, wool, silk or synthetic fibres.

Bias The diagonal grain of a fabric. This is the direction which has the most give or stretch, making it ideal for bindings, especially on curved edges.

Binding A narrow strip of fabric used to finish off the edges of quilts or projects; it can be cut on the straight grain of a fabric or on the bias.

Block A single design unit that when stitched together with other blocks create the quilt top. It is most often a square, hexagon, or rectangle, but it can be any shape. It can be pieced or plain.

Border A frame of fabric stitched to the outer edges of the quilt top. Borders can be narrow or wide, pieced or plain. As well as making the quilt larger, they unify the overall design and draw attention to the central area.

Chalk pencils Available in various colours, they are used for marking lines or spots on fabric.

Cutting mat Designed for use with a rotary cutter, it is made from a special self-healing material that keeps your cutting blade sharp. Cutting mats come in various sizes and are usually marked with a grid to help you line up the edges of fabric and cut out larger pieces.

Design wall Used for laying out fabric patches before sewing. A large wall or folding board covered with flannel fabric or cotton batting in a neutral shade (dull beige or grey work well) will hold fabric in place so that an overall view can be taken of the placement.

Free-motion quilting Curved wavy quilting lines stitched in a random manner. Stitching diagrams are often given for you to follow as a loose guide.

Fussy cutting This is when a template is placed on a particular motif, or stripe, to obtain interesting effects. This method is not as efficient as strip cutting, but yields very interesting results.

Grain The direction in which the threads run in a woven fabric. In a vertical direction it is called the lengthwise grain, which has very little stretch. The horizontal direction, or crosswise grain is slightly stretchy, but diagonally the fabric has a lot of stretch. This grain is called the bias. Wherever possible the grain of a fabric should run in the same direction on a quilt block and borders.

Grain lines These are arrows printed on templates which should be aligned with the fabric grain.

Inset seams or setting-in A patchwork technique whereby one patch (or block) is stitched into a Y shape formed by the joining of two other patches (or blocks).

Patch A small shaped piece of fabric used in the making of a patchwork pattern.

Patchwork The technique of stitching small pieces of fabric (patches) together to create a larger piece of fabric, usually forming a design.

Pieced quilt A quilt composed of patches.

Quilting Traditionally done by hand with running stitches, but for speed modern quilts are often stitched by machine. The stitches are sewn through the top, wadding and backing to hold the three layers together. Quilting stitches are usually worked in some form of design, but they can be random.

Quilting hoop Consists of two wooden circular or oval rings with a screw adjuster on the outer ring. It stabilises the quilt layers, helping to create an even tension.

Reducing glass Used for viewing the complete composition of a quilt at a glance. It works like a magnifier in reverse. A useful tool for checking fabric placement before piecing a quilt.

Rotary cutter A sharp circular blade attached to a handle for quick, accurate cutting. It is a device that can be used to cut several layers of fabric at one time. It must be used in conjunction with a self-healing cutting mat and a thick plastic ruler.

Rotary ruler A thick, clear plastic ruler marked with lines in imperial or metric measurements. Sometimes they also have diagonal lines indicating 45 and 60 degree angles. A rotary ruler is used as a guide when cutting out fabric pieces using a rotary cutter.

Sashing A piece or pieced sections of fabric interspaced between blocks.

Sashing posts When blocks have sashing between them the corner squares are known as sashing posts.

Selvedges Also known as selvages, these are the firmly woven edges down each side of a fabric length. Selvedges should be trimmed off before cutting out your fabric, as they are more liable to shrink when the fabric is washed.

Stitch-in-the-ditch or Ditch quilting Also known as quilting-in-the-ditch. The quilting stitches are worked along the actual seam lines to give a pieced quilt texture.

Template A pattern piece used as a guide for marking and cutting out fabric patches, or marking a quilting, or appliqué design. Usually made from plastic or strong card that can be reused many times. Templates for cutting fabric usually have marked grain lines which should be aligned with the fabric grain.

Threads One hundred percent cotton or cotton-covered polyester is best for hand and machine piecing. Choose a colour that matches your fabric. When sewing different colours and patterns together, choose a medium to light neutral colour, such as grey or ecru. Specialist quilting threads are available for hand and machine quilting.

Walking foot or Quilting foot This is a sewing machine foot with dual feed control. It is very helpful when quilting, as the fabric layers are fed evenly from the top and below, reducing the risk of slippage and puckering.

Yo-Yos A circle of fabric double the size of the finished puff is gathered up into a rosette shape.

Y seams See Inset seams.

ACKNOWLEDGMENTS

I have a small team of makers who patiently sew, quilt and write the instructions for these books, including Liza Prior Lucy, our trusted friend and loyal colleague in the US, with her team of Bobbi Penniman, Sally Davies, Mira Mayer and Judy Baldwin, plus Judy Irish for quilting. In the UK I have the marvellous Janet Haigh of Heart Space Studios, and her team of Ilaria Padovani and Julie Harvey, plus Mary Jane Hutchinson for quilting. Thanks to them all. Were it not for them, these books would not be possible.

Thanks, too, to Bundle Backhouse for taking on the enormous responsibility of the technical editing of the instructions and also for her organizational skills at the Kaffe Fassett Studio; to Anne Wilson for her graphic eye and for her attention to detail on the book layouts; to Steve Jacobson for the technical illustrations and Steven Wooster for the quilt flat shot photography; and to our publishing consultant, Susan Berry of Berry & Co, for managing this series through the process to print, alongside Peter Chapman, executive editor at Taunton Press.

I give enormous thanks to the people of the historic English village of Lavenham in Suffolk for maintaining this wonderful example of past architectural genius. Lavenham served as the perfect backdrop to display our collection of quilts for this book.

Particular thanks to our ever-trusted friend and photographer, Debbie Patterson, who shares not only a similar vision but also our sense of humour. She puts up with Brandon's and my temperamental moods at our photography shoots to arrive at just the magic we were aiming for. And, last but not least, to Brandon, who not only manages the studio, and co-designs with me, but carries the pressure of whirlwind photo shoots in various locations – so glad you hang in there, ensuring the output is of consistently high quality.

The quilts were made and quilted as follows:

Makers
1 *Trip around the Snowball* Ilaria Padovani
2 *Paperweight Checkerboard* Sally Davis
3 *Starry Night* Mira Mayer
4 *Dark Watermelons* Julie Harvey
5 *Peach Sunset* Ilaria Padovani
6 *Woodstock* Liza Prior Lucy
7 *Cottage Garden Flowers* Julie Harvey
8 *Leafy Diamonds* Julie Harvey
9 *Dark Boxes* Julie Harvey
10 *Cotton Candy Pinwheels* Judy Baldwin
11 *Shards* Judy Baldwin
12 *Ancient Glade* Julie Harvey
13 *Bright Weave* Liza Prior Lucy
14 *Marquetry Blocks* Sally Davis
15 *Blooming Columns* Janet Haigh
16 *Opal Crosses* Bobbi Penniman
17 *Mirror Columns* Ilaria Padovani
18 *Tiddlywinks Rosy* Liza Prior Lucy
19 *Shaded Squares* Ilaria Padovani

Quilters (see quilt prefix number)
Janet Haigh 15
Julie Harvey 8, 12
Mary-Jane Hutchinson 1, 4, 5, 7, 9, 17, 19
Judy Irish 2, 3, 6, 10, 11, 13, 14, 16, 18

OTHER TAUNTON TITLES AVAILABLE

Kaffe Fassett's Quilt Romance
Kaffe Fassett's Quilts en Provence
Kaffe Fassett's Quilts in Sweden
Kaffe Quilts Again
Kaffe Fassett's Quilt Grandeur
Kaffe Fassett's Quilts in Morocco
Kaffe Fassett's Heritage Quilts
Kaffe Fassett's Quilts in Italy
Kaffe Fassett's Quilts in Ireland
Kaffe Fassett's Quilts in America
Kaffe Fassett's Quilts in the Cotswolds
Kaffe Fassett's Quilts in Burano

The Taunton Press
Inspiration for hands-on living®

The Taunton Press, Inc., 63 South Main Street,
Newtown, CT 06470
Tel: 800-888-8286 • Email: tp@taunton.com
www.tauntonstore.com

The fabric collection can be viewed online at
www.freespiritfabrics.com

KAFFE FASSETT
for
FreeSpirit

Free Spirit Fabrics
Carmel Park II
11121 Carmel Commons Blvd, Ste 280
Charlotte, NC 28226

distributors and stockists

To find a retailer in the USA and Canada, please go to www.freespiritfabrics.com

For the following countries/territories see contact information below:

AUSTRALIA
XLN Fabrics
2/21 Binney Rd,
Kings Park
NSW 2148
www.xln.com.au
email: allanmurphy@xln.com.au

CHINA, HONG KONG, MACAU
Wan Mei Diy China
1458 GuMei Road, Room 502-14
Shanghai 201102
email: 12178550@qq.com

DENMARK
Industrial Textiles A/S
Engholm Parkvej 1
Alleroed 3450
www.indutex.dk
email: maria@indutex.dk

Stof Fabrics
(see UK/Europe)

HONG KONG
See China

JAPAN
Kiyohara & Co Ltd
4-5-2 Minamikyuhoji-machi
Chuo-ku, Osaka 541-8506
www.kiyohara.co.jp

Mitsuharu Kanda
1-14-10 Nihonbashi Bakuro
Chuo-Ku, Tokyo 103-002
www. kanda.o.oo7.jp/2_1.htm
email: kandacom@nifty.com

Nippon Chuko
1-9-7 Minsmikyuhoji-Machi
Osaka 541-0058
www.nippon-chuko.co.jp
email: k.sanada@nippon-chuko.co.jp

Yamachu-Mengyo Co Ltd
1-10-8 Edobori, Nishi-Ku
Osaka 550-0002
www.yamachu-mengyo.co.jp

MACAO
See China

NEW ZEALAND
Fabco Ltd
Unit 18, 23 Bristol Place,
Te Rapa, Hamilton 3200
www.fabco.co.nz
email: joe@fabco.co.nz

SINGAPORE
Sing Mui Heng Pte Ltd
315 Outram Road
Singapore 169074
www.smhcraft.com
email: mkt@singmuiheng.com

SOUTH AFRICA
Arthur Bales Pty Ltd
62 4th Avenue
Johannesburg 2103
www.arthurbales.co.za
email: nicci@arthurbales.co.za

SOUTH KOREA
J Enterprise Co Ltd
Daerung Techno Town3
115, Gasan Digital 2Ro unit #1008
Geumcheon-Gu, Seoul 08505
www.enjoyquilt.co.kr
email: JinHan@enjoyquilt.co.kr

SPAIN
J. Pujol Maq Conf SA
c/Industria 5
Montgat, Barcelona
www.jpujol.com
email: jpujol@jpujol.com

Jose Rosas Taberner SA
c/o Trafalgar 60
Barcelona
www.castelltort.com
email: info@castelltort.com

TAIWAN
Longteh Trading Co Ltd
No. 71 Hebei W. St
Taichung City 40669
email: longteh.quilt@gmail.com

UK/EUROPE
Rhinetex BV
Maagdenburgstraat 24
ZC Deventer 7421
Netherlands
www.rhinetex.com
email: info@rhinetex.com

Stof Fabrics
Hammershusvej 2 c
Herning 7400
Denmark
www.stoffabrics.com
email: stof@stof.dk

LOCATION OF LAVENHAM, SUFFOLK

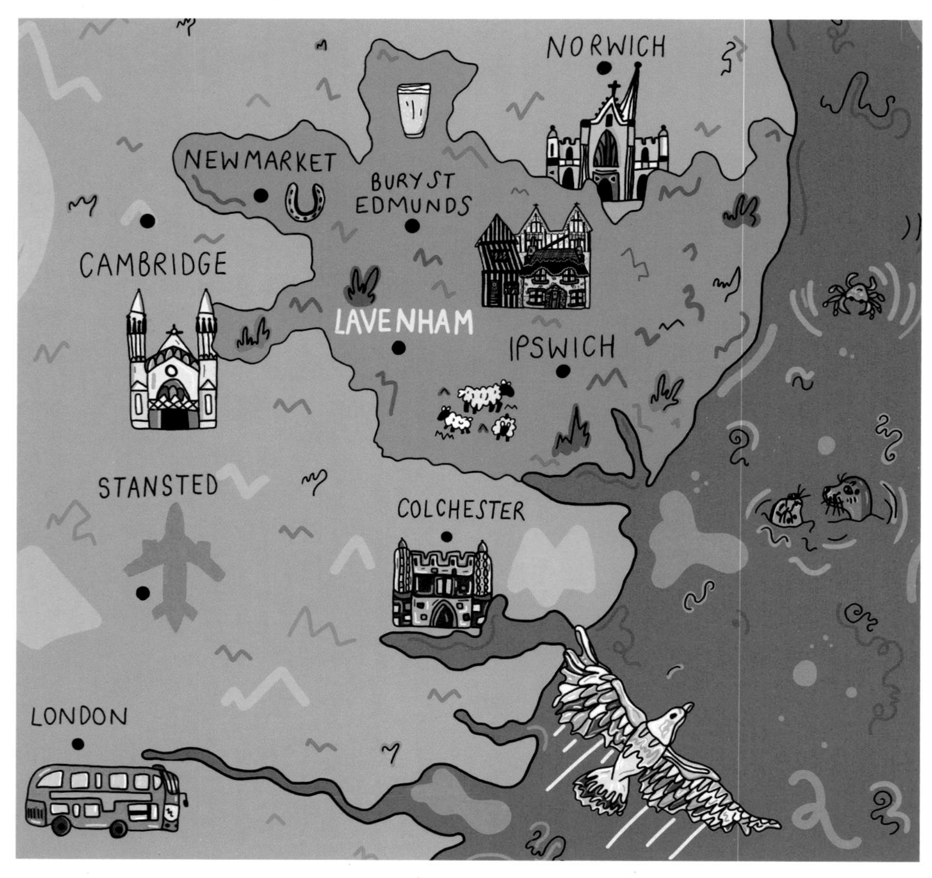